Crisis in Russia 1920

Arthur Ransome

Crisis in Russia 1920

Crisis in Russia 1920 / Arthur Ransome
Published by Redwords, May 1992
Redwords, 31 Cottenham Road London E17 6RP

First published George Allen & Unwin Ltd / 1921
ISBN 1 872208 037
Set in 10:13 Monophoto Bembo
Imagesetting by East End Offset Bureau
Printed and bound in Great Britain by Dotesios Ltd, Trowbridge, Wiltshire
Production and design by Sofie Mason and Roger Huddle

Redwords would like to thank the
following people for making the
publication of this book possible:
John Bell and Sir Rupert Hart-
Davis of the Ransome Estate, Paul
Foot, Sheila McGregor, *Animage*,
Cyrus Gilbert-Rolfe, Elise
Bradbury, Angela Graham, Paul
Cooper, Maxine Lambert, John
Rees, Lindsey German,
Andrew Forbes and
Megan Trudell

Contents / The Crisis in Russia 1920

Introduction

The characteristic of a revolutionary country is that change is a quicker process there than elsewhere. As the revolution recedes into the past the process of change slackens speed. Russia is no longer the dizzying kaleidoscope that it was in 1917. No longer does it change visibly from week to week as it changed in 1918. Already, to get a clear vision of the direction in which it is changing, it is necessary to visit it at intervals of six months, and quite useless to tap the political barometer several times a day as once upon a time one used to do . . . But it is still changing very fast. My journal of *Six Weeks in Russia 1919*, while giving as I believe a fairly accurate picture of the state of affairs in February and March of 1919, pictures a very different stage in the development of the revolution from that which would be found by observers today.

The prolonged state of crisis in which the country has been kept by external war, while strengthening the ruling party by rallying even their enemies to their support, has had the other effects that a national crisis always has on the internal politics of a country. Methods of government which in normal times would no doubt be softened or disguised by ceremonial usage are used nakedly and justified by necessity.

We have seen the same thing in belligerent and non-revolutionary countries, and, for the impartial student, it has been interesting to observe that, when this test of crisis is applied, the actual governmental machine in every country looks very much like that in every other. They wave different flags to stimulate enthusiasm and to justify submission. But that is all. Under the stress of war, 'constitutional safe guards' go by the board 'for the public good', in Moscow as elsewhere. Under that stress it becomes clear that, in spite of its novel constitution, Russia is governed much as other countries are governed, the real directive power lying in the hands of a comparatively small body which is able by hook or crook to infect with its conscious will a population largely indifferent and inert. A visitor to Moscow today would find much of the constitutional machinery that was in full working order in the spring of 1919 now falling into rust and disrepair. He would not be able once a week or so to attend a meeting of the All-Russian Executive and hear discussions in this parliament of the questions of the day. No one tries to shirk the fact that the Executive Committee has fallen into desuetude, from which, when the stress slackens enough to permit ceremony that has not an immediate agitation value, it may some day be revived. The bulk of its members have been at the front or here and there about the country wrestling with the economic problem, and their work is more useful than their chatter. Thus brutally is the thing stated. The continued stress has made the muscles, the actual works, of the revolution more visible than formerly. The working of the machine is not only seen more clearly, but is also more frankly stated (perhaps simply because they too see it now more clearly) by the leaders themselves.

I want in this book to describe the working of the machine as I now see it. But it is not only the machine which is more nakedly visible than it was. The stress to which it is being subjected has also not so much changed its character as become easier of analysis. At least, I seem to myself to see it differently. In the earlier days it seemed quite simply the struggle between a revolutionary and non-revolutionary countries. I now think that that struggle is a foolish, unnecessary, lunatic incident which disguised from us the existence of a far more serious struggle, in which the revolutionary and non-revolutionary governments are fighting on the same side. They fight without co-operation, and throw insults and bullets at each other in the middle of the struggle, but they are fighting for the same thing. They are fighting the same enemy. Their quarrel with each other is for both parties merely a harassing accompaniment of the struggle to which all Europe is committed, for the salvage of what is left of European civilization.

The threat of a complete collapse of civilization is more imminent in Russia than elsewhere. But it is clear enough in Poland, it cannot be disregarded in Germany, there is no doubt of its existence in Italy, France is conscious of it; it is only in England and America that this threat is not among the waking nightmares of everybody. Unless the struggle, which has hitherto been going against us, takes a turn for the better, we shall presently be quite unable to ignore it ourselves.

I have tried to state the position in Russia today; on the one hand to describe the crisis itself, the threat which is forcing these people to an extreme of effort, and on the other hand to describe the organization that is facing that threat; on the one hand to set down what are the main characteristics of the crisis, on the other hand to show how the comparatively small body of persons actually supplying the Russian people with its directives set about the stupendous task of moving that vast inert mass, not along the path of least resistance, but along a path which, while alike unpleasant and extremely difficult, does seem to them to promise some sort of eventual escape.

No book is entirely objective, so I do not in the least mind stating my own reason for writing this one (which has taken time that I should have liked to spend on other and very different things). Knowledge of this reason will permit the reader to make allowances for such bias as I have been unable to avoid, and so, by judicious reading, to make my book perhaps nearly as objective as I should myself wish it to be.

It has been said that when two armies face each other across a battle front and engage in mutual slaughter, they may be considered as a single army engaged in suicide. Now it seems to me that when countries, each one severally doing its best to arrest its private economic ruin, do their utmost to accelerate the economic ruin of each other, we are witnessing something very like the suicide of civilization itself. There are people in both camps who believe that armed and economic conflict between revolutionary and non-revolutionary Europe, or if you like between capitalism and communism, is inevitable. These people, in both camps, are doing their best to make it inevitable. Sturdy pessimists, in Moscow no less than in London and Paris, they go so far as to say 'the sooner the better,' and by all means in their power try to precipitate a conflict.

Now the main effort in Russia today, the struggle which absorbs the chief attention of all but the few communist Churchills and communist Millerands who, blind to all else, demand an immediate pitched battle over the prostrate body of civilization, is directed to finding a way for Russia herself out of the crisis, the severity of which can hardly be realised by people who have not visited the country again and again, and to bringing her as quickly as possible into a state in which she can export her raw materials and import the manufactured goods of which she stands in need. I believe that this struggle is ours as well as Russia's, though we, to whom the threat is less imminent, are less desperately engaged. Victory or defeat in this struggle in Russia, or anywhere else on the world's surface, is victory or defeat for everyone. The purpose of my book is to make that clear. For, bearing that in mind, I cannot but think that every honest man, of whatever party, who cares more for humanity than for politics, must do his utmost to postpone the conflict which a few extremists on each side of the barricades so fanatically desire. If that conflict is indeed inevitable, its consequences will be less devastating to a Europe cured of her wounds than to a Europe scarcely, even by the most hopeful, to be described as convalescent. But the conflict may not be inevitable after all. No man not purblind but sees that communist Europe is changing no less than capitalist Europe. If we succeed in postponing the struggle long enough, we may well succeed in postponing it until the warlike on both sides look in vain for the reasons of their antagonism.

Chapter one / The shortage of things

Nothing can be more futile than to describe conditions in Russia as a sort of divine punishment for revolution, or indeed to describe them at all without emphasising the fact that the crisis in Russia is part of the crisis in Europe, and has been in the main brought about like the revolution itself, by the same forces that have caused, for example, the crisis in Germany or the crisis in Austria.

No country in Europe is capable of complete economic independence. In spite of her huge variety of natural resources, the Russian organism seemed in 1914 to have been built up on the generous assumption that, with Europe at least, the country was to be permanently at peace, or at the most to engage in military squabbles which could be reckoned in months, and would keep up the prestige of the autocracy without seriously hampering imports and exports. Almost every country in Europe, with the exception of England, was better fitted to stand alone, was less completely specialised in a single branch of production. England, fortunately for herself, was not isolated during the war, and will not become isolated unless the development of the crisis abroad deprives her of her markets. England produces practically no food, but great quantities of coal, steel and manufactured goods. Isolate her absolutely, and she will not only starve, but will stop producing manufactured goods, steel and coal, because those who usually produce these things will be getting nothing for their labour except money which they will be unable to use to buy dinners, because there will be no dinners to buy.

That suppositious case is a precise parallel to what has happened in Russia. Russia produced practically no manufactured goods (70 percent of her machinery she received from abroad), but great quantities of food. The blockade isolated her. By the blockade I do not mean merely the childish stupidity committed by ourselves, but the blockade, steadily increasing in strictness, which began in August 1914 and has been unnecessarily prolonged by our stupidity. The war, even while for Russia it was not nominally a blockade, was so actually. The use of tonnage was perforce restricted to the transport of the necessaries of war, and these were narrowly defined as shells, guns and so on, things which do not tend to improve a country economically, but rather the reverse. The imports from Sweden through Finland were no sort of makeweight for the loss of Poland and Germany.

The war meant that Russia's ordinary imports practically ceased. It meant a strain on Russia, comparable to that which would have been put on England if the German submarine campaign had succeeded in putting an end to our imports of food from the Americas. From the moment of the declaration of war, Russia was in the position of one 'holding out', of a city standing a siege without a water supply, for her imports were so necessary to her economy that they may justly be considered as essential irrigation. There could be no question for her of improvement, of strengthening. She was faced with the fact that until the war should end she had to do with what she had, and that the things she had formerly counted on importing would be replaced by guns and shells, to be used, as it turned out, in battering Russian property that happened to be in enemy hands. She even learned that she had to develop gun-making and shell-making at home, at the expense of those other industries which to some small extent might have helped her to keep going. And, just as in England such a state of affairs would lead to a cessation of the output of iron and coal in which England is rich, so in Russia, in spite of her corn lands, it led to a shortage of food.

The Russian peasant formerly produced food for which he was paid in money. With that money, formerly, he was able to clothe himself, to buy the tools of his labour, and further, though no doubt he never observed the fact, to pay for the engines and wagons that took his food to market. A huge percentage of the clothes and the tools and the engines and the wagons and the rails came from abroad, and even those factories in Russia which were capable of producing such things were, in many essentials, themselves dependent upon imports. Russian towns began to be hungry in 1915. In October of that year the Empress reported to the Emperor that the shrewd Rasputin had seen in a vision that it was necessary to bring wagons with flour, butter and sugar from Siberia, and proposed that for three days nothing else should be done. Then there would be no strikes. 'He blesses you for the arrangement of these trains'. In 1916 the peasants were burying their bread instead of bringing it to market. In the autumn of 1916 I remember telling certain most incredulous members of the English government that there would be a most serious food shortage in Russia in the near future. In 1917 came the upheaval of the revolution, in 1918 peace, but for Russia, civil war and the continuance of the blockade. By July 1919 the rarity of manufactured goods was such that it was possible two hundred miles south of Moscow to obtain ten eggs for a box of matches, and the rarity of goods requiring distant transport became such that in November 1919, in western Russia, the peasants would sell me nothing for money, whereas my neighbour in the train bought all he wanted in exchange for small quantities of salt.

It was not even as if, in vital matters, Russia started the war in a satisfactory condition. The most vital of all questions in a country of huge distances must necessarily be that of transport. It is no exaggeration to say that only by fantastic efforts was Russian transport able to save its face and cover its worst deficiencies even before the war began. The extra strain put upon it by the transport of troops and the maintenance of the armies exposed its weakness, and with each succeeding week of war, although in 1916 and 1917 Russia did receive 775 locomotives from abroad, Russian transport went from bad to worse, making inevitable a creeping paralysis of Russian economic life, during the latter already acute stages of which the revolutionaries succeeded to the disease that had crippled their precursors.

In 1914 Russia had in all 20,057 locomotives, of which 15,047 burnt coal, 4,072 burnt oil and 938 wood. But that figure of 20,000 was more impressive for a government official, who had his own reasons for desiring to be impressed, than for a practical railway engineer, since of that number over 5,000 engines were more than 20 years old, over 2,000 were more than 30 years old, 1500 were more than 40 years old, and 147 patriarchs had passed their fiftieth birthday. Of the whole 20,000 only 7,108 were under ten years of age. That was six years ago. In the meantime Russia has been able to make, in quantities decreasing during the last five years by 40 and 50 percent annually, 2,990 new locomotives. In 1914 of the locomotives then in Russia about 17,000 were in working condition. In 1915 there were, in spite of 800 new ones, only 16,500. In 1916 the number of healthy locomotives was slightly higher, owing partly to the manufacture of 903 at home in the preceding year and partly to the arrival of 400 from abroad. In 1917, in spite of the arrival of a further small contingent, the number sank to between 15,000 and 16,000. Early in 1918 the Germans in the Ukraine and elsewhere captured 8,000. Others were lost in the early stages of the civil war. The number of locomotives fell from 14,519 in January to 8,457 in April, after which the artificially instigated revolt of the Czecho-Slovaks made possible the fostering of civil war on a large scale, and the number fell swiftly to 4,679 in December. In 1919 the numbers varied less markedly, but the decline continued, and in December last year 4,141 engines were in working order. In January 1920 the number was 8,969, rising slightly in February, when the number was 4,019. A calculation made before the war showed that in the best possible conditions the maximum Russian output of engines would be not more than 1,800 annually. At this rate in ten years the Russians could restore their collection of engines to something like adequate numbers. Today, 30 years would be an inadequate estimate, for some factories, like the Votkinsky, have been purposely ruined by the Whites; in others the lathes and other machinery for building and repairing locomotives are worn out; many of the skilled engineers were killed in the war with Germany, many others in defending the revolution, and it will be long before it will be possible to restore to the workmen or to the factories the favourable material conditions of 1912-18. Thus the main fact in the present crisis is that Russia possesses one-fifth of the number of locomotives which in 1914 was just sufficient to maintain her railway system in a state of efficiency which to English observers at that time was a joke. For six years she has been unable to import the necessary machinery for making engines or repairing them. Further, coal and oil have been, until recently, cut off by the civil war. The coal mines are left, after the civil war, in such a condition that no considerable output may be expected from them in the near future. Thus, even those engines which exist have had their efficiency lessened by being adapted in a rough and ready manner for burning wood fuel instead of that for which they were designed.

Let us now examine the combined effect of ruined transport and the six years' blockade on Russian life in town and country. First of all was cut off the import of manufactured goods from abroad. That has had a cumulative effect completed, as it were, and rounded off by the breakdown of transport. By making it impossible to bring food, fuel and raw material to the factories, the wreck of transport makes it impossible for Russian industry to produce even that modicum which it contributed to the general supply of manufactured goods which the Russian peasant was accustomed to receive in exchange for his production of food. On the whole, the peasant himself eats rather more than he did before the war. But he has no matches, no salt, no clothes, no boots, no tools. The

Communists are trying to put an end to illiteracy in Russia, and in the villages the most frequent excuse for keeping children from school is a request to come and see them, when they will be found, as I have seen them myself, playing naked about the stove, without boots or anything but a shirt, if that, in which to go and learn to read and write. Clothes and such things as matches are, however, of less vital importance than tools, the lack of which is steadily reducing Russia's actual power of food production. Before the war Russia needed from abroad huge quantities of agricultural implements, not only machines, but simple things like axes, sickles, scythes. In 1915 her own production of these things had fallen to 15.1 percent of her already inadequate peacetime output. In 1917 it had fallen to 2.1 percent The Soviet government is making efforts to raise it, and is planning new factories exclusively for the making of these things, but with transport in such a condition, a new factory means merely a new demand for material and fuel which there are neither engines nor wagons to bring. Meanwhile, all over Russia, spades are worn out, men are ploughing with burnt staves instead of with ploughshares, scratching the surface of the ground, and instead of harrowing with a steel-spiked harrow of some weight, are brushing the ground with light constructions of wooden spikes bound together with wattles.

The actual agricultural productive powers of Russia are consequently sinking. But things are no better if we turn from the rye and corn lands to the forests. Saws are worn out. Axes are worn out. Even apart from that, the shortage of transport cuts the production of wood fuel, the lack of which reacts on transport and on the factories and so on in a circle from which nothing but a large import of engines and wagons will provide an outlet. Timber can be floated down the rivers. Yes, but it must be brought to the rivers. Surely horses can do that. Yes, but horses must be fed, and oats do not grow in the forests. For example, last spring (1920) the best organised timber production was in Perm government. There, 16,000 horses have been mobilised for the work, but further development is impossible for lack of forage. A telegram bitterly reports,

'Two trains of oats from Ekaterinburg are expected day by day. If the oats arrive in time a considerable success will be possible.' And if the oats do not arrive in time? Besides, not horses alone require to be fed. The men who cut the wood cannot do it on empty stomachs. And again rises a cry for trains that do not arrive, for food that exists somewhere, but not in the forest where men work. The general effect of the wreck of transport on food is stated as follows: Less than 12 percent of the oats required, and less than 5 percent of the bread and salt required for really efficient working, were brought to the forests. Nonetheless three times as much wood has been prepared as the available transport has removed.

The towns suffer from lack of transport, and from the combined effect on the country of their productive weakness and of the loss of their old position as centres through which the country received its imports from abroad. Townsfolk and factory workers lack food, fuel, raw materials and much else that in a civilised state is considered a necessary of life. Thus, ten million poods of fish were caught last year, but there were no means of bringing them from the fisheries to the great industrial centres where they were most needed.

Townsfolk are starving, and in winter, cold. People living in rooms in a flat, complete strangers to each other, by general agreement bring all their beds into the kitchen. In the kitchen soup is made once a day. There is a little warmth there beside the natural warmth of several human beings in a small room. There it is possible to sleep. During the whole of last winter, in the case I have in mind, there were no means of heating the other rooms, where the temperature was almost always far below freezing point.

It is difficult to make the conditions real except by individual examples. The lack of medicines, due directly to the blockade, seems to have small effect on the imagination when simply stated as such. Perhaps people will realise what it means when, instead of talking of the wounded undergoing operations without anaesthetics, I record the case of an acquaintance, a Bolshevik, working in a government office, who suffered last summer from a slight derangement of the stomach due to improper and inadequate feeding. His doctor prescribed a medicine, and nearly a dozen different apothecaries were unable to make up the prescription for lack of one or several of the simple ingredients required. Soap has become an article so rare (in Russia as in Germany during the blockade and the war there is a terrible absence of fats) that for the present it is to be treated as a means of safe-guarding labour, to be given to the workmen for washing after and during their work, and in preference to miners, chemical, medical and sanitary workers, for whose efficiency and health it is essential. The proper washing of underclothes is impossible. To induce the population of Moscow to go to the baths during the typhus epidemic, it was a sufficient bribe to promise to each person, beside the free bath, a free scrap of soap.

Houses are falling into disrepair for want of plaster, paint and tools. Nor is it possible to substitute one thing for another, for Russia's industries all suffer alike from their old dependence on the West, as well as from the inadequacy of the transport to bring to the factories the material they need. People remind each other that during the war the Germans, when similarly hard put to it for clothes, made paper dresses, tablecloths, etc. In Russia, the nets used in paper-making are worn out. At last, in April 1920 (so Lenin told me), there seemed to be a hope of getting new ones from abroad. But the condition of the paper industry is typical of all in a country which, it should not be forgotten, could be in a position to supply wood-pulp for other countries besides itself. The factories are able to produce only 60 percent of demands that have previously, by the strictest scrutiny, been reduced to a minimum before they are made. The reasons, apart from the lack of nets and cloths, are summed up in absence of food, forage and finally labour. Even when wood is brought by river the trouble is not yet overcome. The horses are dead and eaten or starved and weak. Factories have to cease working so that the workmen, themselves underfed, can drag the wood from the barges to the mills. It may well be imagined what the effect of hunger, cold, and the disheartement consequent on such conditions of work and the seeming hopelessness of the position have on the productivity of labour, the fall in which reacts on all the industries, on transport, on the general situation, and so again on itself.

Mr J M Keynes, writing with Central Europe in his mind (he is, I think, as ignorant of Russia as I am of Germany), says: 'What then is our picture of Europe? A country population able to support life on the fruits of its own agricultural production, but without the accustomed surplus for the towns, and also (as a result of the lack of imported materials, and so of variety and amount in the saleable manufactures of the towns) without the usual incentives to market food in exchange for other wares; an industrial population unable to keep its strength for lack of food, unable to earn a livelihood for lack of materials, and so unable to make good by imports from abroad the failure of productivity at home.'

Russia is an emphasised engraving, in which every line of that picture is bitten in with repeated washes of acid. Several new lines, however, are added to the drawing, for in Russia the processes at work elsewhere have gone further than in the rest of Europe, and it is possible to see dimly, in faint outline, the new stage of decay which is threatened. The struggle to arrest that decay is the real crisis of the revolution, of Russia, and, not impossibly, of Europe. For each country that develops to the end in this direction is a country lost to the economic comity of Europe. And, as one country follows another over the brink, so will the remaining countries be faced by conditions of increasingly narrow self-dependence, in fact by the very conditions which in Russia, so far, have received their clearest, most forcible illustration.

24

Chapter two / The shortage of men

In the preceding chapter I wrote of Russia's many wants, and of the processes visibly at work, tending to make her condition worse and not better. But I wrote of things, not of people. I wrote of the shortage of this and of that, but not of the most serious of all shortages, which, while itself largely due to those already discussed, daily intensifies them, and points the way to that further stage of decay which is threatened in the near future in Russia and, in the more distant future, in Europe. I did not write of the shortage and deterioration of labour.

Shortage of labour is not peculiar to Russia. It is among the post-war phenomena common to all countries. The war and its accompanying diseases have cost Europe, including Russia, an enormous number of able-bodied men. Many millions of others have lost the habit of regular work. German industrialists complain that they cannot get labour, and that when they get it, it is not productive. I heard complaints on the same subject in England. But just as the economic crisis, due in the first instance to the war and the isolation it imposed, has gone further in Russia than elsewhere, so the shortage of labour, at present a handicap, an annoyance in more fortunate countries, is in Russia perhaps the greatest of the national dangers.

Shortage of labour cannot be measured simply by the

decreasing numbers of the workmen. If it takes two workmen as long to do a particular job in 1920 as it took one man to do in 1914, then, even if the number of workmen has remained the same, the actual supply of labour has been halved. And in Russia the situation is worse than that. For example, in the group of state metal-working factories, those, in fact which may be considered as the weapon with which Russia is trying to cut her way out of her transport difficulties, apart from the fact that in 1916 there were 81,600 workmen, whereas in 1920 there are only 42,500, labour has deteriorated in the most amazing manner. In 1916 in these factories 92 percent of the nominal working hours were actually kept; in 1920 work goes on during only 60 percent of the nominal hours. It is estimated that the labour of a single workman produces now only one-quarter of what it produced in 1916.

To take another example, also from workmen engaged in transport, that is to say, in the most important of all work at the present time: in the Moscow junction of the Moscow–Kazan Railway, between November 1 and February 29 (1920), 292 work-men and clerks missed 12,048 working days, being absent, on an average, forty days per man in the four months. In Moscow passen-ger station on this line, 22 workmen missed in November 106 days, in December 273, in January 338, and in February 380, in an appalling crescendo further illustrated by the wagon department, where 28 workmen missed in November 104 days, and in February 500. In November workmen absented themselves for single days. In February the same workmen were absent for the greater part of the month. The invariable excuse was illness. Many cases of illness there undoubtedly were, since this period was the worst of the typhus epidemic, but besides illness, and besides mere obvious idle-ness, which no doubt accounts for a certain proportion of illegiti-mate holidays, there is another explanation which goes nearer the root of the matter. Much of the time filched from the state was in all probability spent in expeditions in search of food. In Petrograd the Council of Public Economy complain that there is a tendency to turn the eight-hour day into a four-hour day. Attempts are being made to arrest this tendency by making an additional food allowance conditional on the actual fulfilment of working days. In the Donetz coal basin, the monthly output per man was in 1914 750 poods, in 1916 615 poods, in 1919 240 poods (figures taken from Ekaterinoslav government), and in 1920 the output per man is estimated at being something near 220 poods. In the shale mines on the Volga, where food conditions are comparatively good, productivity is comparatively high. Thus in a small mine near Simbirsk there are 230 workmen, of whom 50 to 60 are skilled. The output for the unskilled is 28.9 poods in a shift, for the skilled 68.3. But even there 25 percent of the workmen are regular absentees, and actually the mine works only 17 or 18 days in a month, that is, 70 percent of the normal number of working days. The remaining 30 percent of nominal working time is spent by the workmen in getting food. Another small mine in the same district is worked entirely by unskilled labour, the workers being peasants of the neighbouring villages. In this mine the productivity per man is less, but all the men work full time. They do not have to waste time in securing food because, being local peasants, they are supplied by their own villages and families. In Moscow and Petrograd food is far more difficult to secure, more time is wasted on the hopeless task; even with that waste of time, the workman is not properly fed, and it cannot be wondered at that his productivity is low.

Something, no doubt, is due to the natural character of the Russians, which led Trotsky to define man as an animal distinguished by laziness. Russians are certainly lazy, and probably owe to their climate their remarkable incapacity for prolonged effort. The Russian climate is such that over large areas of Russia the peasant is accustomed, and has been accustomed for hundreds of years, to perform prodigies of labour during two short periods of sowing and harvest, and to spend the immensely long and monotonous winter in a hibernation like that of the snake or the dormouse. There is a much greater difference between a Russian workman's normal output and that of which he is capable for a short time if he sets himself to it, than there is between the normal and exceptional output of an Englishman, whose temperate climate has not taught him to regard a great part of the year as a period of mere waiting for and resting from the extraordinary effort of a few weeks. *

But this uneven working temperament was characteristic of the Russian before the war. It has been said that the revolution removed the stimulus to labour, and left the Russian laziness to have its way. In the first period of the revolution that may have been true. It is becoming day by day less true. The fundamental reasons of low productivity will not be found in any sudden or unusual efflorescence of idleness, but in economic conditions which cannot but reduce the productivity of idle and industrious alike. Insufficient feeding is one such reason. The proportion of working time consumed in foraging is another. But the whole of my first chapter may be taken as a compact mass of reasons why the Russians at the present time should not work with anything like a normal productivity. It is said that bad workmen complain of their

---

* Given any particular motive, any particular enthusiasm, or visible, desirable object, even the hungry Russian workmen of today are capable of sudden and temporary increase of output. The 'Saturdayings' provide endless illustrations of this. They had something in the character of a picnic, they were novel, they were out of the routine, and the productivity of labour during a 'Saturdaying' was invariably higher than on a weekday. For example, there is a shortage of paper for cigarettes. People roll cigarettes in old newspapers. It occurred to the Central Committee of the Papermakers Union to organise a 'Sundaying' with the object of sending cigarette paper to the soldiers in the Red Army. Six factories took part. Here is a table showing the output of these factories during the 'Sundaying' and the average weekday output. The figures are in poods.

Factory	Made on the Sunday	Average Week Output
Krasnogorodskaya	615	450
Griaznovskaya	65	45
Medianskaya	105	90
Dobruzhskaya	286	250
Belgiiskaya	127	85
Ropshinskaya	85	55

tools, but even good ones become disheartened if compelled to work with makeshifts, mended tools, on a stock of materials that runs out from one day to the next, in factories where the machinery may come at any moment to a standstill from lack of fuel.

There would thus be a shortage of labour in Russia, even if the numbers of workmen were the same today as they were before the war. Unfortunately that is not so. Turning from the question of low productivity per man to that of absolute shortage of men: the example given at the beginning of this chapter, showing that in the most important group of factories the number of workmen has fallen 50 percent is by no means exceptional. Walking through the passages of what used to be the Club of the Nobles and is now the house of the trades unions, during the recent Trades Union Congress in Moscow, I observed among a number of pictorial diagrams on the walls one in particular illustrating the rise and fall of the working population of Moscow during a number of years. Each year was represented by the picture of a factory with a chimney which rose and fell with the population. From that diagram I took the figures for 1913, 1918 and 1919. These figures should be constantly borne in mind by anyone who wishes to realise how catastrophic the shortage of labour in Russia actually is, and to judge how sweeping may be the changes in the social configuration of the country if that shortage continues to increase. Here are the figures:

Workmen in Moscow in 1913	159,344
Workmen in Moscow in 1918	157,282
Workmen in Moscow in 1919	105,210

That is to say, that one-third of the workmen of Moscow ceased to live there, or ceased to be workmen, in the course of a single year. A similar phenomenon is observable in each one of the big industrial districts.

What has become of those workmen?

A partial explanation is obvious. The main impulse of the revolution came from the town workers. Of these, the metal workers were the most decided, and those who most freely joined the

Red Guard in the early, and the Red Army in the later, days of the revolution. Many, in those early days, when there was more enthusiasm than discipline, when there were very few experienced officers, and those without much authority, were slaughtered during the German advance of 1918. The first mobilisations, when conscription was introduced, were among the workers in the great industrial districts. The troops from Petrograd and Moscow, exclusively workmen's regiments, have suffered more than any other during the civil war, being the most dependable and being thrown, like the guards of old time, into the worst place at any serious crisis. Many thousands of them have died for the sake of the revolution which, were they living, they would be hard put to it to save. (The special shortage of skilled workers is also partially to be explained by the indiscriminate mobilisations of 1914-15, when great numbers of the most valuable engineers and other skilled workers were thrown into the front line, and it was not until their loss was already felt that the Tsar's government in this matter came belatedly to its senses).

But these explanations are only partial. The more general answer to the question, 'What has become of the workmen?' lies in the very economic crisis which their absence accentuates. Russia is unlike England, where starvation of the towns would be practically starvation of the whole island. In Russia, if a man is hungry, he has only to walk far enough and he will come to a place where there is plenty to eat. Almost every Russian worker retains in some form or other connection with a village, where, if he returns, he will not be an entire stranger, but at worst a poor relation, and quite possibly an honoured guest. It is not surprising that many thousands have 'returned to the land' in this way. Further, if a workman retains his connection, both with a distant village and with a town, he can keep himself and his family fat and prosperous by ceasing to be a workman, and instead, travelling on the buffers or the roof of a railway wagon, and bringing back with him sacks of flour and potatoes for sale in the town at fantastic prices. Thereby he is lost to productive labour, and his uncomfortable but adventurous life becomes directly harmful, tending to increase the strain on transport, since it is obviously more economical to transport a thousand sacks than to transport a thousand sacks with an idle workman attached to each sack. Further, his activities actually make it more difficult for the town population to get food. By keeping open for the village the possibility of selling at fantastic prices, he lessens the readiness of the peasants to part with their flour at the lower prices of the government. Nor do his activities benefit the working population. The food he brings in goes for the most part to those who have plenty of money or have things to exchange for it. And honest men in Russia today have not much money, and those who have things to exchange are not as a rule workmen. The theory of this man's harmfulness is, I know, open to argument, but the practice at least is exactly as I have stated it, and is obviously attractive to the individual who prefers adventure on a full stomach to useful work on an empty one. Setting aside the theory with its latent quarrel between free trade and state control, we can still recognise that each workman engaged in these pursuits has become an unproductive middleman, one of that very parasitic species which the revolutionaries had hoped to make unnecessary. It is bad from the revolutionary point of view if a workman is so employed, but it is no less bad from the point of view of people who do not care twopence about the revolution one way or the other, but do care about getting Russia on her feet again and out of her economic crisis. It is bad enough if an unskilled workman is so employed. It is far worse if a skilled workman finds he can do better for himself as a 'food speculator' than by the exercise of his legitimate craft. From mines, from every kind of factory come complaints of the decreasing proportion of skilled to unskilled workmen. The superior intelligence of the skilled worker offers him definite advantages should he engage in these pursuits, and his actual skill gives him other advantages in the villages. He can leave his factory and go to the village, there on the spot to ply his trade, or variations of it, when as a handy man, repairing tools, etc., he will make an easy living, and by lessening the dependence of the village on the town do as much as the 'food speculator' in worsening the conditions of the workman he has left behind.

And with that we come to the general changes in the social geography of Russia which are threatened if the processes now at work continue unchecked. The relations between town and village are the fundamental problem of the revolution. Town and countryside are in sharp contradiction, daily intensified by the inability of the towns to supply the country's needs. The town may be considered as a single productive organism, with feelers stretching into the country, and actual outposts there in the form of agricultural enterprises taking their directives from the centre and working as definite parts of the state organism. All round this town organism in all its interstices, and also with feelers in the form of 'food speculators' is the anarchic chaos of the country, consisting of a myriad independent units, regulated by no plan, without a brain centre of any kind. Either the organised town will hold its own against and gradually dominate and systematise the country chaos, or that chaos little by little will engulf the town organism. Every workman who leaves the town automatically places himself on the side of the country in that struggle. And when a town like Moscow loses a third of its working population in a year, it is impossible not to see that, so far, the struggle is going in favour of that huge chaotic, unconscious but immensely powerful countryside. There is even a danger that the town may become divided against itself. Just as scarcity of food leads to food speculation, so the shortage of labour is making possible a sort of speculation in labour. The urgent need of labour has led to a resurrection of the methods of the direct recruiting of workmen in the villages by the agents of particular factories, who by exceptional terms, succeed in getting workmen where the government organs fail. And, of course, this recruiting is not confined to the villages. Those enterprises which are situated in the corn districts are naturally able to offer better conditions, for the sake of which workmen are ready to leave their jobs, and skilled workmen to do unskilled work, and the result can only be a drainage of good workmen away from the hungry central industrial districts where they are most of all needed.

Summing up the facts collected in this chapter and in the first on the lack of things and the lack of men, I think the economic crisis in Russia may be fairly stated as follows: Owing to the appalling condition of Russian transport, and owing to the fact that since 1914 Russia has been practically in a state of blockade, the towns have lost their power of supplying, either as middlemen or as producers, the simplest needs of the villages. Partly owing to this, partly again because of the condition of transport, the towns are not receiving the necessaries of life in sufficient quantities. The result of this is a serious fall in the productivity of labour, and a steady flow of skilled and unskilled workmen from the towns towards the villages, and from employments the exercise of which tends to assist the towns in recovering their old position as essential sources of supply to employments that tend to have the opposite effect. If this continues unchecked, it will make impossible the regeneration of Russian industry, and will result in the increasing independence of the villages, which will tend to become entirely self-supporting communities, tilling the ground in a less and less efficient manner, with ruder tools, with less and less incentive to produce more than is wanted for the needs of the village itself. Russia, in these circumstances, may sink into something very like barbarism, for with the decay of the economic importance of the towns would decay also their authority, and freebooting on a small and large scale would become profitable and not very dangerous. It would be possible, no doubt, for foreigners to trade with the Russians as with the natives of the cannibal islands, bartering looking-glasses and cheap tools; but, should such a state of things come to be, it would mean long years of colonisation, with all the new possibilities and risks involved in the subjugation of a free people, before Western Europe could count once more on getting a considerable portion of its food from Russian corn lands.

That is the position, those are the natural tendencies at work. But opposed to these tendencies are the united efforts of the Communists and of those who, leaving the question of communism discreetly aside, work with them for the sake of preventing such collapse of Russian civilisation. They recognise the existence of every one of the tendencies I have described, but they are convinced that every one of these tendencies will be arrested. They believe that the country will not conquer the town but the reverse. So far from expecting the unproductive stagnation described in the last paragraph, they think of Russia as of the natural food supply of Europe, which the Communists among them believe will, in course of time, be made up of 'Working Men's Republics' (though, for the sake of their own Republic, they are not inclined to postpone trade with Europe until that epoch arrives). At the very time when spades and sickles are wearing out or worn out, these men are determined that the food output of Russia shall sooner or later be increased by the introduction of better methods of agriculture and farming on a larger scale. We are witnessing in Russia the first stages of a titanic struggle, with on one side all the forces of nature leading apparently to an inevitable collapse of civilisation, and on the other side nothing but the incalculable force of human will.

Chapter three / The Communist dictatorship

How is that will expressed? What is the organisation welded by adversity which, in this crisis, supersedes even the Soviet Constitution, and stands between this people and chaos?

It is a commonplace to say that Russia is ruled, driven if you like, cold, starving as she is, to effort after effort by the dictatorship of a party. It is a commonplace alike in the mouths of those who wish to make the continued existence of that organisation impossible and in the mouths of the Communists themselves. At the second congress of the Third International, Trotsky remarked, 'A party as such, in the course of the development of a revolution, becomes identical with the revolution.' Lenin, on the same occasion, replying to a critic who said that he differed from the Communists in his understanding of what was meant by the dictatorship of the proletariat, said, 'He says that we understand by the words dictatorship of the proletariat what is actually the dictatorship of its determined and conscious minority. And that is the fact.' Later he asked, 'What is this minority ? It may be called a party. If this minority is actually conscious, *if it is able to draw the masses after it*, if it shows itself capable of replying to every question on the agenda list of the political day, it actually constitutes a party.' And Trotsky again, on the same occasion, illustrated the relative positions of the Soviet Constitution and the Communist Party when he said, 'And today, now that we have received an offer of peace from the Polish Government, who decides the question? Whither are the workers to turn? We have our Council of People's Commissaries, of course, but that, too, must be under a certain control. Whose control? The control of the working class as a formless chaotic mass ? No. The Central Committee of the party is called together to discuss and decide the question. And when we have to wage war, to form new divisions, to find the best elements for them—to whom do we turn ? To the party, to the Central Committee. And it gives directives to the local committees, 'Send Communists to the front.' The case is precisely the same with the agrarian question, with that of supply, and with all other questions whatsoever.'

No one denies these facts, but their mere statement is quite inadequate to explain what is being done in Russia and how it is being done. I do not think it would be a waste of time to set down as briefly as possible, without the comments of praise or blame that would be primarily interested in the problem from the capitalist or communist point of view what, from observation and inquiry, I believe to be the main framework of the organisation whereby that dictatorship of the party works.

The Soviet Constitution is not so much moribund as in abeyance. The Executive Committee, for example, which used to meet once a week or even oftener, now meets on the rarest occasions. Criticism on this account was met with the reply that the members of the Executive Committee were busy on the front and in various parts of Russia, and that their work was more useful than their chatter. As a matter of fact, the work which that Committee used to do is now done by the Central Committee of the Bolshevik Party, so that the bulk of the 150 members the Central Executive are actually free for other work, a saving of something like 130 men. This does not involve any very great change, but merely an economy in the use of men. In the old days, as I well remember, the opening of a session of the Executive Committee was invariably late, the reason being that the various parties composing it had not yet finished their preliminary and private discussions. There is now an overwhelming Communist majority in the Executive, as elsewhere. I think it may be regarded as proved that these majorities are not always legitimately obtained. Non-Communist delegates do undoubtedly find every kind of difficulty put in their way by the rather Jesuitical adherents of the faith. But, no matter how these majorities are obtained, the result is that when the Communist Party has made up its mind on any subject, it is so certain of being able to carry its point that the calling together of the All-Russian Executive Committee is merely a theatrical demonstration of the fact that it can do what it likes. When it does meet, the Communists allow the microscopical opposition great liberty of speech, listen quietly, cheer ironically, and vote like one man, proving on every occasion that the meeting of the Executive Committee was the idlest of forms, intended rather to satisfy purists than for purposes of discussion, since the real discussion has all taken place beforehand among the Communists themselves. Something like this must happen with every representative assembly at which a single party has a great preponderance and a rigid internal discipline. The real interest is in the discussion inside the Party Committees.

This state of affairs would probably be more actively resented if the people were capable of resenting anything but their own hunger, or of fearing anything but a general collapse which would turn that hunger into starvation. It must be remembered that the urgency of the economic crisis has driven political questions into the background. The Communists (compare Rykov's remarks on this subject, p. 105) believe that this is the natural result of social revolution. They think that political parties will disappear altogether and that people will band together, not for the victory of one of several contending political parties, but solely for economic cooperation or joint enterprise in art or science. In support of this they point to the number of their opponents who have become Communists, and to the still greater number of non-Communists who are loyally working with them for the economic reconstruction of the country.

I do not agree with the Communists in this, nor yet with their opponents, who attribute the death of political discussion to fear of the Extraordinary Commission. I think that both the Communists and their opponents underestimate the influence of the economic ruin that affects everybody. The latter particularly, feeling that in some way they must justify themselves to politically minded foreign visitors, seek an excuse for their apathy in the one institution that is almost universally unpopular. I have many non-Communist friends in Russia, but have never detected the least restraint that could be attributed to fear of anybody in their criticisms of the Communist regime. The fear existed alike among Communists and non-Communists, but it was like the fear of people walking about in a particularly bad thunderstorm. The activities and arrests of the Extraordinary Commission are so haphazard, often so utterly illogical, that it is quite idle for anyone to say to himself that by following any given line of conduct he will avoid molestation. Also, there is something in the Russian character which makes any prohibition of discussion almost an invitation to discuss. I have never met a Russian who could be prevented from saying whatever he liked whenever he liked, by any threats or dangers whatsoever. The only way to prevent a Russian from talking is to cut out his tongue. The real reason for the apathy is that, for the moment, for almost everybody, political questions are of infinitesimal importance in comparison with questions of food and warmth. The ferment of political discussion that filled the first years of the revolution has died away, and people talk about little but what they are able to get for dinner, or what somebody else has been able to get. I, like other foreign visitors coming to Russia after feeding up in other countries, am all agog to make people talk. But the sort of questions which interest me, with my full-fed stomach, are brushed aside almost fretfully by men who have been more or less hungry for two or three years on end.

I find, instead of an urgent desire to alter this or that at once, tomorrow, in the political complexion of the country, a general desire to do the best that can be done with things as they are, a general fear of further upheaval of any kind, in fact a general acquiescence in the present state of affairs politically, in the hope of altering the present state of affairs economically. And this is entirely natural. Everybody, Communists included, rails bitterly at the inefficiencies of the present system, but everybody, anti-Communists included, admits that there is nothing whatever capable of taking its place. Its failure is highly undesirable, not because it itself is good, but because such failure would be preceded or followed by a breakdown of all existing organisations. Food distribution, inadequate as it now is, would come to an end. The innumerable non-political committees, which are rather like Boards of Directors controlling the Timber, Fur, Fishery, Steel, Matches or other Trusts (since the nationalised industries can be so considered) would collapse, and with them would collapse not only the one hope of keeping a breath of life in Russian industry, but also the actual livelihoods of a great number of people, both Communists and non-Communists. I do not think it is realised outside Russia how large a proportion of the educated classes have become civil servants of one kind or another. It is a rare thing when a whole family has left Russia, and many of the most embittered partisans of war on Russia have relations inside Russia who have long ago found places under the new system, and consequently fear its collapse as much as anyone. One case occurs to me in which a father was a very important minister in one of the various White governments which have received Allied support, while his son inside Russia was doing pretty well as a responsible official under the Communists. Now in the event of a violent challenge, the Communists would be outlaws with a price on every head, and those who have worked with them, being Russians, know their fellow countrymen well enough to be pretty well convinced that the mere fact that they are without cards of the membership of Communist Party, would not save them in the orgy of slaughter that would follow any such collapse.

People may think that I underestimate the importance of the

Executive Commission. I am perfectly aware that without this police force with its spies, prisons and its troops, the difficulties of the dictatorship would be increased by every kind of disorder, and the chaos, which I still fear may come, would have begun long ago. I believe, too, that the overgrown power of the Executive Commission, and the cure that must sooner or later be applied to it, may, as in the French Revolution, bring about the collapse of the whole system. The Commission depends for its strength on the fear of something else. I have seen it weaken when there was a hope of general peace. I have seen it tighten its grip in the presence of attacks from without and attempted assassination within. It is dreaded by everybody; not even Communists are safe from it; but it does not suffice to explain the dictatorship, and is actually entirely irrelevant to the most important process of that dictatorship, namely, the adoption of a single idea, a single argument, by the whole of a very large body of men. The whole power of the Executive Commission does not affect in the slightest degree discussions inside the Communist Party, and those discussions are the simple fact distinguishing the Communist dictatorship from any of the other dictatorships by which it may be supplanted.

There are 600,000 members of the Communist Party (611,978 on April 2, 1920). There are 19 members of the Central Committee of that party. There are, I believe, five who, when they agree, can usually sway the remaining 14. There is no need to wonder how these 14 can be argued into acceptance of the views of the still smaller inner ring, but the process of persuading the 600,000 of the desirability of, for example, such measures as those involved in industrial conscription which, at first sight, was certainly repugnant to most of them, is the main secret of the dictatorship, and is not in any way affected by the existence of the Executive Commission.

Thus the actual government of Russia at the present time may be not unfairly considered as a small group inside the Central Committee of the Communist Party. This small group is able to persuade the majority of the remaining members of that

Committee. The Committee then sets about persuading the majority of the party. In the case of important measures the process is elaborate. The Committee issues a statement of its case, and the party newspapers, Pravda and its affiliated organs, are deluged with its discussion. When this discussion has had time to spread through the country, congresses of Communists meet in the provincial centres, and members of the Central Committee go down to these conferences to defend the 'theses' which the Committee has issued. These provincial congresses, exclusively Communist, send their delegates to an All-Russian Congress. There the 'theses ' of the Central Committee get altered, confirmed, or, in the case of an obviously unpersuaded and large opposition in the party, are referred back or in other ways shelved. Then the delegates, even those who have been in opposition at the congress, go back to the country pledged to defend the position of the majority. This sometimes has curious results. For example, I heard Communist Trades Unionists fiercely arguing against certain clauses in the theses on industrial conscription at a Communist Congress at the Kremlin; less than a week afterwards I heard these same men defending precisely these clauses at a Trades Union Congress over the way, loyally abiding by the collective opinion of their fellow Communists and subject to particularly uncomfortable heckling from people who vociferously reminded them (since the Communist debates had been published) that they were now defending what, a few days before, they had vehemently attacked.

The great strength of the Communist Party is comparable to the strength of the Jesuits, who, similarly, put themselves and their opinions at the disposal of the body politic of their fellow members. Until a decision had been made, a Communist is perfectly free to do his best to prevent it being made, to urge alterations in it, or to supply a rival decision, but once it has been made he will support it without changing his private opinion. In all mixed congresses, rather than break the party discipline, he will give his vote for it, speak in favour of it, and use against its adversaries the very arguments that have been used against himself. He has his share in electing the local Communist Committee, and, indirectly, in electing the all powerful Central Committee of the party, and he binds himself to do at any moment in his life exactly what these Committees decide for him. These Committees decide the use that is to be made of the lives, not only of the rank and file of the party, but also of their own members. Even a member of the Central Committee does not escape. He may be voted by his fellow members into leaving a job he likes and taking up another he detests in which they think his particular talents still better serve the party's aims. To become a member of the Communist Party involves a kind of intellectual abdication, or, to put it differently, a readiness at any moment to place the collected wisdom of the party's Committee above one's individual instincts or ideas. You may influence its decisions, you may even get it to endorse your own, but Lenin himself, if he were to fail on any occasion to obtain the agreement of a majority in the Central Committee, would have to do precisely what the Committee should tell him. Lenin's opinion carries great weight because he is Lenin, but it carries less weight than that of the Central Committee, of which he forms a nineteenth part. On the other hand, the opinion of Lenin and a very small group of outstanding figures is supported by great prestige inside the Committee, and that of the Committee is supported by overwhelming prestige among the rank and file. The result is that this small group is nearly always sure of being able to use the whole vote of 600,000 Communists in the realisation of its decisions.

Now 600,000 men and women acting on the instructions of a highly centralised directive, all the important decisions of which have been thrashed out and re-thrashed until they have general support within the party; 600,000 men and women prepared, not only to vote in support of these decisions, but with a carefully fostered readiness to sacrifice their lives for them if necessary; 600,000 men and women who are persuaded that by their way alone is humanity to be saved; who are persuaded (to put it as cynically and unsympathetically as possible) that the noblest death one can die is in carrying out a decision of the Central Committee; such a body, even in a country such as Russia, is an enormously strong embodiment of human will, an instrument of struggle capable of working something very like miracles. It can be and is controlled like an army in battle. It can mobilise its members, 10 percent of them, 50 percent, the local Committees choosing them, and send them to the front when the front is in danger, or to the railways and repair shops when it is decided that the weakest point is that of transport. If its only task were to fight those organisations of loosely knit and only momentarily united interests which are opposed to it, those jerrybuilt alliances of reactionaries with liberals, united—indivisible—Russians with Ukrainians, agrarians with sugar-refiners, monarchists with republicans, that task would long ago have been finished. But it has to fight something infinitely stronger than these in fighting the economic ruin of Russia, which, if it is too strong, too powerful to be arrested by the Communists, would make short work of those who are without any such fanatic single-minded and perfectly disciplined organisation.

Chapter four / A conference at Jaroslavl

I have already suggested that although the small Central Committee of the Communist Party does invariably get its own way, there are essential differences between this dictatorship and the dictatorship of, for example, a general. The main difference is that whereas the general merely writes an order about which most people hear for the first time only when it is promulgated, the Central Committee prepares the way for its dictation by a most elaborate series of discussions and counter-discussions throughout the country, whereby it wins the bulk of the Communist Party to its opinion after which it proceeds through local and general congresses to do the same with the trades unions. This done, a further series of propaganda meetings among the people actually to be affected smoothes the way for the introduction of whatever new measure is being carried through at the moment. All this talk, besides lessening the amount of physical force necessary in carrying out a decision, must also avoid, at least in part, the deadening effect that would be caused by mere compulsory obedience to the unexplained orders of a military dictator. Of the reality of the Communist dictatorship I have no sort of doubt. But its methods are such as tend towards the awakening of a political consciousness which, if and when normal conditions — of feeding and peace, for example—are attained, will make dictatorship of any kind almost impossible.

To illustrate these methods of the dictatorship, I cannot do better than copy into this book some pages of my diary written in March 1920, when I was present at one of the provincial conferences which were held in preparation of the All-Russian Communist conference at the end of the month.

At seven in the evening Radek called for me and took me to the Jaroslavl station, where we met Larin, whom I had known in 1918. An old Menshevik, he was the originator and most urgent supporter of the decree annulling the foreign debts. He is a very ill man, partially paralysed, having to use both hands even to get food to his mouth or to turn over the leaves of a book. In spite of this he is one of the hardest workers in Russia, and although his obstinacy, his hatred of compromise, and a sort of mixed originality and perverseness keep him almost permanently at loggerheads with the Central Committee, he retains everybody's respect because of the real heroism with which he conquers physical disabilities which long ago would have overwhelmed a less unbreakable spirit. Both Radek and Larin were going to the Communist conference at Jaroslavl which was to consider the new theses of the Central Committee of the party with regard to industrial conscription. Radek was going to defend the position of the Central Committee, Larin to defend his own. They are old friends. As Radek said to me, he intended to destroy Larin's position, but not, if he could help it, prevent Larin being nominated among the Jaroslavl delegates to the All-Russian conference which was in preparation. Larin, whose work keeps him continually travelling, has his own car, specially arranged so that his uninterrupted labour shall have as little effect as possible on his dangerously frail body. Radek and I travelled in one of the special cars of the Central Executive Committee, of which he is a member.

The car seemed very clean, but, as an additional precaution, we began by rubbing turpentine on our necks and wrists and ankles for the discouragement of lice, now generally known as

'Semyashki' from the name of Semyashko, the Commissar of Public Health, who wages unceasing war for their destruction as the carriers of typhus germs. I rubbed the turpentine so energetically into my neck that it burnt like a collar of fire, and for a long time I was unable to get to sleep.

In the morning Radek, the two conductors who had charge of the wagons and I sat down together to breakfast and had a very merry meal, they providing cheese and bread and I a tin of corned beef providently sent out from home by the Manchester Guardian. We cooked up some coca on a little spirit stove which, in a neat basket together with plates, knives, forks, etc. (now almost unobtainable in Russia), had been a parting present from the German Spartacists to Radek when he was released from prison in Berlin and allowed to leave Germany.

The morning was bright and clear, and we had an excellent view of Jaroslavl when we drove from the station to the town, which is a mile or so off the line of the railway. The sun poured down on the white snow, on the barges still frozen into the Volga River, and on the gilt and painted domes and cupolas of the town. Many of the buildings had been destroyed during the rising artificially provoked in July 1918, and its subsequent suppression. More damage was done then than was necessary, because the town was recaptured by troops which had been deserted by most of their officers, and therefore hammered away with artillery without any very definite plan of attack. The more important of the damaged buildings, such as the waterworks and the power station, have been repaired, the tramway was working, and, after Moscow, the town seemed clean, but plenty of ruins remained as memorials of that wanton and unjustifiable piece of folly which, it was supposed, would be the signal for a general rising.

We drove to the Hotel Bristol, now the headquarters of the Jaroslavl Executive Committee, where Rostopchin, the president, discussed with Larin and Radek the programme arranged for the conference. It was then proposed that we should have something to eat, when a very curious state of affairs (and one extremely

Russian) was revealed. Rostopchin admitted that the Commissariat arrangements of the Soviet and its Executive Committee were very bad. But in the centre of the town there is a nunnery which was very badly damaged during the bombardment and is now used as a sort of prison or concentration camp for a Labour Regiment. Peasants from the surrounding country who have refused to give their proper contribution of corn, or have otherwise disobeyed the laws, are, for punishment, lodged here, and made to expiate their sins by work. It so happens, Rostopchin explained, that the officer in charge of the prison feeding arrangements is a very energetic fellow, who had served in the old army in a similar capacity, and the meals served out to the prisoners are so much better than those produced in the Soviet headquarters, that the members of the Executive Committee make a practice of walking over to the prison to dine. They invited us to do the same. Larin did not feel up to the walk, so he remained in the Soviet House to eat an inferior meal, while Radek and I, with Rostopchin and three other members of the local committee walked round to the prison. The bell tower of the old nunnery had been half shot away by artillery, and is in such a precarious condition that it is proposed to pull it down. But on passing under it we came into a wide courtyard surrounded by two-story whitewashed buildings that seemed scarcely to have suffered at all. We found the refectory in one of these buildings. It was astonishingly clean. There were wooden tables, of course without cloths, and each man had a wooden spoon and a hunk of bread. A great bowl of really excellent soup was put down in the middle of table, and we fell to hungrily enough. I made more mess on the table than anyone else, because it requires considerable practice to convey almost boiling soup from a distant bowl to one's mouth in a shallow wooden spoon four inches in diameter without spilling it, and, having got it to one's mouth, to get any of it in without slopping over on either side. The regular diners there seemed to find no difficulty in it at all. One of the prisoners who mopped up after my disasters said I had better join them for a week, when I should find it quite easy. The soup bowl was followed by a fry of potatoes, quantities of which are grown in the district. For dealing with these I found the wooden spoon quite efficient. After that we had glasses of some sort of substitute for tea.

The conference was held in the town theatre. There was a hint of comedy in the fact that the orchestra was playing the overture to some very cheerful opera before the curtain rang up. Radek characteristically remarked that such music should be followed by something more sensational than a conference, and proposed to me that we should form a tableau to illustrate the new peaceful policy of England with regard to Russia. As it was a party conference, I had really no right to be there, but Radek had arranged with Rostopchin that I should come in with himself, and be allowed to sit in the wings at the side of the stage. On the stage were Rostopchin, Radek, Larin and various members of the Communist Party Committee in the district. Everything was ready, but the orchestra went on with its jig music on the other side of the curtain. A message was sent to them. The music stopped with a jerk. The curtain rose, disclosing a crowded auditorium. Everybody stood up, both on the stage and in the theatre, and sang, accompanied by the orchestra, first the 'Internationale' and then the song for those who had died for the revolution. Then, except for two or three politically-minded musicians, the orchestra vanished away and the conference began.

Unlike many of the meetings and conferences at which I have been present in Russia, this Jaroslavl conference seemed to me to include practically none but men and women who either were or had been actual manual workers. I looked over row after row of faces in the theatre, and could only find two faces which I thought might be Jewish, and none that obviously belonged to the 'intelligentsia'. I found on inquiry that only three of the Communists present, excluding Radek and Larin, were old exiled and imprisoned revolutionaries of the educated class. Of these, two were on the platform. All the rest were from the working class. The great majority of them, of course, had joined he Communists in 1917, but three dozen or so had been in the party as long ago as the first Russian revolution of 1905.

Radek, who was tremendously cheered (his long imprisonment in Germany, during which time few in Russia thought that they would see him alive again, has made him something of a popular hero), made a long, interesting and pugnacious speech setting out the grounds on which the Central Committee base their ideas about industrial conscription. These ideas are embodied in the series of theses issued by the Central Committee in January (see p. 81). Larin, who was very tired after the journey and patently conscious that Radek was a formidable opponent, made a speech setting out his reasons for differing with the Central Committee, and proposed an ingenious resolution which, while expressing approval of the general position of the committee, included four supplementary modifications which, as a matter of fact, nullified that position altogether. It was then about ten at night, and the conference adjourned. We drove round to the prison in sledges, and by way of supper had some more soup and potatoes, and so back to the railway station to sleep in the cars.

Next day the conference opened about noon, when there was a long discussion of the points at issue. Workman after workman came to the platform and gave his view. Some of the speeches were a little naïve, as when one soldier said that Comrades Lenin and Trotsky had often before pointed out difficult roads, and that whenever they had been followed they had shown the way to victory, and that therefore, though there was much in the Central Committee's theses that was hard to digest, he was for giving them complete support, confident that, as Comrades Lenin and Trotsky were in favour of them, they were likely to be right this time, as so often heretofore. But for the most part the speeches were directly concerned with the problem under discussion, and showed a political consciousness which would have been almost incredible three years ago. The Red Army served as a text for many, who said that the methods which had produced that army and its victories over the Whites had been proved successful and should be used to produce a Red Army of Labour and similar victories on the bloodless

50

front against economic disaster. Nobody seemed to question the main idea of compulsory labour. The contest that aroused real bitterness was between the methods of individual and collegiate command. The new proposals led eventually towards individual command, and fears were expressed lest this should mean putting summary powers into the hands of bourgeois specialists, thus nullifying 'workers' control.' In reply, it was pointed out that individual command had proved necessary in the army and had resulted in victory for the revolution. The question was not between specialists and no specialists. Everybody knew that specialists were necessary. The question was how to get the most out of them. Effective political control had secured that bourgeois specialists, old officers, led the army of the Red Republic to victory. The same result could be secured in the factories in the same way. It was pointed out that in one year they had succeeded in training 32,000 Red Commanders, that is to say, officers from the working class itself, and that it was not Utopian to hope and work for a similar output of workmen specialists, technically trained, and therefore themselves qualified for individual command in the factories. Meanwhile there was nothing against the employment of Political Commissars in the factories as formerly in the regiments, to control in other than technical matters the doings of the specialists. On the other hand, it was said that the appointment of Commissars would tend to make Communists unpopular, since inevitably in many cases they would have to support the specialists against the workmen, and that the collegiate system made the workmen feel that they were actually the masters, and so gave possibilities of enthusiastic work not otherwise obtainable. This last point was hotly challenged. It was said that collegiate control meant little in effect, except waste of time and efficiency, because at worst work was delayed by disputes and at best the work men members of the college merely countersigned the orders decided upon by the specialists. The enthusiastic work was said to be a fairy story. If it were really to be found then there would be no need for a conference to discover how to get it.

The most serious opposition, or at least the most serious

argument put forward, for there was less opposition than actual discussion, came from some of the representatives of the trades unionists. A good deal was said about the position of the trades unions in a socialist state. There was general recognition that since the trades unions themselves controlled the conditions of labour and wages, the whole of their old work of organising strikes against capitalists had ceased to have any meaning, since to strike now would be to strike against their own decisions. At the same time, certain tendencies to syndicalism were still in existence, tendencies which might well lead to conflict between different unions, so that, for example, the match makers or the metal workers might wish to strike a bargain with the state, as of one country with another, and this might easily lead to a complete collapse of the socialist system.

The one thing on which the speakers were in complete agreement was the absolute need of an effort in industry equal to, if not greater than, the effort made in the army. I thought it significant that in many of the speeches the importance of this effort was urged as the only possible means of retaining the support of the peasants. There was a tacit recognition that the conference represented town workers only. Larin, who had belonged to the old school which had grown up with its eyes on the industrial countries of the West and believed that revolution could be brought about by the town workers alone, that it was exclusively their affair, and that all else was of minor importance, unguardedly spoke of the peasant as 'our neighbour'. In Jaroslavl, country and town are too near to allow the main problem of the revolution to be thus easily dismissed. It was instantly pointed out that the relation was much more intimate, and that, even if it were only 'neighbourly', peace could not long be preserved if it were continually necessary for one neighbour to steal the chickens of the other. These town workers of a district for the most part agricultural were very sure that the most urgent of all tasks was to raise industry to the point at which the town would really be able to supply the village with its needs.

Larin and Radek severally summed up and made final attacks on each other's positions, after which Radek's resolution approving the theses of the Central Committee was passed almost unanimously. Larin's four amendments received one, three, seven and one vote apiece. This result was received with cheering throughout the theatre, and showed the importance of such conferences in smoothing the way of the dictatorship, since it had been quite obvious when the discussion began that a very much larger proportion of the delegates than finally voted for his resolution had been more or less in sympathy with Lenin in his opposition to the Central Committee.

There followed elections to the Party conference in Moscow. Rostopchin, the president, read a list which had been submitted by the various *ouezds* in the Jaroslavl Government. They were to send to Moscow 15 delegates with the right to vote, together with another 15 with the right to speak but not to vote. Larin, who had done much work in the district, was mentioned as one of the 15 voting delegates, but he stood up and said that as the conference had so clearly expressed its disagreement with his views, he thought it better to withdraw his candidature. Rostopchin put it to the conference that although they disagreed with Larin, yet it would be as well that he should have the opportunity of stating his views at the All-Russian conference, so that discussion there should be as final and as many-sided as possible. The conference expressed its agreement with this. Larin withdrew his withdrawal, and was presently elected. The main object of these conferences in unifying opinion and in arming Communists with argument for the defence of this unified opinion among the masses was again illustrated when the conference, in leaving it to the *ouezds* to choose for themselves the non-voting delegates, urged them to select wherever possible people who would have the best opportunities of explaining on their return to the district whatever results might be reached in Moscow.

It was now pretty late in the evening, and after another very satisfactory visit to the prison we drove back to the station. Larin, who was very disheartened, realising that he had lost much support in the course of the discussion, settled down to work, and buried himself in a mass of statistics. I prepared to go to bed, but we had hardly got into the car when there was a tap at the door and a couple of railwaymen came in. They explained that a few hundred yards away along the line a concert and entertainment arranged by the Jaroslavl railwaymen was going on, and that their committee, hearing that Radek was at the station, had sent them to ask him to come over and say a few words to them if he was not too tired.

'Come along', said Radek, and we walked in the dark along the railway lines to a big one-story wooden shanty, where an electric lamp lit a great placard, 'Railwaymen's Reading Room'. We went into a packed hall. Every seat was occupied by railway workers and their wives and children. The gangways on either side were full of those who had not found room on the benches. We wriggled and pushed our way through this crowd, who were watching a play staged and acted by the railwaymen themselves, to a side door, through which we climbed up into the wings, and slid across the stage behind the scenery into a tiny dressing room. Here Radek was laid hold of by the Master of the Ceremonies, who, it seemed, was also part editor of a railwaymen's newspaper, and made to give a long account of the present situation of Soviet Russia's foreign affairs. The little box of a room filled to a solid mass as policemen, generals and ladies of the old regime threw off their costumes, and, in their working clothes, plain signalmen and engine-drivers pressed round to listen. When the act ended, one of the railwaymen went to the front of the stage and announced that Radek, who had lately come back after imprisonment in Germany for the cause of revolution, was going to talk to them about the general state of affairs. I saw Radek grin at this forecast of his speech. I understood why, when he began to speak. He led off by a direct and furious onslaught on the railway workers in general, demanding work, work and more work, telling them that as the Red Army had been the vanguard of the revolution hitherto, and had starved and fought and given lives to save those at home from Denikin and Kolchak, so now it was the turn of the railway workers on whose efforts not only the Red Army but also the whole future of Russia depended. He addressed himself to the women, telling them in very bad Russian that unless their men worked superhumanly they would see their babies die from starvation next winter. I saw women nudge their husbands as they listened. In stead of giving them a pleasant, interesting sketch of the international position, which, no doubt, was what they had expected, he took the opportunity to tell them exactly how things stood at home. And the amazing thing was that they seemed to be pleased. They listened with extreme attention, wanted to turn out someone who had a sneezing fit at the far end of the hall, and nearly lifted the roof off with cheering when Radek had done. I wondered what sort of reception a man would have who in another country interrupted a play to hammer home truths about the need of work into an audience of working men who had gathered solely for the purpose of legitimate recreation. It was not as if he sugared the medicine he gave them. His speech was nothing but demands for discipline and work, coupled with prophecy of disaster in case work and discipline failed. It was delivered like all his speeches, with a strong Polish accent and a steady succession of mistakes in grammar.

As we walked home along the railway lines, half a dozen of the railwaymen pressed around Radek, and almost fought with each other as to whom should walk next to him. And Radek, entirely happy, delighted at his success in giving them a bombshell instead of a bouquet, with one stout fellow on one arm, another on the other, two or three more listening in front and behind, continued rubbing it into them until we reached our wagon, when, after a general handshaking, they disappeared into the night.

Chapter five / The trades unions

Trades unions in Russia are in a different position from that which is common to all other trades unions in the world. In other countries the trades unions are a force with whose opposition the government must reckon. In Russia, the government reckons not on the possible opposition of the trades unions, but on their help for realising its most difficult measures, and for undermining and overwhelming any opposition which those measures may encounter. The trades unions in Russia, instead of being an organisation outside the state, protecting the interests of a class against the governing class, have become a part of the state organisation. Since, during the present period of the revolution the backbone of the state organisation is the Communist Party, the trades unions have come to be practically an extension of the party organisation. This, of course, would be indignantly denied both by trades unionists and Communists. Still, in the preface to the All-Russian trades Union Reports for 1919, Glebov, one of the best known trades union leaders whom I remember in the spring of last year objecting to the use of bourgeois specialists in their proper places, admits as much in the following muddle-headed statement:

'The base of the proletarian dictatorship is the Communist Party, which in general directs all the political and economic work of the state, leaning, first of all, on the Soviets as on the more revolutionary arm of dictatorship of the proletariat, and secondly on the trades unions, as organisations which economically unite the proletariat of factory and workshop as the vanguard of the revolution, and as organisations of the new socialistic construction of state. Thus the trades unions must be considered as a base of the Soviet state, as an organic form complementary to the other forms of the proletarian dictatorship.' The first and last sentence in this constitute an admission of what I have just said.

Trades unionists of other countries must regard the fate of their Russian colleagues with horror or with satisfaction, according to their views of events in Russia taken as a whole. If they do not believe that there has been a socialist revolution in Russia, they must regard the present position of the Russian trades unions as the reward of a complete defeat of trade unionism, in which a capitalist government as been able to lay violent hands on the organisation which was protecting the workers against it. If, on the other hand, they believe that there has been a social revolution, so that the class organised in trades unions is now identical with the governing class (of employers, etc.) against which the unions once struggled, then they must regard the present position as a natural and satisfactory result of victory.

When I was in Moscow in the spring of 1920, the Russian trades unions received a telegram from the trades union congress at Amsterdam, a telegram which admirably illustrated the impossibility of separating judgment of the present position of the unions from judgments of the Russian revolution as a whole. It encouraged the unions 'in their struggle' and promised support in that struggle. The Communists immediately asked, 'What struggle? Against the capitalist system in Russia which does not exist? Or against capitalist systems outside Russia?' They said that either the telegram meant this latter only, or it meant that its writers did not believe that there had been a social revolution in Russia. The point is arguable. If one believes that revolution is an impossibility, one can reason from that belief and say that in spite of certain upheavals in Russia, the fundamental arrangement of society is the same there as in other countries, so that the position of the trades unions there must be the same, and, as in other countries, they must be still engaged in augmenting the dinners of their members at the expense of the dinners of the capitalists which, in the long run (if that were possible) they would abolish. If, on the other hand, one believes that social revolution has actually occurred, to speak of trades unions continuing the struggle in which they conquered something like three years ago, is to urge them to a sterile fanaticism which has been neatly described by Professor Santayana as a redoubling of your effort when you have forgotten your aim.

It is probably true that the aim of the trades unions was more clearly defined in Russia than elsewhere. In England, during the greater part of their history, the trades unions have not been in conscious opposition to the state. In Russia this position was forced on the trades unions almost before they had had time to get to work. They were born, so to speak, with red flags in their hands. They grew up under circumstances of extreme difficulty and persecution. From 1905 on they were in decided opposition to the existing system and were revolutionary rather than merely mitigatory organisations.

Before 1905 they were little more than associations for mutual help, very weak, spending most of their energies in self-preservation from the police, and hiding their character as class organisations by electing more or less liberal managers and employers as 'honorary members'. 1905, however, settled their revolutionary character. In September of that year there was a conference at Moscow, where it was decided to call an All-Russian Trades Union Congress. Reaction in Russia made this impossible, and the most they could do was to have another small conference in February 1906, which, however, defined their object as that of creating a general trade union movement organised on All-Russian lines. The temper of the trades unions then, and the condition of the country at that time, may be judged from the fact that although they were merely working for the right to form unions, the right to strike, etc., they passed the following significant resolution: 'Neither from the present government *nor from the future State Duma* can be expected realisation of freedom of coalition . . . This conference considers the legalisation of the trades unions under present conditions absolutely impossible.' The conference was right. For 12 years after that there were no trades unions conferences in Russia. Not until June 1917, three months after the March Revolution, was the third trade union conference able to meet. This conference reaffirmed the revolutionary character of the Russian trades unions.

At that time the dominant party in the Soviets was that of the Mensheviks, who were opposed to the formation of a Soviet government, and were supporting the provisional Cabinet of Kerensky. The trades unions were actually at that time more revolutionary than the Soviets. This third Conference passed several resolutions, which show clearly enough that the present position of the unions has not been brought about by any violence of the Communists from without, but was definitely promised by tendencies inside the unions at a time when the Communists were probably the least authoritative party in Russia. This conference of June 1917 resolved that the trades unions should not only 'remain militant class organisations . . . but . . . should support the activities of the Soviets of soldiers and workers' deputies.' They thus clearly showed on which side they stood in the struggle then proceeding. Nor was this all. They also, though the Mensheviks were still the dominant party, resolved on that system of internal organisations and grouping which has been actually realised under the Communists. I quote again from the resolution of this conference:

'The evolution of the economic struggle demands from the workers such forms of professional organisation, as, basing themselves on the connection between various groups of workers in the process of production, should unite within a general organisation, and under general leadership, as large masses of workers as possible occupied in enterprises of the same kind, or similar professions. With this object the workers should organise themselves professionally, not by shops or trades, but by productions, so that all the workers in a given enterprise should belong to one union, even if

they belong to different professions and even different productions.'
That which was then no more than a design is now an accurate
description of trades union organisation in Russia. Further, much
that at present surprises the foreign inquirer was planned and considered desirable then, before the Communists had won a majority
either in the unions or in the Soviet. Thus this same third conference resolved that 'in the interests of greater efficiency and success
in the economic struggle, a professional organisation should be built
on the principle of *democratic centralism*, assuring to every member a
share in the affairs of the organisation and, at the same time, obtaining unity in the leadership of the struggle.' Finally, 'Unity in the
direction (leadership) of the economic struggle demands unity in
the exchequer of the trades unions.'

The point I wish to make in thus illustrating the pre-
Communist tendencies of the Russian trades unions is not simply
that if their present position is undesirable they have only themselves to thank for it, but in Russia the trade union movement
before the October revolution was working in the direction of such
a revolution, that the events of October represented something like
a trade union victory, so that the present position of the unions as
part of the organisation defending that victory, as part of the system
of government set up by that revolution, is logical and was to be
expected. I have illustrated this from resolutions, because these give
statements in words easily comparable with what has come to pass.
It would be equally easy to point to deeds instead of words if we
need more forcible though less accurate illustrations.

Thus, at the time of the Moscow congress the Soviets, then
Mensheviks, who were represented at the congress (the object of
the congress was to whip up support for the coalition government)
were against strikes of protest. The trades unions took a point of
view nearer that of the Bolsheviks, and the strikes in Moscow took
place in spite of the Soviets. After the Kornilov affair, when the
Mensheviks were still struggling for coalition with the bourgeois
parties, the trades unions quite definitely took the Bolshevik standpoint. At the so-called Democratic Conference, intended as a sort

of lifebelt for the sinking Provisional government, only eight of the trades union delegates voted for a continuance of the coalition, whereas 73 voted against.

This consciously revolutionary character throughout their much shorter existence has distinguished Russian from, for example, English trades unions. It has set their course for them.

In October 1917, they got the revolution for which they had been asking since March. Since then, one congress after another has illustrated the natural and inevitable development of trades unions inside a revolutionary state which, like most if not all revolutionary states, is attacked simultaneously by hostile armies from without and by economic paralysis from within. The excited and lighthearted trades unionists of three years ago, who believed that the mere decreeing of workers' control would bring all difficulties automatically to an end, are now unrecognisable. We have seen illusion after illusion scraped from them by the pumice stone of experience, while the appalling state of the industries which they now largely control, and the ruin of the country in which they attained that control, have forced them to alter their immediate aims to meet immediate dangers, and have accelerated the process of adaptation made inevitable by their victory.

The process of adaptation has had the natural result of producing new internal cleavages. Change after change in the programme and theory of the Russian trades unionists has been due to the pressure of life itself, to the urgency of struggling against the worsening of conditions already almost unbearable. It is perfectly natural that those unions which hold back from adaptation and resent the changes are precisely those which, like that of the printers, are not intimately concerned in any productive process, are consequently outside the central struggle, and, while feeling the discomforts of change, do not feel its need.

The opposition inside the productive trades unions is of two kinds. There is the opposition, which is of merely psychological interest, of old trades union leaders who have always thought of themselves as in opposition to the government, and feel themselves like watches without mainsprings in their new role of government supporters. These are men in whom a natural intellectual stiffness makes difficult the complete change of front which was the logical result of the revolution for which they had been working. But beside that there is a much more interesting opposition based on political considerations. The Menshevik standpoint is one of disbelief in the permanence of the revolution, or rather in the permanence of the victory of the town workers. They point to the divergence in interests between the town and country populations, and are convinced that sooner or later the peasants will alter the government to suit themselves, when, once more, it will be a government against which the town workers will have to defend their interests. The Mensheviks object to the identification of the trades unions with the government apparatus on the ground that when this change which they expect comes about, the trade union movement will be so far emasculated as to be incapable of defending the town workers against the peasants who will then be the ruling class. Thus they attack the present trades Union leaders for being directly influenced by the government in fixing the rate of wages, on the ground that this establishes a precedent from which, when the change comes, it will be difficult to break away. The Communists answer them by insisting that it is to everybody's interest to pull Russia through the crisis, and that if the trades unions were for such academic reasons to insist on their complete independence instead of in every possible way collaborating with the government, they would be not only increasing the difficulties of the revolution in its economic crisis, but actually hastening that change which the Mensheviks, though they regard it as inevitable, cannot be supposed to desire. This Menshevik opposition is strongest in the Ukraine. Its strength may be judged from the figures of the congress in Moscow this spring, when, of 1,300 delegates, over 1,000 were Communists or sympathisers with them, 63 were Mensheviks and 200 were non-party, the bulk of whom, I fancy, on this point would agree with the Mensheviks.

But apart from opposition to the statification of the trades unions, there is a cleavage cutting across the Communist Party itself and uniting in opinion, though not in voting, the Mensheviks and a section of their Communist opponents. This cleavage is over the question of workers' control. Most of those who, before the revolution, looked forward to the workers' control, thought of it as meaning that the actual workers in a given factory would themselves control that factory, just as a board of directors controls a factory under the ordinary capitalist system. The Communists, I think, even today admit the ultimate desirability of this, but insist that the important question is not who shall give the orders, but in whose interest the orders shall be given. I have nowhere found this matter properly thrashed out, though feeling upon it is extremely strong. Everybody whom I asked about it began at once to address me as if I were a public meeting, so that I found it extremely difficult to get from either side a statement not free from electioneering bias. I think, however, that it may be fairly said that all but a few lunatics have abandoned the ideas of 1917, which resulted in the workmen in a factory deposing any technical expert or manager whose orders were in the least irksome to them. These ideas and the miseries and unfairness they caused, the stoppages of work, the managers sewn up in sacks, ducked in ponds and trundled in wheel barrows, have taken their places as curiosities of history. The change in these ideas has been gradual. The first step was the recognition that the state as a whole was interested in the efficiency of each factory, and therefore that the workmen of each factory had no right to arrange things with no thought except for themselves. The committee idea was still strong, and the difficulty was got over by assuring that the technical staff should be represented on the committee, and that the casting vote between workers and technical experts or managers should belong to the central economic organ of the state. The next stage was when the management of a workshop was given a so-called collegiate character, the workmen appointing representatives to share the responsibility of the bourgeois specialist. The bitter controversy now going on concerns the seemingly inevitable transition to a later stage in which, for all practical purposes, the bourgeois specialist will be responsible solely to the state. Many Communists, including some of the best known, while recognising the need of greater efficiency if the revolution is to survive at all, regard this step as definitely retrograde and likely in the long run to make the revolution not worth preserving.*

The enormous importance attached by everybody to this question of individual or collegiate control, may be judged from the fact that at every conference I attended, and every discussion to which I listened, this point, which might seem of minor importance, completely overshadowed the question of industrial conscription which, at least inside the Communist Party, seemed generally taken for granted. It may be taken now as certain that the majority of the Communists are in favour of individual control. They say that the object of workers' control before the revolution was to ensure that factories should be run in the interests of workers as well as of employers. In Russia now there are no employers other than the state as a whole, which is exclusively made up of employees. (I am stating now the view of the majority at the last trades union congress at which I was present, April 1920.) They say that 'workers' control' exists in a larger and more efficient manner than was suggested by the old pre-revolutionary statements on that question. Further, they say that if workers' control ought to be identified with trade union control, the trades unions are certainly supreme in all those matters with which they have chiefly concerned themselves, since they dominate the Commisariat of Labour, are very largely represented on the Supreme Council of Public Economy, and fix the rates of pay for their own members.*

The enormous Communist majority, together with the fact

---

*Thus Rykov, President of the Supreme Council of Public Economy: 'There is a possibility of so constructing a state that in it there will be a ruling caste consisting chiefly of administrative engineers, technicians, etc.; that is, we should get a form of state economy based on a small group of a ruling caste whose privilege in this case would be the management of the workers and peasants.' That criticism of individual control, from a Communist, goes a good deal further than most of the criticism from people avowedly in opposition.

that however much they may quarrel with each other inside the party, the Communists will go to almost any length to avoid breaking the party discipline, means that at present, the resolutions of trades union congresses will not be different from those of Communist congresses on the same subjects. Consequently, the questions which really agitate the members, the actual cleavages inside that Communist majority, are comparatively invisible at a trades union congress. They are fought over with great bitterness, but they are not fought over in the Hall of the unions—once the Club of the Nobility, with on its walls on congress days the hammer and spanner of the engineers, the pestle and trowel of the builders, and so on—but in the Communist congresses in the Kremlin and throughout the country. And, in the problem with which in this book we are mainly concerned, neither the regular business of the unions nor their internal squabbles affect the cardinal fact that in the present crisis the trades unions are chiefly important as part of that organisation of human will with which the Communists are attempting to arrest the steady progress of Russia's economic ruin. Putting it brutally, so as to offend trades unionists and Communists alike, they are an important part of the Communist system of internal propaganda, and their whole organisation acts as a gigantic megaphone through which the Communist Party makes known its fears, its hopes and its decisions to the great masses of the industrial workers.

---

* The wages of workmen are decided by the trades unions, who draw up 'tariffs' for the whole country, basing their calculations on three criteria: (1) The price of food in the open market in the district where a workman is employed, (2) the price of food supplied by the state on the card system, (3) the quality of the workman. This last is decided by a special section of the Factory Committee, which in each factory is an organ of the trades unions.

Chapter six / The propaganda trains

When I crossed the Russian front in October 1919, the first thing I noticed in peasants' cottages, in the villages, in the little town where I took the railway to Moscow, in every railway station along the line, was the elaborate pictorial propaganda concerned with the war. There were posters showing Denikin standing straddled over Russia's coal, while the factory chimneys were smokeless and the engines idle in the yards, with the simplest wording to show why it was necessary to beat Denikin in order to get coal; there were posters illustrating the treatment of the peasants by the Whites; posters against desertion; posters illustrating the Russian struggle against the rest of the world, showing a workman, a peasant, a sailor and a soldier fighting in self defence against an enormous capitalistic Hydra. There were also—and this I took as a sign of what might be—posters encouraging the sowing of corn, and posters explaining in simple pictures improved methods of agriculture. Our own recruiting propaganda during the war, good as that was, was never developed to such a point of excellence, and knowing the general slowness with which the Russian centre reacts on its periphery, I was amazed not only at the actual posters, but at their efficient distribution thus far from Moscow.

I have had an opportunity of seeing two of the propaganda trains, the object of which is to reduce the size of Russia politically by bringing Moscow to the front and to the out-of-the-way districts, and so to lessen the difficulty of obtaining that general unity of purpose which it is the object of propaganda to produce. The fact that there is some hope that in the near future the whole of this apparatus may be turned over to the propaganda of industry makes it perhaps worthwhile to describe these trains in detail.

Russia, for purposes of this internal propaganda, is divided into five sections, and each section has its own train, prepared for the particular political ends of the section it serves, bearing its own name, carrying its regular crew—a propaganda unit, as corporate as the crew of a ship. The five trains at present in existence are the 'Lenin', the 'Sverdlov', the 'October Revolution', the 'Red East', which is now in Turkestan, and the 'Red Cossack', which, ready to start for Rostov and the Don, was standing in the sidings at the Kursk station, together with the 'Lenin', returned for refitting and painting.

Burov, the organiser of these trains, a ruddy, enthusiastic little man in a patched leather coat and breeches, took a party of foreigners—a Swede, a Norwegian, two Czechs, a German and myself—to visit his trains, together with Radek, in the hope that Radek would induce Lenin to visit them, in which case Lenin would be cinematographed for the delight of the villagers, and possibly the Central Committee would, if Lenin were interested, lend them more lively support.

We walked along the 'Lenin' first, at Burov's special request. Burov, it seems, had only recently escaped from what he considered a bitter affliction due to the Department of Proletarian Culture, who, in the beginning, for the decoration of his trains, had delivered him bound hand and foot to a number of Futurists. For that reason he wanted us to see the 'Lenin' first, in order that we might compare it with the result of his emancipation, the 'Red Cossack', painted when the artists 'had been brought under proper control'. The 'Lenin' had been painted a year and a half ago when, as fading hoarding in the streets of Moscow still testify, revolutionary art was dominated by the Futurist movement. Every carriage is decorated with most striking but not very comprehensible pictures in the brightest colours, and the proletariat was called upon to enjoy what the pre-revolutionary artistic public had for the most part failed to understand. Its pictures are 'art for art's sake', and cannot have done more than astonish, and perhaps terrify, the peasants and the workmen of the country towns who had the luck to see them. The 'Red Cossack' is quite different. As Burov put it with deep satisfaction, 'At first we were in the artists' hands, and now the artists are in our hands', a sentence suggesting the most horrible possibilities of official art under socialism, although, of course, bad art flourishes pretty well even under other systems.

I inquired exactly how Burov and his friends kept the artists in the right way, and received the fullest explanation. The political section of the organisation works out the main idea and aim for each picture, which covers the whole side of a wagon. The idea is then submitted to a 'collective' of artists, who are jointly responsible for its realisation in paint. The artists compete with each other for a prize which is awarded for the best design, the judges being the artists themselves. It is the art of the poster, art with a purpose of the most definite kind. The result is sometimes amusing, interesting, startling, which, whatever else it does, hammers home a plain idea.

Thus the picture on the side of the wagon is divided into two sections. On the left is a representation of the peasants and workmen of the Soviet Republic. Under it are the words, 'Let us not find ourselves again . . .' and then, in gigantic lettering under the right-hand section of the picture, '. . . in the HEAVEN OF THE WHITES'. This heaven is shown by an epauletted officer hitting a soldier in the face, as was done in the Tsar's army and in at least one army of the counter-revolutionaries, and workmen tied to stakes, as was done by the Whites in certain towns in the south. Then another wagon illustrating the methods of Tsardom, with a state vodka shop selling its wares to wretched folk, who, when drunk on the state vodka, are flogged by the state police. Then there is a wagon showing the different Cossacks—of the Don,

Terek, Kuban, Ural—riding in pairs. The Cossack infantry is represented on the other side of this wagon. On another wagon is a very jolly picture of Stenka Razin in his boat with little old-fashioned brass cannon, rowing up the river. Underneath is written the words: 'I attack only the rich, with the poor I divide everything'. On one side are the poor folk running from their huts to join him, on the other, the rich folk firing at his from their castle. One wagon is treated purely decoratively, with a broad, effective, characteristically south Russian design, framing a huge inscription to the effect that the Cossacks need not fear that the Soviet Republic will interfere with their religion, since under its regime every man is to be free to believe exactly what he likes.

Then there is an entertaining wagon showing Kolchak sitting inside a fence in Siberia with a Red soldier on guard, Yudenitch sitting in a little circle with a signpost to show it is Estonia, and Denikin running at full speed to the asylum indicated by another signpost on which is the crescent of the Turkish Empire. Another lively picture shows the young Cossack girls learning to read, with a most realistic old Cossack woman telling them they had better not. But there is no point in describing every wagon. There are 16 wagons in the 'Red Cossack', and every one is painted all over on both sides.

The internal arrangements of the train are sufficient proof that Russians are capable of organisation if they set their minds to it. We went through it wagon by wagon. One wagon contains a wireless telegraphy station capable of receiving news from such distant stations as those of Carnarvon or Lyons.

Another is fitted up as a newspaper office, with a mechanical press capable of printing an edition of 15,000 daily, so that the district served by the train, however out of the way, gets its news simultaneously with Moscow, many days sometimes before the belated Izvestia or Pravda finds its way to them. And with its latest news it gets its latest propaganda, and in order to get the one it cannot help getting the other. Next door to that there is a cinematograph wagon, with benches to seat about 150 persons. But indoor performances are only given to children, who must come during the daytime, or in summer when the evenings are too light to permit an open-air performance. In the ordinary way, at night, a great screen is fixed up in the open. There is a special hole cut in the side of the wagon, and through this the cinematograph throws its picture on the great screen outside, so that several thousands can see it at once. The enthusiastic Burov insisted on working through a couple of films for us, showing the Communist boy scouts in their country camps, children's meetings in Petrograd, and the big demonstrations of 1919 in honour of the Third International. He was extremely disappointed that Radek, being in a hurry, refused to wait for a performance of 'The Father and his Son', a drama which, he assured us with tears in his eyes, was so thrilling that we should not regret being late for our appointments if we stayed to witness it. Another wagon is fitted up as an electric power station, lighting the train, working the cinematograph and the printing machine, etc. Then there is a clean little kitchen and dining room, where, before being cinematographed—a horrible experience when one is first quite seriously begged (of course by Burov) to assume an expression of intelligent interest—we had soup, a plate of meat and cabbage, and tea. Then there is a wagon book shop, where, while customers buy books, a gramophone sings the revolutionary songs of Demian Biedny, or speaks with the eloquence of Trotsky or the logic of Lenin. Other wagons are the living rooms of the personnel, divided up according to their duties—political, military, instructional, and so forth. For the train has not merely an agitational purpose. It carries with it a staff to give advice to local authorities, to explain what has not been understood, and so in every way to bring the ideas of the centre quickly to the backwoods of the Republic. It works also in the opposite direction, helping to make the voice of the backwoods heard at Moscow. This is illustrated by a painted pillar-box on one of the wagons, with a slot for letters, labelled, 'For Complaints of Every Kind'. Anybody anywhere who has a grievance, thinks he is being unfairly treated, or has a suggestion to make, can speak with the centre in this way. When the train is on a voyage telegrams announce its arrival beforehand, so that the local Soviets can make full use of its advantages, arranging meetings, cinematograph shows, lectures. It arrives, this amazing picture-train, and proceeds to publish and distribute its newspaper, sell its books (the bookshop, they tell me, is literally stormed at every stopping place), send books and posters for 40 versts on either side of the line in the motor-cars which it carries with it and enliven the population with its cinematograph.

I doubt if a more effective instrument of propaganda has ever been devised. And in considering the question whether or not the Russians will be able after organising their military defence to tackle with similar comparative success the much more difficult problem of industrial rebirth, the existence of such instruments, the use of such propaganda is a factor not to be neglected. In the spring of 1919, when the civil war seemed to be ending, when there was a general belief that the Poles would accept the peace that Russia offered (they ignored this offer, advanced, took Kiev, were driven back to Warsaw, advanced again, and finally agreed to terms which they could have had in March without bloodshed of any kind), two of these propaganda trains were already being repainted with a new purpose. It was hoped that in the near future all five trains would be explaining not the need to fight but the need to work. Undoubtedly, at the first possible moment, the whole machinery of agitation, of posters, of broadsheets and of trains, will be turned over to the task of explaining the government's plans for reconstruction, and the need for extraordinary concentration, now on transport, now on something else, that these plans involve.

Chapter seven / Saturdayings

So much for the organisation, with its Communist Party, its system of meetings and counter-meetings, its adapted trades unions, its infinitely various propaganda, which is doing its best to make headway against ruin. I want now to describe, however briefly, the methods it has adopted in tackling the worst of all Russia's problems—the non-productivity and absolute shortage of labour.

I find a sort of analogy between these methods and those which we used in England in tackling the similar cumulative problem of finding men for war. Just as we did not proceed at once to conscription, but began by a great propaganda of voluntary effort, so the Communists, faced with a need at least equally vital, did not turn at once to industrial conscription. It was understood from the beginning that the Communists themselves were to set an example of hard work, and I dare say a considerable proportion of them did so. Every factory had its little Communist Committee, which was supposed to leaven the factory with enthusiasm, just as similar groups of Communists drafted into the armies in moments of extreme danger did, on more than one occasion, as the non-Communist Commander-in-Chief admits, turn a rout into a stand and snatch victory from what looked perilously like defeat. But this was not enough, arrears of work accumulated, enthusiasm waned, productivity decreased, and some new move was obviously necessary. This first move in the direction of industrial conscription, although no one perceived its tendency at the time, was the inauguration of what have become known as Saturdayings.

Early in 1919, the Central Committee of the Communist Party put out a circular letter calling upon the Communists 'to work revolutionally', to emulate in the rear the heroism of their brothers on the front, pointing out that nothing but the most determined efforts and an increase in the productivity of labour would enable Russia to win through her difficulties of transport, etc. Kolchak, to quote from English newspapers, was 'sweeping on to Moscow' and the situation was pretty threatening. As a direct result of this letter, on May 7, a meeting of Communists in the sub-district of the Moscow-Kazan railway passed a resolution that, in view of the imminent danger to the Republic, Communists and their sympathisers should give up an hour a day of their leisure, and, lumping these hours together, do every Saturday six hours of manual labour; and further, that these Communist Saturdayings should be continued 'until complete victory over Kolchak should be assured.' That decision of a local committee was the actual beginning of a movement which spread all over Russia, and though the complete victory over Kolchak was long ago obtained, is likely to continue so long as Soviet Russia is threatened by anyone else.

The decision was put into effect on May 10 when the first Communist 'saturdaying' in Russia took place on the Moscow-Kazan railway. The commissar of the railway, Communist clerks from the offices, and everyone else who wished to help, marched to work, 182 in all, and put in 1,012 hours of manual labour, in which they finished the repairs of four locomotives and sixteen wagons and loaded and unloaded 9,300 poods of engine and wagon parts and material. It was found that the productivity of labour in loading and unloading shown on this occasion was about 270 percent of the normal, and a similar superiority of effort was shown in the other kinds of work. This example was immediately copied on other railways. The Alexandrovsk railway had its first Saturdaying on May 17. Ninety-eight persons worked for five hours, and here also did two or three times as much as the usual amount of work done in the same number of working hours under ordinary circumstances. One of the workmen, in giving an account of the performance, wrote: 'The comrades explain this by saying that in ordinary times the work was dull and they were sick of it, whereas on this occasion they were working willingly and with excitement. But now it will be shameful in ordinary hours to do less than in the Communist Saturdaying.' The hope implied in this last sentence has not been realised.

In Pravda of June 7 there is an article describing one of these early Saturdayings, which gives a clear picture of the infectious character of the proceedings, telling how people who came out of curiosity to look on found themselves joining in the work, and how a soldier with an accordion, after staring for a long time open-mouthed at these lunatics working on a Saturday afternoon, put up a tune for them on his instrument, and, delighted by their delight, played on while the workers all sang together.

The idea of the Saturdayings spread quickly from railways to factories, and by the middle of the summer reports of similar efforts were coming from all over Russia. Then Lenin became interested, seeing in these Saturdayings not only a special effort in the face of common danger, but an actual beginning of communism and a sign that socialism could bring about a greater productivity of labour than could be obtained under capitalism. He wrote: 'This is a work of great difficulty and requiring much time, but it has begun, and that is the main thing. If in hungry Moscow in the summer of 1919 hungry workmen who have lived through the difficult four years of the imperialistic war, and then the year and a half of the still more difficult civil war, have been able to begin this great work, what will not be its further development when we conquer in the civil war and win peace.' He sees in it a promise of work being done not for the sake of individual gain, but because of a recognition that such work is necessary for the general good, and in all he wrote and spoke about it he emphasised the fact that people worked better and harder when working thus than under any of the conditions (piece-work, premiums for good work, etc.) imposed by the revolution in its desperate attempts to raise the productivity of labour. For this reason alone, he wrote, the first Saturdaying on the Moscow-Kazan railway was an event of historical significance, and not for Russia alone.

Whether Lenin was right or wrong in so thinking, Saturdayings became a regular institution, like Dorcas meetings in Victorian England, like the thousands of collective working parties instituted in England during the war with Germany. It remains to be seen how long they will continue, and if they will survive peace when that comes. At present the most interesting point about them is the large proportion of non-Communists who take an enthusiastic part in them. In many cases not more than 10 percent of Communists are concerned, though they take the initiative in organising the parties and in finding the work to be done. The movement spread like fire in dry grass, like the craze for rollerskating which swept over England some years ago, and efforts were made to control it, so that the fullest use may be made of it. In Moscow it was found worthwhile to set up a special bureau for Saturdayings. Hospitals, railways, factories, or any other concerns working for the public good, notify this bureau that they need the sort of work a 'saturdaying' provides. The bureau informs the local Communists where their services are required, and thus there is a minimum of wasted energy. The local Communists arrange the Saturdayings, and any one else who wants can join in. These Saturdayings are a hardship to none because they are voluntary, except for members of the Communist Party, who are considered to have broken the party discipline if they refrain. But they can avoid the Saturdayings if they wish to by leaving the party. Indeed, Lenin points out that the Saturdayings are likely to assist in clearing out of the party those elements which joined it with the hope of personal gain. He observes that the privileges of a Communist now consist in doing more work than other people in the rear, and, on the front, in having the certainty of being killed when other folk are merely taken prisoners.

The following are a few examples of the sort of work done in the Saturdayings. Briansk hospitals were improperly heated because of lack of the local transport necessary to bring them wood. The Communists organised a Saturdaying, in which 900 persons took part, including military specialists (officers of the old army serving in the new), soldiers, a chief of staff, workmen and women. Having no horses, they harnessed themselves to sledges in groups of ten and brought in the wood required. At Nijni, 800 persons spent their Saturday afternoon in unloading barges. In the Basman district of Moscow there was a gigantic Saturdaying and Sundaying, in which 2,000 persons (in this case all but a little over 500 being Communists) worked in the heavy artillery shops, shifting materials, cleaning tramlines for bringing in fuel, etc. Then there was a Saturdaying the main object of which was a general autumn cleaning of the hospitals for the wounded. One form of Saturdaying for women is going to the hospitals, talking with the wounded and writing letters for them, mending their clothes, washing sheets, etc. The majority of Saturdayings at present are concerned with transport work and with getting and shifting wood, because at the moment these are the chief difficulties. I have talked to many Saturdaying, Communist and non-Communist, and all alike spoke of these Saturday afternoons as of a kind of picnic. On the other hand, I have met Communists who were accustomed to use every kind of ingenuity to find excuses not to take part in them and yet preserve the good opinion of their local committee.

But even if the whole of the Communist Party did actually indulge in a working picnic once a week, it would not suffice to meet Russia's tremendous needs. And, as I pointed out in the chapter specially devoted to the shortage of labour, the most serious need at present is to keep skilled workers at their jobs instead of letting them drift away into non-productive labour. No amount of Saturday picnics could do that, and it was obvious long ago that some other means would have to be devised.

Chapter eight / Industrial conscription

The general principle of industrial conscription is recognised by the Russian Constitution, section ii, chapter v, paragraph 18, which reads: 'The Russian Socialist Federate Soviet Republic recognises that work is an obligation on every citizen of the Republic and proclaims, He who does not work shall not eat.' It is, however, one thing to proclaim such a principle and quite another to put it into action.

On December 17, 1919, the moment it became clear that there was a real possibility that the civil war was drawing to an end, Trotsky allowed the Pravda to print a memorandum of his, consisting of theses or reasoned notes about industrial conscription and the militia system. He points out that a socialist state demands a general plan for the utilisation of all the resources of a country, including its human energy. At the same time, 'in the present economic chaos in which are mingled the broken fragments of the past and the beginnings of the future,' a sudden jump to a complete centralised economy of the country as a whole is impossible. Local initiative, local effort must not be sacrificed for the sake of a plan. At the same time industrial conscription is necessary for complete socialisation. It cannot be regardless of individuality like military conscription. He suggests a subdivision of the state into territorial productive districts which should coincide with the territorial districts of the militia system which shall replace the regular army. Registration of labour is necessary. Necessary also to co-ordinate military and industrial registration. At demobilisation, the cadres of regiments, divisions, etc., should form the fundamental cadres of the militia. Instruction to this end should be included in the courses for workers and peasants who are training to become officers in every district. Transition to the militia system must be carefully and gradually accomplished so as not for a moment to leave the Republic defenceless. While not losing sight of these ultimate aims, it is necessary to decide on immediate needs and to ascertain exactly what amount of labour is necessary for their limited realisation. He suggests the registration of skilled labour in the army. He suggests that a commission under the general direction of the Council of Public Economy should work out a preliminary plan and then hand it over to the War Department, so that means should be worked out for using the military apparatus for this new industrial purpose.

Trotsky's 24 theses or notes must have been written in odd moments, now here now there, on the way from one front to another. They do not form a connected whole. Contradictions jostle each other, and it is quite clear that Trotsky himself had no very definite plan in his head. But his notes annoyed and stimulated so many other people that they did perhaps precisely the work they were intended to do. Pravda printed them with a note from the editor inviting discussion. The *Ekonomitcheskaya Jizn* printed letter after letter from workmen, officials and others, attacking, approving and bringing new suggestions. Larin, Semyashko, Pyatakov, Bukharin all took a hand in the discussion. Larin saw in the proposals the beginning of the end of the revolution, being convinced that authority would pass from the democracy of the workers into the hands of the specialists. Rykov fell upon them with sturdy blows on behalf of the trades unions. All, however, agreed on the one point—that something of the sort was necessary. On December 27 a commission for studying the question of industrial conscription was formed under the presidency of Trotsky. This commission included the People's Commissars, or Ministers, of Labour, Ways of Communication, Supply, Agriculture, War, and the Presidents of the Central Council of the trades unions and of the Supreme Council of Public Economy. They compiled a list of the principal questions before them, and invited anybody interested to bring them suggestions and material for discussion.

But the discussion was not limited to the newspapers or to this commission. The question was discussed in Soviets and conferences of every kind all over the country. Thus, on January 1 an All-Russian conference of local departments for the registration and distribution of labour, after prolonged argument, contributed their views. They pointed out (1) the need of bringing to work numbers of persons who, instead of doing the skilled labour for which they were qualified, were engaged in petty profiteering, etc. (2) that the evaporation of skilled labour into unproductive speculation could at least be checked by the introduction of labour books, which would give some sort of registration of each citizen's work (3) that workmen can be brought back from the villages only for enterprises which are supplied with provisions or are situated in districts where there is plenty ('The opinion that, in the absence of these preliminary conditions, it will be possible to draw workmen from the villages by measures of compulsion or mobilisation is profoundly mistaken') (4) that there should be a census of labour and that the trades unions should be invited to protect the interests of the conscripted. Finally, this conference approved the idea of using the already existing military organisation for carrying out a labour census of the Red Army, and for the turning over to labour of parts of the army during demobilisation, but opposed the idea of giving the military organisation the work of labour registration and industrial conscription in general.

On January 22, 1920, the Central Committee of the Communist Party, after prolonged discussion of Trotsky's rough memorandum, finally adopted and published a new edition of the theses, expanded, altered, almost unrecognisable, a reasoned body of theory entirely different from the bundle of arrows loosed at a venture by Trotsky. They definitely accepted the principle of industrial conscription, pointing out the immediate reasons for it in the fact that Russia cannot look for much help from without and must somehow or other help herself.

Long before the All-Russian Congress of the Communist Party approved the theses of the committee, one form of industrial conscription was already being tested at work. Very early in January, when the discussion on the subject was at its height, the Soviet of the Third Army addressed itself to the Council of Defence of the Republic with an invitation to make use of this army (which at least for the moment had finished its military task) and to experiment with it as a labour army. The Council of Defence agreed. Representatives of the Commissariats of Supply, Agriculture, Ways and Communications, Labour, and the Supreme Council of Public Economy were sent to assist the Army Soviet. The army was proudly renamed The First Revolutionary Army of Labour and began to issue communiqués 'from the Labour fronts', precisely like the communiqués of an army in the field. I translate as a curiosity the first communiqué issued by a Labour Army's Soviet:

'Wood prepared in the districts of Ishim, Karatulskaya, Omutinskaya, Zavodoutovskaya, Yalutorovska, Iushaly, Kamuishlovo, Turinsk, Altynai, Oshtchenkovo, Shadrinsk, 10,180 cubic *sazhins*. Working days, 52,651. Taken to the railway stations, 5,334 cubic *sazhins*. Working days on transport, 22,840. One hundred carpenters detailed for the Kizelovsk mines. One hundred carpenters detailed for the bridge at Ufa. One engineer specialist detailed to the government Council of Public Economy for repairing the mills in Chelyabinsk government. One instructor accountant detailed for auditing the accounts of the economic organisations of Kamuishlovo. Repair of locomotives proceeding in the works at Ekaterinburg. January 20, 1920, midnight.'

The Labour Army's Soviet received a report on the state of the district covered by the army with regard to supply and needed work. By the end of January it had already carried out a labour census of the army, and found that it included over 50,000 labourers, of whom a considerable number were skilled. It decided on a general plan of work in re-establishing industry in the Urals, which suffered severely during the Kolchak regime and the ebb and flow of the civil war, and was considering a suggestion of one of its members that if the scheme worked well the army should be increased to 300,000 men by way of mobilisation.

On January 23 the Council of Defence of the Republic, encouraged to proceed further, decided to make use of the Reserve Army for the improvement of railway transport on the Moscow-Kazan railway, one of the chief arteries between the eastern food districts and Moscow. The main object was to be the re-establishment of through traffic between Moscow and Ekaterinburg and the repair of the Kazan-Ekaterinburg line, which particularly suffered during the war. An attempt was to be made to rebuild the bridge over the Kama River before the ice melted. The Commander of the Reserve Army was appointed Commissar of the eastern part of the Moscow-Kazan railway, retaining his position as Commander of the Army. With a view of co-ordination between the army Soviet and the railway authorities, a member of the Soviet was also appointed Commissar of the railway. On January 25 it was announced that a similar experiment was being made in the Ukraine. A month before the ice broke the first train actually crossed the Kama River by the rebuilt bridge.

By April, 1920, the organisation of industrial conscription had gone far beyond the original labour armies. A decree of February 5 had created a Chief Labour Committee, consisting of five members, Serebryakov and Danilov, from the Commissariat of War; Vasiliev, from the Commissariat of the Interior; Anikst, from the Commissariat of Labour; Dzerzhinsky, from the Commissariat of Internal Affairs. Dzerzhinsky was President, and his appointment was possibly made in the hope that the reputation he had won as President of the Extraordinary Committee for Fighting Counter-Revolution would frighten people into taking this committee seriously. Throughout the country in each government or province similar committees, called troikas, were created, each of three members, one from the Commissariat of War, one from the Department of Labour, one from the Department of Management, in each case from the local Commissariats and departments attached to the local Soviet. Representatives of the Central Statistical Office and its local organs had a right to be present at the meeting of these committees of three, or troikas, but had not the right to vote.

An organisation or a factory requiring labour was to apply to the Labour Department of the local Soviet. This department was supposed to do its best to satisfy demands upon it by voluntary methods first. If these proved insufficient they were to apply to the local troika, or Labour Conscription Committee. If this found that its resources also were insufficient, it was to refer back the request to the Labour Department of the Soviet, which was then to apply to its corresponding department in the government Soviet, which again, first voluntarily and then through the government Committee of Labour Conscription, was to try to satisfy the demands. I fancy the object of this arrangement was to prevent local troikas from referring to government troikas, and so directly to Dzerzhinsky's Central Committee. If they had been able to do this there would obviously have been danger lest a new network of independent and powerful organisations should be formed. Experience with the overgrown and insuppressible Committees for Fighting Counter-Revolution had taught people how serious such a development might be. Such was the main outline of the scheme for conscripting labour. A similar scheme was prepared for superintending and safeguarding labour when conscripted. In every factory of over 1,000 workmen, clerks, etc., there was formed a commission (to distinguish it from the committee) of Industrial Conscription. Smaller factories shared such commissions or were joined for the purpose to larger factories nearby. These commissions were to be under the direct control of a Factory Committee, thereby preventing squabbles between conscripted and non-conscripted labour. They were to be elected for six months, but their members could be withdrawn and replaced by the Factory Committee with the approval of the local troika. These commissions, like the troikas, consisted of three members: one from the management of the factory, one from the Factory Committee, one from the executive committee of the workers. (It was suggested in the directions that one of these should be from the group which 'has been organising Saturdayings, that is to say that he or she should be a Communist). The payment of conscripted workers was to be by production, with prizes for specially good work. Specially bad work was also foreseen in the detailed scheme of possible punishments. Offenders were to be brought before the People's Court (equivalent to the ordinary Civil Court), or, in the case of repeated or very bad offences, were to be brought before the far more dreaded Revolutionary Tribunals. Six categories of possible offences were placed upon the new code:

(1) Avoiding registration, absenteeism, or desertion.

(2) The preparation of false documents or the use of such.

(3) Officials giving false information to facilitate these crimes.

(4) Purposeful damage of instruments or material.

(5) Uneconomical or careless work.

(6) (Probably the most serious of all) Instigation to any of these actions.

The troikas have the right to deal administratively with the less important crimes by deprival of freedom for not more than two weeks. No one can be brought to control except by the Committee for Industrial Conscription on the initiative of the responsible director of work, and with the approval either of the local labour inspection authorities or with that of the local Executive Committee.

No one with the slightest knowledge of Russia will suppose for a moment that this elaborate mechanism sprang suddenly into existence when the decree was signed. On the contrary, all stages of industrial conscription exist simultaneously even today, and it would be possible by going from one part of Russia to another to collect a series of specimens of industrial conscription at every stage of evolution, just as one can collect all stages of man from a baboon to a company director or a Communist. Some of the more primitive kinds of conscription were not among the least successful. For example, at the time (in the spring of this year) when the Russians still hoped that the Poles would be content with the huge area of non-Polish territory they had already seized, the army on the western front was, without any elaborate system of decrees, being turned into a labour army. The work done was at first ordinary country work, mainly wood-cutting. They tried to collaborate with the local troikas, sending help when these committees asked for it. This, however, proved unsatisfactory, so, disregarding the troikas, they organised things for themselves in the whole area immediately behind the front. They divided up the forests into definite districts, and they worked these with soldiers and with deserters. Gradually their work developed, and they built themselves narrow-gauge railways for the transport of the wood. Then they needed wagons and locomotives, and of course immediately found themselves at loggerheads with the railway authorities. Finally, they struck a bargain with the railwaymen, and were allowed to take broken down wagons which the railway people were not in a position to mend. Using such skilled labour as they had, they mended such wagons as were given them, and later made a practice of going to the railway yards and inspecting 'sick' wagons for themselves, taking out any that they thought had a chance even of temporary convalescence. Incidentally they caused great scandal by finding in the Smolensk sidings, among the locomotives and wagons supposed to be sick six good locomotives and 70 perfectly healthy wagons. Then they began to improve the feeding of their army by sending the wood they had cut, in the trains they had mended, to people who wanted wood and could give them provisions. One such train went to Turkestan and back from the army near Smolensk. Their work continually increased, and since they had to remember that they were an army and not merely a sort of nomadic factory, they began themselves to mobilise, exclusively for purposes of work, sections of the civil population. I asked Unshlicht, who had much to do with this organisation, if the peasants came willingly. He said, 'Not very', but added that they did not mind when they found that they got well fed and were given packets of salt as prizes for good work. 'The peasants,' he said, 'do not grumble against the government when it shows the sort of common sense that they themselves can understand. We found that when we said definitely how many carts and men a village must provide, and used them without delay for a definite purpose, they were perfectly satisfied and considered it right and proper. In every case, however, when they saw people being mobilised and sent hither and thither without obvious purpose or result, they became hostile at once.' I asked Unshlicht how it was that their army still contained skilled workmen when one of the objects of industrial conscription was to get the skilled workmen back into the factories?. He said, 'We have an accurate census of the army, and when we get asked for skilled men for such and such a factory, they go there knowing that they still belong to the army.'

That, of course, is the army point of view, and indicates one of the main squabbles which industrial conscription has produced. Trotsky would like the various armies to turn into units of a territorial militia, and at the same time to be an important part of the labour organisation of each district. His opponents do not regard the labour armies as a permanent manifestation, and many of them have declared that the productivity of labour in one of these armies is lower than among ordinary workmen. Both sides produce figures on this point, and Trotsky goes so far as to say that if his opponents are right, then not only are labour armies damned, but also the whole principle of industrial conscription. 'If compulsory labour—independently of social conditions—is unproductive, that is a condemnation not of the labour armies, but of industrial conscription in general, and with it the whole Soviet system, the further development of which is unthinkable except on a basis of universal industrial conscription.'

But, of course, the question of the permanence of the labour armies is not so important as the question of getting the skilled workers back to the factories. The comparative success or failure of soldiers or mobilised peasants in cutting wood is quite irrelevant to this recovery of the vanished workmen. And that recovery will take time, and will be entirely useless unless it is possible to feed these workers when they have been collected. There have already been several attempts, not wholly successful, to collect the straying workers of particular industries. Thus, after the freeing of the oil wells from the Whites, there was a general mobilisation of naphtha workers. Many of these had bolted on or after the arrival of Krasnov or Denikin and gone far into Central Russia, settling where they could. So many months passed before the Red Army definitely pushed the area of civil war beyond the oil wells, that many of these refugees had taken new root and were unwilling to return. I believe that in spite of the mobilisation, the oil wells are still short of men. In the coal districts also, which have passed through similar experiences, the proportion of skilled to unskilled labour is very much smaller than it was before the war. There have also been two mobilisations of railway workers, and these, I think, may be partly responsible for the undoubted improvement notice-able during the year, although this is partly at least due to other things beside conscription. In the first place Trotsky carried with him into the Commisariat of Transport the same ferocious energy that he has shown in the Commissariat of War, together with the prestige that he had gained there. Further, he was well able in the councils of the Republic to defend the needs of his particular com-missariat against those of all others. He was, for example, able to persuade the Communist Party to treat the transport crisis precisely as they had treated each crisis on the front—that is to say, to mobilise great numbers of professed Communists to meet it, giving them in this case the especial task of getting engines mended and, somehow or other, of keeping trains on the move.

But neither the bridges mended and the wood cut by the labour armies, nor the improvement in transport, are any final proof of the success of industrial conscription. Industrial conscrip-tion in the proper sense of the words is impossible until a govern-ment knows what it has to conscript. A beginning was made early in 1919 by the introduction of labour books, showing what work people were doing and where, and serving as industrial passports. But by April these had not yet become general in Moscow, although the less unwieldy population of Petrograd was already supplied with them. It will be long, even if it is possible at all, before any considerable proportion of the people not living in these two cities are registered in this way. A more useful step was taken at the end of August, in a general census throughout Russia. There has been no Russian census since 1897. There was to have been another about the time the war began. It was postponed for obvious reasons. If the Communists carry through the census with even moderate success (they will of course have to meet every kind of evasion), they will at least get some of the information without which industrial conscription on a national scale must be little more than a farce. The census should show them where the skilled workers are. Industrial conscription should enable them to collect them and put them at their own skilled work. Then if, besides transplanting them, they are able to feed them, it will be possible to judge the success or failure of a scheme which in most countries would bring a government toppling to the ground.

In most countries yes, but then the economic crisis has gone further in Russia than in most countries. There is talk of introducing industrial conscription (one year's service) in Germany, where things have not gone nearly so far. And perhaps industrial conscription, like communism itself, becomes a thing of desperate hope only in a country actually face to face with ruin. I remember saying to Trotsky, when talking of possible opposition, that I, as an Englishman, with the tendencies to practical anarchism belonging to my race, should certainly object most strongly if I were mobilised and set to work in a particular factory, and might even want to work in some other factory just for the sake of not doing what I was forced to do. Trotsky replied: 'You would now. But you would not if you had been through a revolution, and seen your country in such a state that only the united, concentrated effort of everybody could possibly re-establish it. That is the position here. Everybody knows the position and that there is no other way.'

Chapter nine / What the Communists
are trying to do in Russia

We come now to the Communist plans for reconstruction. We have seen, in the first two chapters, something of the appalling paralysis which is the most striking factor in the economic problem today. We have seen how Russia is suffering from a lack of things and from a lack of labour, how these two shortages react on each other, and how nothing but a vast improvement in transport can again set in motion what was one of the great food producing machines of the world. We have also seen something of the political organisation which, with far wider ambitions before it, is at present struggling to prevent temporary paralysis from turning into permanent atrophy. We have seen that it consists of a political party so far dominant that the trades unions and all that is articulate in the country may be considered as part of a machinery of propaganda for getting those things done which that political party considers should be done. In a country fighting, literally, for its life, no man can call his soul his own, and we have seen how this fact—a fact that has become obvious again and again in the history of the world, whenever a nation has had its back to the wall—is expressed in Russia in terms of industrial conscription; in measures, that is to say, which would be impossible in any country not reduced to such extremities; in measures which may prove to be the inevitable accompaniment of national crisis, when such crisis is economic rather than military. Let us now see what the Russians, with that machinery at their disposal, are trying to do.

It is obvious that, since this machinery is dominated by a political party, it will be impossible to understand the Russian plans without understanding that particular political party's estimate of the situation in general. It is obvious that the Communists' plans for Russia must be largely affected by their view of Europe as a whole. This view is gloomy in the extreme. The Communists believe that Europe is steadily shaking itself to pieces. They believe that this process has already gone so far that, even given goodwill on the part of European governments, the manufacturers of Western countries are already incapable of supplying them with all the things which Russia was importing before the war, still less make up the enormous arrears which have resulted from six years of blockade. They do not agree with M. Clemenceau that 'revolution is a disease attacking defeated countries only.' Or, to put it as I have heard it stated in Moscow, they believe that President Wilson's aspiration towards a peace in which there should be neither conqueror nor conquered has been at least partially realised in the sense that every country ended the struggle economically defeated, with the possible exception of America, whose signature, after all, is still to be ratified. They believe that even in seemingly prosperous countries the seeds of economic disaster are already fertilised. They think that the demands of labour will become greater and more difficult to fulfil until at last they become incompatible with a continuance of the capitalist system. They think that strike after strike, irrespective of whether it is successful or not, will gradually widen the cracks and flaws already apparent in the damaged economic structure of Western Europe. They believe that conflicting interests will involve our nations in new national wars, and that each of these will deepen the cleavage between capital and labour. They think that even if exhaustion makes mutual warfare on a large scale impossible, these conflicting interests will produce such economic conflicts, such refusals of co-operation, as will turn exhaustion to despair. They believe, to put it briefly, that Russia has passed through the worst stages of a process to which every country in Europe will be submitted in turn by its desperate and embittered inhabitants.

We may disagree with them, but we shall not understand them if we refuse to take that belief into account. If, as they imagine, the next five years are to be years of disturbance and growing revolution, Russia will get very little from abroad. If, for example, there is to be a serious struggle in England, Russia will get practically nothing. They not only believe that these things are going to be, but make the logical deductions as to the effect of such disturbances on their own chances of importing what they need. For example, Lenin said to me that 'the shock of revolution in England would ensure the final defeat of capitalism,' but he said at the same time that it would be felt at once throughout the world and cause such reverberations as would paralyse industry everywhere. And that is why, although Russia is an agricultural country, the Communists' plans for her reconstruction are concerned first of all not with agriculture, but with industry. In their schemes for the future of the world, Russia's part is that of a gigantic farm, but in their schemes for the immediate future of Russia, their eyes are fixed continually on the nearer object of making her so far self-supporting that, even if Western Europe is unable to help them, they may be able to crawl out of their economic difficulties, as Krassin put it to me before he left Moscow, 'if necessary on all fours, but somehow or other, crawl out.'

Some idea of the larger ambitions of the Communists with regard to the development of Russia are given in a conversation with Rykov, which follows this chapter. The most important characteristic of them is that they are ambitions which cannot but find an echo in Russians of any kind, quite regardless of their political convictions. The old anomalies of Russian industry, for example, the distances of the industrial districts from their sources of fuel and raw material are to be done away with. These anomalies were largely due to historical accidents, such as the caprice of Peter the Great, and not to any economic reasons. The revolution, destructive as it has been, has at least cleaned the slate and made it possible, if it is possible to rebuild at all, to rebuild Russia on foundations laid by common sense. It may be said that the Communists are merely doing flamboyantly and with a lot of flag-waving, what any other Russian government would be doing in its place. And without the flamboyance and the flag-waving, it is doubtful whether in an exhausted country it would be possible to get anything done at all. The result of this is that in their work of economic reconstruction the Communists get the support of most of the best engineers and other technicians in the country, men who take no interest whatsoever in the ideas of Karl Marx, but have a professional interest in doing the best they can with their knowledge, and a patriotic satisfaction in using that knowledge for Russia. These men, caring not at all about communism, want to make Russia once more a comfortably habitable place, no matter under what government. Their attitude is precisely comparable to that of the officers of the old army who have contributed so much to the success of the new. These officers were not Communists, but they disliked civil war, and fought to put an end to it. As Sergei Kamenev, the Commander-in-Chief, and not a Communist, said to me, 'I have not looked on the civil war as on a struggle between two political ideas, for the Whites have no definitive idea. I have considered it simply as a struggle between the Russian government and a number of mutineers.' Precisely so do these bourgeois technicians now working throughout Russia regard the task before them. It will be small satisfaction to them if famine makes the position of any government impossible. For them the struggle is quite simply a struggle between Russia and the economic forces tending towards a complete collapse of civilization.

The Communists have thus practically the whole intelligence of the country to help them in their task of reconstruction, or of salvage. But the educated classes alone cannot save a nation. Muscle is wanted besides brain, and the great bulk of those who can provide muscle are difficult to move to enthusiasm by any broad schemes of economic rearrangement that do not promise immediate improvement in their own material conditions. Industrial conscription cannot be enforced in Russia unless there is among the conscripted themselves an understanding, although a resentful understanding, of its necessity. The Russians have not got an army of Martians to enforce effort on an alien people. The army and the people are one. 'We are bound to admit,' says Trotsky, 'that no wide industrial mobilisation will succeed, if we do not capture all that is honourable, spiritual in the peasant working masses in explaining our plan.' And the plan that he referred to was not the grandiose (but obviously sensible) plan for the eventual electrification of all Russia, but a programme of the struggle before them in actually getting their feet clear of the morass of industrial decay in which they are at present involved. Such a programme has actually been decided upon—a programme the definite object of which is to reconcile the workers to work not simply hand to mouth, each for himself, but to concerntrate first on those labours which will eventually bring their reward in making other labours easier and improving the position as a whole.

Early in 1920 a comparatively unknown Bolshevik called Gusev, to whom nobody had attributed any particular intelligence, wrote, while busy on the staff of an army on the south east front, which was at the time being used partly as a labour army, a pamphlet which has had an extraordinary influence in getting such a programme drawn up. The pamphlet is based on Gusev's personal observations both of a labour army at work and of the attitude of the peasants towards industrial conscription. It was extremely frank, and contained so much that might have been used by hostile critics, that it was not published in the ordinary way but printed at the army press on the Caucasian front and issued exclusively to members of the Communist Party. I got hold of a copy of this pamphlet through a friend. It is called Urgent Questions of Economic Construction. Gusev sets out in detail the sort of opposition he had met, and says: 'The Anarchists, Social Revolutionaries and Mensheviks have a clear, simple economic plan which the great masses can understand: "Go about your own business and work freely for yourself in your own place." They have a criticism of labour mobilisations equally clear for the masses. They say to them, "They are putting Simeon in Peter's place, and Peter in Simeon's. They are sending the men of Saratov to dig the ground in the government of Stavropol, and the Stavropol men to the Saratov government for the same purpose." Then besides that there is "non-party" criticism: "When it is time to sow they will be shifting muck, and when it is time to reap they will be told to cut timber." That is a particularly clear expression of the peasants' disbelief in our ability to draw up a proper economic plan. This belief is clearly at the bottom of such questions as, "Comrade Gusev, have you ever done any ploughing?" or "Comrade Orator, do you know anything about peasant work?" Disbelief in the townsman who understands nothing about peasants is natural to the peasant, and we shall have to conquer it, to get through it, to get rid of it by showing the peasant, with a clear plan in our hands that he can understand, that we are not altogether fools in this matter and that we understand more than he does.' He then sets out the argument which he himself had found successful in persuading the peasants to do things the reward for which would not be obvious the moment they were done. He says, 'I compared our state economy to a colossal building with scores of stories and tens of thousands of rooms. The whole building has been half smashed; in places the roof has tumbled down, the beams have rotted, the ceilings are tumbling, the drains and water pipes are burst, the stoves are falling to pieces, the partitions are shattered, and, finally, the walls and foundations are unsafe and the whole building is threatened with collapse. I asked, how must one set about the repair of this building? With what kind of economic plan? To this question inhabitants of different stories, and even of different rooms on one and the same story, will reply variously. Those who live on the top floor will shout that the rafters are rotten and the roof falling; that it is impossible to live there any longer, and that it is immediately necessary, first of all, to put up new beams and to repair the roof. And from their point of view they will be perfectly right. Certainly it is not possible to live any longer on that floor. Certainly the repair of the roof is necessary. The inhabitants of one of the lower stories in which the water pipes have burst will cry out that it is impossible to live without water, and therefore, first of all, the water pipes must be mended. And they from their point of view, will be perfectly right, since it certainly is impossible to live without water. The inhabitants of the floor where the stoves have fallen to pieces will insist on an immediate mending of the stoves, since they and their children are dying of cold because there is nothing on which they can hot up water or boil *kasha* for the children; and they, too, will be quite right. But in spite of all these just demands, which arrive in thousands from all sides, it is impossible to forget the most important of all, that the foundation is shattered and that the building is threatened with a collapse, which will bury all the inhabitants of the house together and that, therefore, the *only* immediate task is the strengthening of the foundation and the walls. Extraordinary firmness, extraordinary courage is necessary, not only not to listen to the cries and groans of old men, women, children and sick, coming from every floor, but also to decide on taking from the inhabitants of all floors the instruments and materials necessary for the strengthening of the foundations and walls, and to force them to leave their corners and hearths, which they are doing the best they can to make habitable, in order to drive them to work on the strengthening of the walls and foundations.'

Gusev's main idea was that the Communists were asking new sacrifices from a weary and exhausted people, that without such sacrifices these people would presently find themselves in even worse conditions, and that, to persuade them to make the effort necessary to save themselves, it was necessary to have a perfectly clear and easily understandable plan which could be dinned into the whole nation and silence the criticism of all possible opponents. Copies of his little book came to Moscow. Lenin read it and caused excruciating jealousy in the minds of several other Communists, who had also been trying to find the philosopher's stone that should turn discouragement into hope, by singling out Gusev for his special praise and insisting that his plans should be fully discussed at the Supreme Council in the Kremlin. Trotsky followed Lenin's lead, and in the end a general programme for Russian reconstruction was drawn up, differing only slightly from that which Gusev had proposed. I give this scheme in Trotsky's words, because they are a little fuller than those of others, and knowledge of this plan will explain not only what the Communists are trying to do in Russia, but what they would like to get from us today and what they will want to get tomorrow. Trotsky says:

'The fundamental task at this moment is improvement in the condition of our transport, prevention of its further deterioration and preparation of the most elementary stores of food, raw material and fuel. The whole of the first period of our reconstruction will be completely occupied in the concentration of labour on the solution of these problems, which is a condition of further progress.

'The second period (it will be difficult to say now whether it will be measured in months or years, since that depends on many factors beginning with the international situation and ending with the unanimity or the lack of it in our own party) will be a period occupied in the building of machines in the interest of transport, and the getting of raw materials and provisions.

'The third period will be occupied in building machinery, with a view to the production of articles in general demand, and, finally, the fourth period will be that in which we are able to produce these articles.'

Does it not occur, even to the most casual reader, that there is very little politics in that programme, and that, no matter what kind of government should be in Russia, it would have to endorse that programme word for word? I would ask any who doubt this to turn again to my first two chapters describing the nature of the economic crisis in Russia, and to remind themselves how not only the lack of things but the lack of men is intimately connected with the lack of transport, which keeps labourers ill fed, factories ill supplied with material, and in this way keeps the towns incapable of supplying the needs of the country, with the result that the country is most unwilling to supply the needs of the town. No Russian government unwilling to allow Russia to subside definitely to a lower level of civilization can do otherwise than to concentrate upon the improvement of transport. Labour in Russia must be used first of all for that, in order to increase its own productivity. And, if purchase of help from abroad is to be allowed, Russia must 'control' the outflow of her limited assets, so that, by healing transport first of all, she may increase her power of making new assets. She must spend in such a way as eventually to increase her power of spending. She must prevent the frittering away of her small purse on things which, profitable to the vendor and doubtless desirable by the purchaser, satisfy only individual needs and do not raise the producing power of the community as a whole.

Chapter ten / Rykov on the economic plans and on the transformation of the Communist Party

Alexei Rykov, the President of the Supreme Council of Public Economy, is one of the hardest worked men in Russia, and the only time I was able to have a long talk with him (although more than once he snatched moments to answer particular questions) was on a holiday, when the old Siberian Hotel, now the offices of the council, was deserted, and I walked through empty corridors until I found the President and his secretary at work as usual.

After telling of the building of the new railway from Alexandrovsk Gai to the Emba, the prospects of developing the oil industry in that district, the relative values of those deposits and of those at Baku, and the possible decreasing significance of Baku in Russian industry generally, we passed to broader perspectives. I asked him what he thought of the relations between agriculture and industry in Russia, and supposed that he did not imagine that Russia would ever become a great industrial country. His answer was characteristic of the tremendous hopes that nerve these people in their almost impossible task, and I set it down as nearly as I can in his own words. For him, of course, the economic problem was the first, and he spoke of it as the director of a huge trust might have spoken. But, as he passed on to talk of what he thought would result from the Communist method of tackling that problem, and spoke of the eventual disappearance of political parties, I felt I was trying to read a kind of palimpsest of the Economist and News from Nowhere, or listening to a strange compound of William Morris and, for example, Sir Eric Geddes. He said:

'We may have to wait a long time before the inevitable arrives and there is a Supreme Economic Council dealing with Europe as with a single economic whole. If that should come about we should, of course, from the very nature of our country, be called upon in the first place to provide food for Europe, while enormously improving our agriculture, working on a larger and larger scale, using mechanical ploughs and tractors, which would be supplied us by the West. But in the meantime we have to face the fact that events may cause us to be, for all practical purposes, in a state of blockade for perhaps a score of years, and, so far as we can, we must be ready to depend on ourselves alone. For example, we want mechanical ploughs which could be procured abroad. We have had to start making them ourselves. The first electric plough made in Russia and used in Russia started work last year, and this year we shall have a number of such ploughs made in our country, not because it is economic so to make them, but because we could get them in no other way. In so far as is possible, we shall have to make ourselves self-supporting, so as somehow or other to get along even if the blockade, formal or perhaps willy-nilly (imposed by the inability of the West to supply us), compels us to postpone co-operation with the rest of Europe. Every day of such postponement is one in which the resources of Europe are not being used in the most efficient manner to supply the needs not only of our own country but of all.'

I referred to what he had told me last year about the intended electrification of Moscow by a station using turf fuel.

'That,' he said, 'is one of the plans which, in spite of the war, has gone a very long way towards completion. We have built the station in the Ryezan government, on the Shudul peat mosses, about 110 *versts* from Moscow. Before the end of May that station should be actually at work. (It was completed, opened and partially destroyed by a gigantic fire). Another station at Kashira in the Tula government (on the Oka), using the small coal produced in the Moscow coalfields, will be at work before the autumn. This year similar stations are being built at Ivano-Voznesensk and at Nijni-Novgorod. Also, with a view to making the most economic use of what we already possess, we have finished both in Petrograd and in Moscow a general unification of all the private power stations, which now supply their current to a single main cable. Similar unification is nearly finished at Tula and at Kostroma. The big water power station on the rapids of the Volkhov is finished in so far as land construction goes, but we can proceed no further until we have obtained the turbines, which we hope to get from abroad. As you know, we are basing our plans in general on the assumption that in the course of time we shall supply the whole of Russian industry with electricity, of which we also hope to make great use in agriculture. That, of course, will take a great number of years.'

(Nothing could have been much more artificial than the industrial geography of old Russia. The caprice of history had planted great industrial centres literally at the greatest possible distance from the sources of their raw materials. There was Moscow bringing its coal from Donetz, and Petrograd, still further away, having to eke out a living by importing coal from England. The difficulty of transport alone must have forced the Russians to consider how they could do away with such anomalies. Their main idea is that the transport of coal in a modern state is an almost inexcusable barbarism. They have set themselves, these ragged engineers, working in rooms which they can hardly keep above freezing point and walking home through the snow in boots without soles, no less a task than the electrification of the whole of Russia. There is a state committee presided over by an extraordinary optimist called Krzhizohanovsky, entrusted by the Supreme Council of Public Economy and Commissariat of Agriculture with the working out of a general plan. This committee includes, besides a number of well known practical engineers, Professors Latsinsky, Klassen, Dreier, Alexandrov, Tcharnovsky, Dend and Pavlov. They are investigating the water power available in different districts in Russia, the possibilities of using turf, and a dozen similar questions including, perhaps not the least important, investigation to discover where they can do most with least dependence on help from abroad).

Considering the question of the import of machinery from abroad, I asked him whether in existing conditions of transport Russia was actually in a position to export the raw materials with which alone the Russians could hope to buy what they want. He said:

'Actually we have in hand about two million poods (a pood is a little over 36 English pounds) of flax, and any quantity of light leather (goat, etc.), but the main districts where we have raw material for ourselves or for export are far way. Hides, for example, we have in great quantities in Siberia, in the districts of Orenburg and the Ural River and in Tashkent. I have myself made the suggestion that we should offer to sell this stuff where it is, that is to say not delivered at a seaport, and that the buyers should provide their own trains, which we should eventually buy from them with the raw material itself, so that after a certain number of journeys the trains should become ours. In the same districts we have any quantity of wool, and in some of these districts corn. We cannot, in the present condition of our transport, even get this corn for ourselves. In the same way we have great quantities of rice in Turkestan, and are actually being offered rice from Sweden, because we cannot transport our own. Then we have over a million poods of copper, ready for export on the same conditions. But it is clear that if the Western countries are unable to help in the transport, they cannot expect to get raw materials from us.'

I asked about platinum. He laughed.

'That is a different matter. In platinum we have a world monopoly, and can consequently afford to wait. Diamonds and gold, they can have as much as they want of such rubbish; but platinum is different, and we are in no hurry to part with it. But diamonds and gold ornaments, the jewellry of the Tsars, we are ready to give to any king in Europe who fancies them, if he can give us some less ornamental but more useful locomotives instead.'

I asked if Kolchak had damaged the platinum mines. He replied, 'Not at all. On the contrary, he was promising platinum to everybody who wanted it, and he set the mines going, so we arrived to find them in good condition, with a considerable yield of platinum ready for use.'

(I am inclined to think that in spite of Rykov's rather intransigent attitude on the question, the Russians would none the less be willing to export platinum, if only on account of the fact in comparison with its great value it requires little transport, and so would make possible for them an immediate bargain with some of the machinery they most urgently need).

Finally we talked of the growing importance of the Council of Public Economy. Rykov was of the opinion that it would eventually become the centre of the whole state organism, 'It and the trades unions organising the actual producers in each branch.'

'Then you think that as your further plans develop, with the creation of more and more industrial centres, with special productive populations concentrated round them, the councils of the trades unions will tend to become identical with the Soviets elected in the same districts by the same industrial units?'

'Precisely,' said Rykov, 'and in that way the Soviets, useful during the period of transition as an instrument of struggle and dictatorship, will be merged with the unions.' (One important factor, as Lenin pointed out when considering the same question, is here left out of count, namely the political development of the enormous agricultural as opposed to industrial population).

'But if this merging of political Soviets with productive unions occurs, the questions that concern people will cease to be political questions, but will be purely questions of economics.'

'Certainly. And we shall see the disappearance of political parties. That process is already apparent. In the present huge Trade Union Conference there are only 60 Mensheviks. The Communists are swallowing one party after another. Those who were not drawn over to us during the period of struggle are now joining us during the process of construction, and we find that our differences now are not political at all, but concerned only with the practical details of construction.' He illustrated this by pointing out the present constitution of the Supreme Council of Public Economy. There are under it 53 departments or centres (textile, soap, wool, timber, flax, etc.), each controlled by a 'college' of three or more persons. There are 232 members of these colleges or boards in all, and of them 83 are workmen, 79 are engineers, one was an ex-director, 50 were from the clerical staff, and 19 unclassified. Politically, 115 were Communists, 105 were non-party, and 12 were of non-Communist parties. He continued, 'Further, in swallowing the other parties, the Communists themselves will cease to exist as a political party. Think only that youths coming to their manhood during this year in Russia and in the future will not be able to confirm from their own experience the reasoning of Karl Marx, because they will have had no experience of a capitalist country. What can they make of the class struggle? The class struggle here is already over, and the distinctions of class have already gone altogether. In the old days, members of our party were men who had read, or tried to read, Marx's Capital, who knew the Communist Manifesto by heart, and were occupied in continual criticism of the basis of capitalist society. Look at the new members of our party. Marx is quite unnecessary to them. They join us, not for struggle in the interests of an oppressed class, but simply because they understand our aims in constructive work. And, as this process continues, we old social democrats shall disappear, and our places will be filled by people of entirely different character grown up under entirely new conditions.'

Chapter eleven / Non-partyism

Rykov's prophecies of the disappearance of political parties may be falsified by a development of that very non-partyism on which he bases them. It is true that the parties openly hostile to the Communists in Russia have practically disappeared. Many old-time Mensheviks have joined the Communist Party. Here and there in the country may be found a Social Revolutionary stronghold. Here and there in the Ukraine the Mensheviks retain a footing, but I doubt whether either of these parties has in it the vitality to make itself once again a serious political factor. There is, however, a movement which, in the long run, may alter Russia's political complexion. More and more delegates to Soviets or congresses of all kinds are explicitly described as non-party. Non-partyism is perhaps a sign of revolt against rigid discipline of any kind. Now and then, of course, a clever Menshevik or Social Revolutionary, by trimming his sails carefully to the wind, gets himself elected on a non-party ticket. When this happens there is usually a great hullabaloo as soon as he declares himself. A section of his electors agitates for his recall and presently someone else is elected in his stead. But non-partyism is much more than a mere cloak of invisibility for enemies or conditional supporters of the Communists. I know of considerable country districts which, in the face of every kind of agitation, insist on returning exclusively non-party delegates. The local Soviets in the districts are also non-party, and they elect usually a local Bolshevik to some responsible post to act, as it were, as a buffer between themselves and the central authority. They manage local affairs in their own way, and, through the use of tact on both sides, avoid falling foul of the more rigid doctrinaires in Moscow.

Eager reactionaries outside Russia will no doubt point to non-partyism as a symptom of friendship for themselves. It is nothing of the sort. On all questions of the defence of the Republic the non-party voting is invariably solid with that of the Communists. The non-party men do not want Denikin. They do not want Baron Wrangel. They have never heard of Professor Struve. They do not particularly like the Communists. They principally want to be left alone, and they principally fear any enforced continuation of war of any kind. If, in the course of time, they come to have a definite political programme, I think it not impossible that they may turn into a new kind of constitutional democrat. That does not mean that they will have any use for Miliukov or for a monarch with whom Miliukov might be ready to supply them. The constitution for which they will work will be that very Soviet Constitution which is now in abeyance, and the democracy which they associate with it will be that form of democracy which, were it to be accurately observed in the present state of Russia, that constitution would provide. The capitalist in Russia has long ago earned the position in which, according to the constitution, he has a right to vote, since he has long ago ceased to be a capitalist. Supposing the Soviet Constitution were today to be literally applied, it would be found that practically no class except the priests would be excluded from the franchise. And when this agitation swells in volume, it will be an agitation extremely difficult to resist, supposing Russia to be at peace, so that there will be no valid excuse with which to meet it. These new constitutional democrats will be in the position of saying to the Communists, 'Give us, without change, that very Constitution which you yourselves drew up.' I think they will find many friends inside the Communist Party, particularly among those Communists who are also trades unionists. I heard something very like the arguments of this new variety of constitutional democrat in the Kremlin itself at an All-Russian Conference of the Communist Party. A workman, Sapronov, turned suddenly aside in a speech on quite another matter, and said with great violence that the present system was in danger of running to seed and turning into oligarchy, if not autocracy. Until the moment when he put his listeners against him by a personal attack on Lenin, there was no doubt that he had with him the sympathies of quite a considerable section of an exclusively Communist audience.

Given peace, given an approximate return to normal conditions, non-partyism may well profoundly modify the activities of the Communists. It would certainly be strong enough to prevent the rasher spirits among them from jeopardising peace or from risking Russia's chance of convalescence for the sake of promoting in any way the growth of revolution abroad. Of course, so long as it is perfectly obvious that Soviet Russia is attacked, no serious growth of non-partyism is to be expected, but it is obvious that any act of aggression on the part of the Soviet government, once Russia had attained peace—which she has not known since 1914—would provide just the basis of angry discontent which might divide even the disciplined ranks of the Communists and give non-partyism an active, instead of a comparatively passive, backing throughout the country.

Non-partyism is already the peasants' way of expressing their aloofness from the revolution and, at the same time, their readiness to defend that revolution against anybody who attacks it from outside. Lenin, talking to me about the general attitude of the peasants, said: 'Hegel wrote "What is the People? The people is that part of the nation which does not know what it wants." That is a good description of the Russian peasantry at the present time, and it applies equally well to your Arthur Hendersons and Sidney Webbs in England, and to all other people like yourself who want incompatible things. The peasantry are individualists, but they support us.

We have, in some degree, to thank Kolchak and Denikin for that. They are in favour of the Soviet government, but hanker after free trade, not understanding that the two things are contradictory. Of course, if they were a united political force they could swamp us, but they are disunited both in their interests and geographically. The interests of the poorer and middle class peasants are in contradiction to those of the rich peasant farmer who employs labourers. The poorer and middle class see that we support them against the rich peasant, and also see that he is ready to support what is obviously not in their interests.' I said, 'If state agriculture in Russia comes to be on a larger scale, will there not be a sort of proletarianisation of the peasants so that, in the long run, their interests will come to be more or less identical with those of the workers in other than agricultural industry?' He replied, 'Something in that direction is being done, but it will have to be done very carefully and must take a very long time. When we are getting many thousands of tractors from abroad, then something of the sort would become possible.' Finally I asked him point-blank, 'Did he think they would pull through far enough economically to be able to satisfy the needs of the peasantry before that same peasantry had organised a real political opposition that should overwhelm them?' Lenin laughed. 'If I could answer that question,' he said, 'I could answer everything, for on the answer to that question everything depends. I think we can. Yes, I think we can. But I do not know that we can.'

Non-partyism may well be the protoplasmic stage of the future political opposition of the peasants.

Chapter twelve / Possibilities

I have done my best to indicate the essential facts in Russia's problem today, and to describe the organisation and methods with which she is attempting its solution. I can give no opinion as to whether by these means the Russians will succeed in finding their way out of the quagmire of industrial ruin in which they are involved. I can only say that they are unlikely to find their way out by any other means. I think this is instinctively felt in Russia. Not otherwise would it have been possible for the existing organisation, battling with one hand to save the towns from starvation, to destroy with the other the various forces clothed and armed by Western Europe, which have attempted its undoing. The mere fact of continued war has, of course, made progress in the solution of the economic problem almost impossible, but the fact that the economic problem was unsolved must have made war impossible, if it were not that the instinct of the people was definitely against Russian or foreign invaders.

Consider for one moment the military position.

Although the enthusiasm for the Polish war began to subside (even among the Communists) as soon as the Poles had been driven back from Kiev to their own frontiers, although the Poles are occupying an enormous area of non-Polish territory, although the Communists have had to conclude with Poland a peace obviously unstable, the military position of Soviet Russia is infinitely better at this time than it was in 1918 or 1919. In 1918 the Ukraine was held by German troops and the district east of the Ukraine was in the hands of General Krasnov, the author of a flattering letter to the Kaiser. In the north-west the Germans were at Pskov, Vitebsk and Mohilev. We ourselves were at Murmansk and Archangel. In the east, the front which became known as that of Kolchak, was on the Volga. Soviet Russia was a little hungry island with every prospect of submersion. A year later the Germans had vanished, the flatterers of the Kaiser had joined hands with those who were temporarily flattering the Allies, Yudenitch's troops were within sight of Petrograd, Denikin was at Orel, almost within striking distance of Moscow; there had been a stampede of desertion from the Red Army. There was danger that Finland might strike at any moment. Although in the east Kolchak had been swept over the Urals to his ultimate disaster, the situation of Soviet Russia seemed even more desperate than in the year before. What is the position today? Estonia, Latvia, Lithuania, and Finland are at peace with Russia. The Polish peace brings comparative quiet to the western front, although the Poles, keeping the letter rather than the spirit of their agreement, have given Balahovitch the opportunity of establishing himself in Minsk, where it is said that the progroms of unlucky Jews show that he has learnt nothing since his ejection from Pskov.

Balahovitch's force is not important in itself, but its existence will make it easy to start the war afresh along the whole new frontier of Poland; and that frontier shuts into Poland so large an anti-Polish population that a moment may still come when desperate Polish statesmen may again choose war as the least of many threatening evils. Still, for the moment, Russia's western frontier is comparatively quiet. Her northern frontier is again the Arctic Sea. Her eastern frontier is in the neighbourhood of the Pacific. The Ukraine is disorderly, but occupied by no enemy; the only front on which serious fighting is proceeding is the small semi-circle north of the Crimea. There Denikin's successor, supported by the French but exultantly described by a German conservative newspaper as a

'German baron in Cherkass uniform', is holding the Crimea and a territory slightly larger than the peninsula on the mainland. Only to the immense efficiency of anti-Bolshevik propaganda can be ascribed the opinion, common in England but comic to any one who takes the trouble to look at a map, that Soviet Russia is on the eve of military collapse.

In any case it is easy in a revolution to magnify the influence of military events on internal affairs. In the first place, no one who has not actually crossed the Russian front during the period of active operations can well realise how different are the revolutionary wars from that which ended in 1918. Advance on a broad front no longer means that a belt of men in touch with each other has moved definitely forward. It means that there have been a series of forward movements at widely separated points, and with the very haziest of mutual connections. There will be violent fighting for a village or a railway station or the passage of a river. Small hostile groups will engage in mortal combat to decide the possession of a desirable hut in which to sleep, but, except at these rare points of actual contact, the number of prisoners is far in excess of the number of casualties. Parties on each side will be perfectly ignorant of events to right or left of them, ignorant even of their gains and losses. Last year I ran into Whites in a village which the Reds had assured me was strongly held by themselves, and these same Whites refused to believe that the village where I had spent the preceding night was in the possession of the Reds. It is largely an affair of scouting parties, of patrols dodging each other through the forest tracks, of swift raids, of sudden conviction (often entirely erroneous) on the part of one side or the other, that it or the enemy has been 'encircled.' The actual number of combatants to a mile of front is infinitely less than during the German war. Further, since an immense proportion of these combatants on both sides have no wish to fight at all, being without patriotic or political convictions and very badly fed and clothed, and since it is more profitable to desert than to be taken prisoner, desertion in bulk is not uncommon, and the deserters, hurriedly enrolled to fight on the other side, indignantly re-desert when opportunity offers. In this way the armies of Denikin and Yudenitch swelled like mushrooms and sank with similar rapidity. Military events of this kind, however spectacular they may seem abroad, do not have the political effect that might be expected. I was in Moscow at the worst moment of the crisis in 1919 when practically everybody outside the government believed that Petrograd had already fallen, and I could not but realise that the government was stronger then than it had been in February of the same year, when it had had a series of victories, and peace with the Allies seemed for a moment to be in sight. A sort of fate seems to impel the Whites to neutralise with extraordinary rapidity any good will for themselves which they may find among the population. This is true of both sides, but seems to affect the Whites especially. Although General Baron Wrangel does indeed seem to have striven more successfully than his predecessors not to set the population against him and to preserve the loyalty of his army, it may be said with absolute certainty that a large success on his part would bring crowding to his banner the same crowd of stupid reactionary officers who brought to nothing any mild desire for moderation that may have been felt by General Denikin. If the area he controls increases, his power of control over his subordinates will decrease, and the forces that led to Denikin's collapse will be set in motion in his case also.* And, of course, should hostilities flare up again on the Polish frontier, should the lions and lambs and jackals and eagles of Cossack, Russian, Ukrainian and Polish nationalists temporarily join forces, no miracles of diplomacy will

---

*On the day on which I send this book to the printers news comes of Wrangel's collapse and flight. I leave standing what I have written concerning him, since it will apply to any successor he may have. Each general who has stepped into Kolchak's shoes has eventually had to run away in them, and always for the same reasons. It may be taken almost as an axiom that the history of a great country is that of its centre, not of its periphery. The main course of English history throughout the troubled seventeenth and eighteenth centuries was never deflected from London. French history did not desert Paris, to make a new start at Toulon or at Quiberon Bay. And only a fanatic could suppose that Russian history would run away from

keep them from coming to blows. For all these reasons a military collapse of the Soviet government at the present time, even a concerted military advance of its enemies, is unlikely.

It is undoubtedly true that the food situation in the towns is likely to be worse this winter than it has yet been. Forcible attempts to get food from the peasantry will increase the existing hostility between town and country. There has been a very bad harvest in Russia. The bringing of food from Siberia or the Kuban (if military activities do not make that impossible) will impose an almost intolerable strain on the inadequate transport. Yet I think internal collapse unlikely. It may be said almost with certainty that governments do not collapse until there is no one left to defend them. That moment had arrived in the case of the Tsar. It had arrived in the case of Kerensky. It has not arrived in the case of the Soviet government for certain obvious reasons. For one thing, a collapse of the Soviet government at the present time would be disconcerting, if not disastrous, to its more respectable enemies. It would, of course, open the way to a practically unopposed military advance, but at the same time it would present its enemies with enormous territory, which would overwhelm the organising powers which they have shown again and again to be quite inadequate to much smaller tasks. Nor would collapse of the present government turn a bad harvest into a good one. Such a collapse would mean the breakdown of all existing organisations, and would intensify the horrors of famine for every town dweller.

Consequently, though the desperation of hunger and resent-

Moscow, to begin again in in a semi-Tartar peninsula in the Black Sea. Moscow changes continually, and may so change as to make easy the return of the 'refugees'. Some have already returned. But the refugees will not return as conquerors. Should a Russian Napoleon (an unlikely figure, even in spite of our efforts) appear, he will not throw away the invaluable asset of a revolutionary war-cry. He will have to fight someone, or he will not be a Napoleon. And whom will he fight but the very people who, by keeping up the friction, have rubbed Aladdin's ring so hard and so long that a Djinn, by no means kindly disposed towards them, bursts forth at last to avenge the breaking of his sleep?

ment against inevitable requisitions may breed riots and revolts here and there throughout the country, the men who, in other circumstances, might co-ordinate such events, will refrain from doing anything of the sort. I do not say that collapse is impossible. I do say that it would be extremely undesirable from the point of view of almost everybody in Russia. Collapse of the present government would mean at best a reproduction of the circumstances of 1917, with the difference that no intervention from without would be necessary to stimulate indiscriminate slaughter within. I say 'at best' because I think it more likely that collapse would be followed by a period of actual chaos. Any government that followed the Communists would be faced by the same economic problem, and would have to choose between imposing measures very like those of the Communists or allowing Russia to subside into a new area for colonisation. There are people who look upon this as a natural, even a desirable, result of the revolution. They forget that the Russians have never been a subject race, that they have immense powers of passive resistance, that they respond very readily to any idea that they understand, and that the idea of revolt against foreigners is difficult not to understand. Any country that takes advantage of the Russian people in a moment of helplessness will find, sooner or later, first that it has united Russia against it, and secondly that it has given all Russians a single and undesirable view of the history of the last three years. There will not be a Russian who will not believe that the artificial incubation of civil war within the frontiers of old Russia was not deliberately undertaken by Western Europe with the object of so far weakening Russia as to make her exploitation easy. Those who look with equanimity even on this prospect forget that the creation in Europe of a new area for colonisation, a knocking out of one of the sovereign nations, will create a vacuum, and that the effort to fill this vacuum will set at loggerheads nations at present friendly and so produce a struggle which may well do for Western Europe what Western Europe will have done for Russia.

It is of course possible that in some such way the Russian

Revolution may prove to be no more than the last desperate gesture of a stricken civilization. My point is that if that is so, civilization in Russia will not die without infecting us with its disease. It seems to me that our own civilization is ill already, slightly demented perhaps, and liable, like a man in delirium, to do things which tend to aggravate the malady. I think that the whole of the Russian war, waged directly or indirectly by Western Europe, is an example of this sort of dementia, but I cannot help believing that sanity will reassert itself in time. At the present moment, to use a modification of Gusev's metaphor, Europe may be compared to a burning house and the governments of Europe to fire brigades, each one engaged in trying to save a wing or a room of the building. It seems a pity that these fire brigades should be fighting each other, and forgetting the fire in their resentment of the fact that some of them wear red uniforms and some wear blue. Any single room to which the fire gains complete control increases the danger of the whole building, and I hope that before the roof falls in the firemen will come to their senses.

But turning from grim recognition of the danger, and from speculations as to the chance of the Russian government collapsing, and as to the changes in it that time may bring, let us consider what is likely to happen supposing it does not collapse. I have already said that I think collapse unlikely. Do the Russians show any signs of being able to carry out their programme, or has the fire gone so far during the quarrelling of the firemen as to make that task impossible?

I think that there is still a hope. There is as yet no sign of a general improvement in Russia, nor is such an improvement possible until the Russians have at least carried out the first stage of their programme. It would not even be surprising if things in general were to continue to go to the bad during the carrying out of that first stage. Shortages of food, of men, of tools, of materials, are so acute that they have had to choose those factories which are absolutely indispensable for the carrying out of this stage, and make of them 'shock' factories, like the 'shock' troops of the war, giving

them equipment over and above their rightful share of the impov-
erished stock, feeding their workmen even at the cost of letting
others go hungry. That means that other factories suffer. No matter, say the Russians, if only that first stage makes progress.
Consequently, the only test that can be fairly applied is that of
transport. Are they or are they not gaining on ruin in the matter of
wagons and engines? Here are the figures of wagon repairs in the
seven chief repairing shops up to the month of June:

December 1919	475	wagons were repaired
January 1920	656	wagons were repaired
February	697	wagons were repaired
March	1,104	wagons were repaired
April	1,141	wagons were repaired
May	1,154	wagons were repaired
June	1,161	wagons were repaired

After elaborate investigation last year Trotsky, as temporary
Commissar of Transport, put out an order explaining that the railways, to keep up their present condition, must repair roughly 800
engines every month. During the first six months of 1920 they ful-
filled this task in the following percentages:

January	32	percent
February	50	percent
March	66	percent
April	78	percent
May	98	percent
June	104	percent

I think that it is proof that, supposing normal relations existed
between Russia and ourselves, the Russians would be able to tackle
the first stage of the problem that lies before them, and would lie
before them whatever their government might be. Unfortunately
there is no proof that this steady improvement can be continued,
except under conditions of trade with Western Europe. There are
Russians who think they can pull through without us, and, remem-

bering the miracles of which man is capable when his back is to the wall, it would be rash to say that this is impossible. But other Russians point out gloomily that they have been using certain parts taken from dead engines (engines past repair) in order to mend sick engines. They are now coming to the mending, not of sick engines merely, but of engines on which post-mortems have already been held. They are actually mending engines, parts of which have already been taken out and used for mending other engines. There are consequently abnormal demands for such things as shafts and piston rings. They are particularly short of Babbit metal and boiler tubes. In normal times the average number of new tubes wanted for each engine put through the repair shops was 25 (ten to 15 for engines used in the more northerly districts, and 30 to 40 for engines in the south where the water is not so good). This number must now be taken as much higher, because during recent years tubes have not been regularly renewed. Further, the railways have been widely making use of tubes taken from dead engines, that is to say, tubes already worn. Putting things at their very best, assuming that the average demand for tubes per engine will be that of normal times, then, if 1,000 engines are to be repaired monthly, 150,000 tubes will be wanted every six months. Now on the June 15 the total stock of tubes ready for use was 58,000, and the railways could not expect to get more than another 13,000 in the near future. Unless the factories are able to do better (and their improvement depends on improvement in transport), railway repairs must again deteriorate, since the main source of materials for it in Russia, namely the dead engines, will presently be exhausted.

On this there is only one thing to be said. If, whether because we do not trade with them, or from some other cause, the Russians are unable to proceed even in this first stage of their pro-gramme, it means an indefinite postponement of the moment when Russia will be able to export anything, and, consequently, that when at last we learn that we need Russia as a market, she will be a market willing to receive gifts, but unable to pay for anything at all. And that is a state of affairs a great deal more serious to ourselves than to the Russians, who can, after all, live by wandering about their country and scratching the ground, whereas we depend on the sale of our manufactured goods for the possibility of buying the food we cannot grow ourselves. If the Russians fail, their failure will affect not us alone. It will, by depriving her of a market, lessen Germany's power of recuperation, and consequently her power of fulfilling her engagements. What, then, is to happen to France? And, if we are to lose our market in Russia, and find very much weakened markets in Germany and France, we shall be faced with an ever-increasing burden of unemployment, with the growth, in fact, of the very conditions in which alone we shall ourselves be unable to recover from the war. In such conditions, upheaval in England would be possible, and, for the dispassionate observer, there is a strange irony in the fact that the Communists desire that upheaval, and, at the same time, desire a rebirth of the Russian market which would tend to make that upheaval unlikely, while those who most fear upheaval are precisely those who urge us, by making recovery in Russia impossible, to improve the chances of collapse at home. The peasants in Russia are not alone in wanting incompatible things.

Six weeks in Russia 1919

Arthur Ransome

Six weeks
in Russia 1919

Six weeks in Russia 1919 / Arthur Ransome

Published by Redwords, May 1992

Redwords 31 Cottenham Road London E17 6RP

ISBN 1 872208 029

Set in 10:13 Monophoto Bembo

Imagesetting by East End Offset Bureau

Printed and bound in Great Britain by

Dotesios Ltd., Trowbridge, Wiltshire

Production and design: Sofie Mason and Roger Huddle

Redwords would like to thank the following people for making the publication of this book possible: John Bell and Sir Rupert Hart-Davis of the Ransome Estate, Paul Foot, Sheila McGregor, *Animage*, Cyrus Gilbert-Rolfe, Elise Bradbury, Angela Graham, Paul Cooper, Maxine Lambert, John Rees, Lindsey German, Andrew Forbes and Megan Trudell

Contents / Six weeks in Russia 1919

PAUL FOOT

Arthur Ransome in revolutionary Russia

Millions of people in the English-speaking world have heard of Arthur Ransome. His books for children, most of them adventure stories based on messing about in boats, were a staggering success almost from the moment he started writing them. They have fascinated children of both sexes and all classes for more than sixty years. Ransome died, aged 83, in 1967, but his books are still being republished in paperback editions, tape-recordings and television serials.

Even the most pedantic Ransome addict would be hard pressed to find in any of these children's books a single word about politics. The subject simply doesn't arise. There is nothing even of the implied radicalism of that other great children's story-writer, whom Arthur Ransome much admired, E Nesbit. The children's world in Ransome's books is, quite deliberately, hived off from the adult world outside. Though all the famous books were written in times of slump, war or postwar reconstruction, there is hardly a whisper of any of this in any of them.

Ransome did not develop this mastery of the separate children's world until his late middle age. The first of the long string of famous children's stories, *Swallows and Amazons*, was published in 1930, when Ransome was 46. Though he hankered after writing children's books as early as 1906, most of his youth was spent as a journalist and foreign correspondent. His few attempts at writing for children, though not unsuccessful, were entirely overshadowed by his work as a journalist. Most of that work was carried out in Russia where he fled in 1913 from a disastrous marriage. He quickly taught himself Russian, and before long was taken on by the liberal Daily News. Though he lived in different places, he wrote copiously on Russia for the News and later for the Manchester Guardian for 14 years.

From 1914 to 1918 he was in Russia almost all the time. When he started there, his main aim was to put the Russian case to her Allies in the Great War effort. But before long he became absorbed by the political developments in Russia, and started to predict the end of the suffocating dictatorship of Tsar Nicholas.

The two books and the pamphlet reprinted here for the first time since the 1920s are Ransome's contemporary account and analysis of the two Russian revolutions of 1917 and the events which followed. They are exceptional for a number of reasons. First, Ransome's writing style is as plain and clear as in any of his children's books. His prose, in Orwell's famous phrase, is 'like a window pane'. There were other English writers who visited Russia both during and after the revolution whose writing style was every bit as irresistible as Ransome's: Bertrand Russell, for instance, or H G Wells. There are also a series of brilliant accounts of revolutionary Russia from committed sympathisers. John Reed's *Ten Days That Shook the World* is an obvious example, as is Victor Serge's *Year One of the Russian Revolution* or Alfred Rosmer's *Lenin's Moscow*.

Ransome's contribution is quite different. Unlike Wells and Russell, he had been in Russia since the start of the First World War and knew it well. His interviews with the Bolshevik leaders were not one-off affairs, conducted by the travelling journalist eager to get back home. He came to know people like Lenin, Trotsky and Chicherin almost as personal friends. In 1918, he fell in love with Evgenia Petrovna Shelepina, Trotsky's secretary, whom he married as soon as his divorce came through. He lived for a time in the same house as the Bolshevik leader, Karl Radek.

He differed from men like Reed, Rosmer and Serge in another way. All three of them were convinced revolutionaries when they came to Russia. Reed had taken part in and reported the Mexican revolution, and had campaigned for socialism across the United States. Rosmer and Serge were, in their different ways, convinced of the case for the overthrow of capitalism. Ransome was extraordinary in that both before and after his involvement in Russia he does not seem to have had any ideological commitment to socialism.

This can be exaggerated. In his excellent and painstaking biography, *The Life of Arthur Ransome,* published by Cape in the hundredth year after Ransome's birth, 1984, Hugh Brogan refers to Ransome's 'vast ignorance of politics'. This seems unlikely. Hugh Brogan tells us that one of the most formative influences on Ransome's youth was J W Mackail's biography of William Morris. Anyone turned on by William Morris cannot possibly have had a 'vast ignorance' of politics. Again, even before he left for Russia, Ransome had built up an enormous library, and had written work-manlike, if uninspiring, books on Edgar Allen Poe and Oscar Wilde. He was not ignorant of politics. What he lacked was any sort of clear commitment. Perhaps he yearned for the sort of world which William Morris painted in *News from Nowhere*, but felt that the reality of Britain in the first 14 years of the century was so far distant from anything Morris had hoped for that there was no point in taking up a political position.

So Ransome went to Russia entirely without political enthusiasms or commitment. He had not joined the newly-formed Labour Party or shown the slightest interest in any of the great issues which racked prewar Britain: women's suffrage, Irish independence or the great strikes of 1911 and 1912 which effectively destroyed the Liberal Party and shook the Tories to their foundations.

It is this detachment from previous political commitment which gives to Arthur Ransome's reports of revolutionary Russia their singular fascination and verve. He saw the world as it was, or rather as it was changing. What he saw excited him so much that he became for the first and last time in his life politically committed.

The three works published here span a period of three years, from 1917 to 1920. Ransome was in Petrograd during the 1917 February revolution. Infuriatingly for him and for us, he returned to Britain on holiday in September and so missed the October revolution. As soon as he heard about it, he returned to Russia as quickly as he could, arriving in Petrograd on Christmas Day. He threw himself at once into investigating and reporting what was happening in Russia. His reports were greeted with contempt and fury by the British government, which regarded the new Russian government as a threat to their alliance and the war effort. Ransome's dispatches were systematically censored by the British government and their security services which (then as now) were controlled by a wildly hysterical anti-communist right. At one stage, MI5 proposed that Ransome should be prosecuted as a traitor under the Defence of the Realm Act.

Nothing infuriated Ransome more than what he called 'the intellectual sloth, the gross mental indolence' which infected the British government and their newspapers whenever anyone mentioned Russia. No one seemed capable of making the leap in imagination necessary to understand even a little of the stupendous events in revolutionary Russia. In April 1918, Ransome was approached by an American journalist, Raymond Robins, with an idea for a pamphlet for the American people on what was really happening in Russia. To avoid the censor, Robins suggested he take it back to the States with him on his next visit. Nothing much happened for a week or two, when suddenly Robins arrived at Ransome's lodgings to announce that he was off in 36 hours and the pamphlet had better be written by then. Ransome sat down and, almost without stopping, typed out *The Truth About Russia*. Robins arrived to collect it just as it was being finished. So it is almost unchecked, a result of the free flow of Ransome's uninhibited and even unedited prose style, and probably much the better for it.

Hugh Brogan devotes only two pages of his biography to this remarkable pamphlet, which he obviously regards as a bit embarrassing. An honest biographer, Brogan takes great care not to distort the facts or the views of those with whom he disagrees. But he had little sympathy with the Bolsheviks and it is hard for him properly to convey Arthur Ransome's untrammelled enthusiasm for them.

The Truth About Russia starts with Ransome's feelings as he hurried round Petrograd, often in great danger, during the February revolution. His language is extreme: 'I do not think I shall ever be so happy in my life as I was during those first days when I saw working men and peasant soldiers sending representatives of their class and not of mine. I remembered Shelley's:

Shake your chains to earth like dew
Which in sleep had fallen on you.
Ye are many - they are few'.

The key to his excitement was the new democracy. Representatives of a new class, previously dispossessed of property and power, were suddenly entering the political arena. News from Nowhere was News from Everywhere. Here at once Ransome parted company with the ephemeral enthusiasts who described these events in the liberal press. The liberals were excited by the prospect of the old Tsarist tyranny being replaced by safe parliamentary institutions like those in England or France or the United States. Ransome noticed at once that the real democratic force introduced by the Russian Revolution - the workers' council, the soviet - was a hundred thousand times more democratic than the parliaments of the West, which had never really interested him.

The soviets were directly elected. Their delegates were recallable. They were therefore responsive and sensitive to the working people. The Provisional government and its parliament were none of these things. The two sources of power were locked in a life-and-death struggle, which, Ransome observed, was continually being won by the soviets.

As the power struggle became more and more intense, it had to be resolved. Inside the soviets the mood changed. They were controlled originally by parliamentarians, by Mensheviks and Social Revolutionaries who wanted to be subservient to the Provisional government. The Bolsheviks on the other hand wanted to take power in the name of the people they represented. Arthur Ransome, who had been sceptical, even dismissive of Lenin and the Bolsheviks, swung round in their support.

This led him to the main thrust of his argument in *The Truth About Russia*. Liberals then and now (Hugh Brogan chimes in as well) argued that the dissolution of the elected Constituent Assembly (parliament) by the Bolsheviks in January 1918 was the decisive moment at which Bolshevism parted company with democracy. On the contrary, Ransome argued, the only way democracy could possibly proceed was through the soviets. In fact, as he also records and was plain from the near-unanimous reports at the time (though not in the memory of latter-day liberals) the Constituent Assembly in the reality of Russia in early 1918 was a complete irrelevance and passed away without incident and without mourning. In its place was the living, vibrant democracy of the soviets. Watching Trotsky in action explaining the government's policies to hundreds of freezing soviet delegates in crude clothes, this moderate and restrained reporter, trained in the reserved language of British upper class education, wrote this:

'I felt I would willingly give the rest of my life if it could be divided into minutes and given to men in England and France so that those of little faith who say that the Russian Revolution is discredited could share for one minute each that wonderful experience'.

The riddle of how this unlikely revolutionary had become such an enthusiastic one is to some extent solved in a revealing passage in *The Truth about Russia*: 'Socialists especially who had long dreamed of revolution found it particularly difficult to recognise in this clouded tremendous struggle the thing which their dreams had softened for them into something more docile, less self-willed'.

Those, unlike Ransome, who had become socialists by working out utopias, by imagining that socialism would all be dancing round a maypole for the common people, while intelligent and benevolent governments handed down plans for industry and welfare, were a bit shocked by the rough and ready soviets, and by the fact that everything did not come right all of a sudden. Ransome, who had never been impressed by utopias or dreams, was inspired by the reality in front of him, especially the way in which the will of the people was being brought to bear on the political process.

This enthusiasm intensified as the World War ended and the war of intervention on Russia by the Western powers became clear for what it was - a blatant attempt by capitalist powers to drown socialist Russia in blood. Ransome was outraged by the continued hostility of his own government to the Russian regime and continued to defend the Bolsheviks in his reports. He and Evgenia, by now devoted to the Bolshevik government though she had been a Menshevik in 1917, left Russia for Stockholm in 1918, soon after *The Truth About Russia* was published. They were thrown out of Sweden by a combination of red-baiting governments, and ended up in Tallin, Estonia, from where Ransome repeatedly travelled to Russia as a reporter.

In the spring of 1919, on a trip to England, he wrote *Six Weeks in Russia in 1919*. Much of the warm glow of triumph in *The Truth About Russia* has vanished from this kaleidoscope of revolutionary pictures. Instead, pervading everything, there are the cold and hunger of the cities, the apparently insuperable problems of transport and food supply, all of them directly attributable to the blockade and the war. Yet Ransome's enthusiasm for the achievement of the Bolsheviks and their system of government is not at all diminished by the terrible privations of the Russian people.

The most consistent theme of these thirty reports is the survival of the Bolshevik regime in the face of everything which has being thrown against it. People were hungry, but there was little or no exploitation in their hunger. There were free meals for every school child. Housing policy was based on the 'rough and ready' principle that until everyone had one room, no one should have two. Universities and libraries were growing. A night at the opera where the audience was all roughly-dressed working men and women, freezing in their tattered overcoats, was far more exhilarating than in the old days when all was tinsel and glitter. It was not true that opposition was cut out of public life. Even in spite of the war and the blockade, opponents of Bolshevism like Sukhanov and Martov were still at work, expressing their views with all their accustomed vehemence. In an interview, Martov conceded that his paper should have been shut down for excessive opposition to a government harassed on all sides by rampaging White armies. Martov did not like the Bolsheviks, but he preferred them any day to the White generals.

Ransome's lack of ideology was not always useful to him. He never even started to understand the central Bolshevik strategy of exporting revolution to other European countries. But his report of the decision to form the Third International, and the huge meeting which inaugurated it, is perhaps the most thrilling episode in this thrilling little book.

Six Weeks In Russia published by Allen and Unwin, was a

great success. It was published in America, where it sold widely. It coincided with the upsurge of socialist thinking on both sides of the Atlantic and the growing working class impatience with their government's war against Russia. Many radical publishers reprinted the book. Ransome, who was born in Leeds, must have been specially delighted with the paperback edition printed at the relatively cheap price of half a crown by the Yorkshire Reformers' Bookshop in Bradford. But *Six Weeks In Russia* was not a popular book in the sixty years from 1930 to 1990. Like John Reed's *Ten Days That Shook the World*, it did not mention the man who according to the folklore of the left for half a century was as important a figure in the Russian Revolution as Lenin or Trotsky. It did not mention Stalin. It shuffled him off where he belonged, to the fringe of the revolution. This was intolerable to Communist Party orthodoxy. Lawrence and Wishart, the Party's publishers, eventually republished John Reed's book (with Stalinist footnotes) in 1960. Ransome's *Six Weeks in Russia* has not been reprinted since the 1920s.

Nor has *Crisis in Russia*, which was written almost a year after *Six Weeks*, and takes the revolution forward to the early months of 1920. This was never reprinted by anyone. It came out in 1921, as the postwar upsurge in socialist agitation started to die down and the ruling class on both sides of the Atlantic began to breathe more confidently. Yet it is in my view the best of Ransome's work on revolutionary Russia.

By now the cold and hunger had entered into the very heart of the Russian cities. With his usual skill and humility, Arthur Ransome lets us know that everyone he meets is hungry and cold before everything else, and that well-fed foreign journalists are not well placed to lecture the Russians about their political failures.

He notices one of the key elements of the collapse of the Russian economy: the flight to the countryside by industrial workers who cannot find any other way of getting something to eat. He predicts that the future for Russia was 'something like barbarism'.

Either the industrial production would collapse through the voluntary movement of workers to the countryside, or that production would have to be restored by entirely over-ruling all voluntary movement: by a dictatorship over the proletariat not of the proletariat. He sees and mourns the rapid disappearance of the class which made the revolution and kept it going: the industrial working class. Most of that class had been killed in the wars; another large part of it had become the administration and now almost all that was left was vanishing, starving, into the countryside, Yet the book is not all gloomy. It is in many ways a much clearer and more persuasive argument for the Bolsheviks either than the grand revolutionary rhetoric of *The Truth about Russia* or the patchwork of vignettes, *Six Weeks in Russia*.

Crisis in Russia has a consistent theme, which harks back to Ransome's original enthusiasm for the revolution. The whole of Russia, it reports, is held together by the 600,000 members of the Communist Party. It is this 'enormously strong embodiment of the human will' which has made it possible to create an army to defeat the Whites, and to retain in office a revolutionary regime which by all that was logical should have been smashed to pieces months if not years before.

The key to the strength and power of the party was its internal democracy. Ransome summons all his journalistic skill to describe without a word of jargon the practical ways in which Communist Party democracy worked; the exhaustive discussions, the arrival at decisions and the respecting of those decisions.

The high water mark of all three books is Ransome's account of a conference at Jaroslavl. He went there in early 1920 with Radek, recently released from prison in Germany, and Larin, who opposed the party majority line on industrial conscription. Larin was elderly and ill with a crippling disease. He and Radek opposed each other at the conference, and Radek won the vote. Then the conference had to elect delegates to another conference. Larin promptly withdrew his name from the list of candidates on the grounds that he had been defeated on an important issue. At once the conference renominated him and in due course elected him. Here in a single story from a besieged and starving country was an example of representative democracy incomparably more democratic and representative than anything thrown up in a hundred years of parliamentary democracy. The delegates did not want their representatives elected once every five years who would forget their electorate as soon as they trotted off to some distant scene of ancestor-worship in the capital; nor did they want mindless delegates who would act as rubber stamps. They wanted something much richer, more truly democratic, and they got it.

The conference was a long and difficult one and Ransome and his friends were glad to retire that night to their hotel. As they prepared for bed there was a knock on the door. A railwayman stood outside, begging them to come to a performance of a local play written and performed by local workers and their families. Ransome's description of what follows - especially his account of Radek's speech to the railwaymen and their families, is an electrifying piece of writing. I read it first in 1976, and return to it again and again whenever I feel dispirited. This passage, indeed all the book, needs to be read carefully by all those people who argue that 'Lenin led to Stalin'; that there was some continuous bond which linked the Bolshevik regime from 1917 to 1924 with the Stalinist tyranny which followed it. Passages like this written at the time by someone who was not a Bolshevik help to prove that even in 1920 the regime in Russia was not the harbinger of Stalinism but the precise opposite of it; that in order to establish a tyrannous state capitalism Stalin and his henchmen had to smash every vestige of the democracy and spirit of public service which inspired the Communist Party Arthur Ransome described.

All through this period, Arthur Ransome was accused of bias and partiality. He was always in trouble with his editors for 'taking sides'. Facts are sacred, comment is free was the prevailing cliche at the Manchester Guardian, and it was thrown again and again at

Ransome as editors tried to curb his enthusiasm for the Bolsheviks.

He replied furiously. For all his mild manners, he was as tough as the pike he fought with in his beloved Lakes. When the Liberal editor of the News, A G Gardiner, wrote to his Russian correspondent demanding more impartiality, he was rebuked with this magnificent reply:

'I do think I have earned a right to my opinion. I contradicted everybody about the coming of the Revolution, and I was right. Early last year I said it was idle to watch the Duma and the Provisional government, because the future would be decided not by them but by the soviets who had the real power. I was right. My point is that if my telegrams have been partial, they have been partial for the truth. And now again I am perfectly content to disagree with everybody, and perfectly convinced that within the year the position will be clearer and my judgement vindicated'.

He was partial, because he found himself in the middle of a 'titanic struggle', and could not avoid taking sides. This did not entitle him to tell lies or make up facts. Indeed, it was precisely the facts, his partiality for the truth, which had convinced him in the first place to take up sides. So his partial reporting is a million times more readable and more persuasive than the deluge of anti-Bolshevik reports from hacks who were praised for their objectivity but were in fact indulging in the most partisan of all journalistic undertakings: swimming with the stream.

Like George Orwell, with whom Arthur Ransome had a great deal in common, he observed that everyone is in their own way partial, and that the best way for the writer to deal with the partiality problem is to admit where he stands and report what he sees and how he feels. That approach inspired Orwell's reporting of the Spanish revolution in 1936 and Ransome's of the Russian revolution nearly twenty years earlier.

Another charge against Ransome, made more than once by Hugh Brogan, is 'pervasive sentimentalising' of Lenin. In fact, as the reader can judge from what follows, Ransome was not at all sentimental about Lenin. He was impressed not just by Lenin's intellect, but by his lack of ambition, his ordinariness, even his Russianness. Ransome reported these things lucidly, sometimes even coldly, but never with a trace of sentimentality. What he brings out about Lenin is the Bolshevik leader's sense of humour. Of all Lenin's qualities this was the one his detractors have most wanted to suppress. So here almost for the first and only time is Lenin's perennial chuckle, his observation and enjoyment of the ridiculous - perhaps the least likely qualities in a dictator and therefore the ones which the countless historians who caricatured Lenin as a dictator most wished to write out of the history books.

From 1929 to his death in 1967, Arthur Ransome lived with Evgenia in England, becoming increasingly rich and famous for his children's books. In 1924 he visited parliament (appropriately enough he was taken there by the Labour Party leader, Ramsay Macdonald) but he never showed the slightest interest in what went on there. He hardly ever again wrote a word about Russia - partly no doubt because he didn't want to cause trouble for his wife's family, partly because he was obviously sickened by Stalin. It was only in the 1950s when he started to write his autobiography that the old enthusiasms stirred in him again.

Was there any link at all between his delightful tales of middle class children in the Lake District and in Suffolk and the great events which shook the world in 1917? There is perhaps a clue in something wrote when he was only 22. Hugh Brogan recounts:

'The essence of the child, he held, is its imagination, the way in which, left to itself, and not withered by obtuse or manipulative adults, "it adopts any material at hand, and weaves for itself a web of imaginative life, building the world again in splendid pageantry, and all without ever (or hardly ever) blurring its sense of the actual" '.

This combination of the unleashing of the imagination without ever losing grip on reality is the hallmark of Arthur Ransome's marvellous reports from revolutionary Russia.

A common leftist criticism of Ransome's children's books is

that they deal only with middle class children with nannies and boathouses and so on. Ransome had a sharp answer to that too. When an Edwina Spart of the time criticised one of his books in these terms, the librarian of a county secondary school in Shropshire wrote in to complain. She'd observed that all the children (especially the girls) read the books again and again so that they had constantly to be rebound. There was no class divide in the readership, she insisted. Ransome thanked her warmly:

'In Russia, in the early years of the revolution there,' he wrote in a letter 'young devotees quite honestly believed that after 1917 literature must concern itself exclusively with the proletariat, and some of them went even further and believed that it must be written only by the proletariat. It was a sterile and short-lived movement and was killed by the proletariat itself which preferred to read the best books it could get. Within a very few years that movement became a memory and a joke...'

The veteran book-lover, then almost 60, looked back a quarter of a century and remembered the astonishing way in which great literature became, for the first time ever, the property of the masses. He recalled how he himself had reread the British classics, Shakespeare, Burns, Milton, Wordsworth, Coleridge, Shelley, Byron, and discovered their full glories in the bright revolutionary light in which they were being read and in which they had been written.

Why, finally, are we republishing these forgotten tracts so long after they were written? The reason is simple and compelling. After the collapse of Stalinism in Russia and Central Europe, reactionaries and liberals all over the world cheerfully tolled the death-knell of all revolutions.

They exulted that the 20th century history of what were known as 'socialist countries' showed that socialism was no longer an option; that the Bolshevik revolution was inherently responsible for the Stalinist horrors which followed it. There is no better option, their argument concludes, to a future of endless capitalism in which most men and women will be tossed forever on the waves of a market system they cannot control. It follows that rich people will always be rich and poor people, in increasing numbers, will always be poor. To risk a revolution again is to risk a further round of tyranny and horror even worse than the tyranny and horror we know, and that there is nothing for the young but to accept the hideous world created for them by their elders and betters.

In all this despair and reaction, a clear small voice calls out dissent. The Russian Revolution, it says, was the greatest event of the 20th century. Stalinism was not the inevitable consequence of revolution, but its gravedigger. Stalin took power not because there was too much revolution but because there was not enough of it, because Lenin, Trotsky and the Bolsheviks were isolated in their small enclave and their legitimate hopes that their revolution would spread to the industrial countries of the West were dashed. Every time since that the workers have risen and momentarily toppled their oppressors, they have resorted to the same living democracy which inspired Arthur Ransome in 1918 and 1919: in Spain in 1936, in Hungary in 1956, in France in 1968, in Portugal in 1975, in Poland in 1981. To defeat this democracy, reactionary parliamentary regimes or Stalinist tyrannies have had to resort to the most deadly warfare or the most disgusting oppression. The Russian Revolution is not just the most important event of the 20th century. It is a beacon for the 21st. For English-speaking socialists there is no more eloquent or accurate assertion of that than these passionate essays by one of the century's great writers.

'Let the revolution fail' wrote Arthur Ransome in 1918. 'No matter. If only in America, in England, in France, in Germany people know why it has failed, and how it failed, who betrayed it, who murdered it. Man does not live by his deeds so much as the purpose of his deeds. We have seen the flight of the young eagles. Nothing can destroy that fact, even if, later in the day the eagles fall to earth one by one, with broken wings'.

The truth about Russia

Every day brings a ship,
Every ship brings a word;
Well for those who have no fear,
Looking seaward well assured
that the word the vessel brings
is the word they wish to hear.

Emerson wrote the poem I have stolen
for the headpiece to this pamphlet, and Emerson wrote the best
commentary on that poem, 'If there is any period one would desire
to be born in - is it not the age of Revolution; when the old and
the new stand side by side, and admit of being compared; when the
energies of all men are searched by fear and hope; when the his-
toric glories of the old can be compensated by the rich possibilities
of the new era? This time, like all times, is a very good one, if we
but know what to do with it.' Revolution divides men by character far more sharply than they are divided by war. Those whom the
gods love take the youth of their hearts and throw themselves glad-
ly on that side, even if, clearsighted, they perceive that the fires of
revolution will burn up perhaps the very things that, for themselves
they hold most dear. Those others, wise, circumspect, foolish with
the folly of wisdom, refrain, and are burned up none the less. It is
the same with nations, and I send this pamphlet to America because
America supported the French Revolution when England con-
demned it, and because now also America seems to me to look
towards Russia with better will to understand, with less suspicion,
without the easy cynicism that prepares the disaster at which it is
afterwards ready to smile.

Not that I think all this is due to some special virtue in America. I have no doubt it is due to geographical and economic conditions. America is further from this bloody cockpit of Europe, for one thing. For another, even rich Americans dependent for their full pockets on the continuance of the present capitalist system, can wholeheartedly admire the story of the Bolshevik adventure, and even wish for its success, without fearing any serious damage to the edifice in which they live, on which they feed, like parasites in cheese. Or it may be, that knowing so little about America, I let myself think too well of it. Perhaps there too men go about repeating easy lies, poisoning the wells of truth from simple lack of attention to the hygiene of the mind. I do not know. I only know that, from the point of view of the Russian Revolution, England seems to be a vast nightmare of blind folly, separated from the continent, indeed from the world, by the sea, and beyond that by the trenches, and deprived, by some fairy godmother who was not invited to her christening, of the imagination to realise what is happening beyond. Shouting in daily telegrams across the wires from Russia I feel I am shouting at a drunk man asleep in the road in front of a steamroller. And then the newspapers of six weeks ago arrive, and I seem to see that drunk sleeping fool make a motion as if to brush a fly from his nose, and take no further notice of the monstrous thing bearing steadily towards him. I love the real England, but I hate, more than I hate anything on earth (except cowardice in looking at the truth) the intellectual sloth, the gross mental indolence that prevents the English from making an effort of imagination and realising how shameful will be their position in history when the tale of this last year in the biography of democracy comes to be written. How shameful, and how foolish, for they will one day be forced to realise how appalling are the mistakes they committed, even from the mere bestial standpoint of self interest and expediency. Shameful, foolish and tragic beyond tears— for the toll will be paid in English blood. English lads will die and English lads have died, not one or two, but hundreds of thousands, because their elders listen to men who think little things, and tell them little things, which are so terribly easy to repeat. At least half of our worst mistakes have been due to the underestimation of some person or force outside England, and disturbing to little men who will not realise that chaos is once again and that giants are waking in the world. They look across Europe and see huge things, monstrous figures, and, to save themselves, and from respect for other little lazy minds, they leap for the easiest tawdry explanation, and say, 'Ah, yes, bogies made in Germany with candles inside turnip heads!' Then having found their miserable little atheistical explanation they din it into everybody, so that other people shall make the same mistakes, and they have company in folly, and so be excused. And in the end it becomes difficult for even honest-minded sturdy folk in England to look those bogies squarely in their turnip faces and see that they are not bogies at all, but the real article, giants, whose movements in the mist are of greater import for the future of the world than anything else that is happening in our day.

I think it possible that the revolution will fail. If so, then its failure will not mean that it loses its importance. The French Revolution gave a measure of freedom to every nation in Europe, although it failed most notably in France and ended in a dictator, and a defeated dictator at that, and for the brave, clearsighted France, foreseen by Diderot and Rousseau, substituted a France in which thought died and everyone was left to grub money with a view to enslaving everybody else. The failure of the French Revolution did not lessen the ardour which the ideas which sprang from it poured into the minds that came to their maturity after 1795. And perhaps it was that failure which sharpened the conflict of the first half of the nineteenth century, when, after all, many candles were lit and fiercely, successfully guarded in the windy night which followed the revolutionary sunset. Let the revolution fail. No matter, if only in America, in England, in France, in Germany men know what it was that failed, and how it failed, who betrayed it, who murdered it. Man does not live by his deeds so much as by the purpose of his deeds. We have seen the flight of the young eagles. Nothing can destroy that fact, even if, later in the day, the eagles fall to earth one by one, with broken wings.

It is hard here, where the tragedy is so close at hand, so intimate, not to forget the immediate practical purpose of my writing. It is this; to set down, as shortly as possible, the story of the development of the Soviet power in Russia, to show what forces in Russia worked against that power and why, to explain what exactly the Soviet government is, and how the end of the Soviet government will mean the end of the revolution, whatever may be the apparent character of any form of government which succeeds it.

Circumstances of the March revolution

Revolutions are not definite political acts carried out by the majority in a nation who are unanimous in desiring a single definite object. Revolutionaries and their historians often try to give them that character afterwards, but that is only an illustration of man's general tendency to supply his instinctive acts with family pedigrees of irreproachable, orderly reasoning. It would be less dignified but more honest to admit that revolution is a kind of speeding up of the political flux, during which tendencies that in ordinary times would perhaps only become noticeable in the course of years, come to full fruition in a few weeks or days. Revolution turns the slow river of political development into a rapid in which the slightest action has an immediate effect, and the canoe of government answers more violently to a paddle dipped for a moment than in more ordinary times to the organised and prolonged effort of its whole crew.

Those servants of the autocracy who fermented disorder in Petrograd in March 1917 believed that by creating and suppressing an artificial, premature revolt they could forestall and perhaps altogether prevent the more serious revolt which they had good reason to expect in the future. They were wrong, because revolution is not an act of political life but a state of political life. Hoping to crush a political act, they created the state in which the old means of control slipped from their hands and they became incapable of the suppression of any acts whatsoever.

Their immediate political opponents made the same mistake as the servants of the autocracy. They believed that the autocracy would carry out its plan and therefore did their best to prevent the revolution. Thus, in the days when the revolution of March 1917 began we had the spectacle of the autocracy wrestling with the bourgeoisie, both far removed from the actual people, both gambling with the lives of the people with entirely different objects. The autocracy was trying to create a revolution which would fail. The bourgeoisie was trying to prevent the autocracy from creating a revolution at all. Looking back over a year, it is almost laughable to think that it was the autocracy that arrested the whole labour group of the Central War Industries Committee, because that group of patriotic socialists had shown themselves capable of preventing trouble with the workmen. It is more than laughable to remember that Miliukov, the Cadet leader, sent a statement to the papers alleging that someone pretending to be Miliukov had been urging the workmen to come out into the streets, but that actually begged the workmen, for their own sakes, to do nothing of the kind.

This is not the place in which to give detailed accounts of the methods whereby the autocracy prepared the artificial fireworks, which, unfortunately for them, turned into a very genuine volcano.

It is enough to say that for several months before the revolution they had been running kindergarten classes for policemen in the use of machine guns, just outside Petrograd that armoured cars had been kept back from the front with a view to moving target practice in the streets of the capital, and that weeks before the actual disorders, Petrograd had been turned into a fortified battleground, with machine gun embrasures in the garrets of the houses at points of strategic advantage. Meanwhile, the food shortage, already serious in the preceding September, had been steadily emphasised. The whole labour of the country had been mobilised, out in uniforms, armed, and taken from the land, thus insuring starvation for the nation as a whole in the not distant future. Starvation in the present was inspired by the complete breakdown in the always inadequate transport. Dissatisfaction with the government was common to every class of the population, although it had different causes. Thus the bourgeoisie were dissatisfied with the government because it put difficulties in the way of a successful waging of the war that was to give Russia Constantinople. The aristocracy were dissatisfied with the Tsar on account of his inability to keep his family in order, or to hide the fact that it was in disorder. The folk, the great bulk of the nation, were dissatisfied with the government because they held the government responsible for their increasingly difficult conditions. They were dissatisfied with the government for waging the war, while the classes above them were dissatisfied with the government for not waging it well enough.

For one moment these various discontents were united, and in one matter. When the revolution had begun, when the flux had already gathered speed, when the banks of the hitherto placid stream were already crumbling under the pressure of the torrent, there was not a single class in the nation that was not dissatisfied with the Tsar. The Tsar, accordingly, left the stage as politely as he could, as painlessly as a person in a play. And seeing the bloodless character of his removal, and mistaking his removal for the object and end of the revolution, English, Americans and French united in applauding the most moderate, the biggest, the most surprising revolution in the world. The bourgeois classes in the fighting countries, and those of the labouring classes who had been tamed by reading the newspapers, to a happy acquiescence in bourgeois ideas, were a little troubled lest the disturbance in Russia should affect their war; they having forgotten that they were fighting for democracy, and that the enfranchisement of 180 million souls was in itself a greater victory than they had set out to gain, so that, from that moment, the main object of the war should have been to save that victory. But if the bourgeois classes in the Allied countries were a little troubled, their disquiet was as nothing in comparison with the helpless terror of the bourgeois classes in Russia. They had taken no part in the actual starting of the revolution. Miliukov, as he openly confessed to his party, had seen from his window the soldiers pouring out into the street with red flags to fight for the people instead of for their masters, and he had said to himself, 'there goes the Russian Revolution, and it will be crushed in a quarter of an hour'. A little later he had seen more soldiers in the streets and decided that it would not be crushed so easily. It was only when the risks had already been taken by plain soldiers and workmen, by Cossacks who refused to fire on them; it was only when the revolution had begun, that the already existing organ of the bourgeoisie, the Duma, threw itself into line, and, foam on the crest of an irresistible wave, tried vainly to pretend that it had the power to control and direct the wave itself.

Already a newer, more vital organ was forming. While Miliukov was formulating his ideas about the preservation of the dynasty, or in other words, the transfer of the autocracy to the bourgeoisie, the Soviet of Workmen's Deputies, at first merely a small group of Duma labour members, had formulated quite other ideas, and declared that the revolution belonged to those who made it, not to those who stood aside and then sought to profit by it, and had stated that neither Miliukov nor the outworn Duma had the right to decide their future who had won their freedom, but that that task would be undertaken by a constituent assembly which should represent all Russia. The subsequent history illustrated the necessary opportunism of all parties in a time of revolution, since within a few weeks Miliukov and his party had declared for a republic, and, when the constituent assembly met, it had already earned itself a place, like that of the Duma, among the relics of the past, and was gently set aside by the Soviet which had been the first cause of its summoning.

The Provisional government and the Soviet

There were thus formed two bodies, each of which claimed to represent the revolutionary nation. The first of these was the Provisional government, appointed by an executive committee of the Duma, and so did indirectly represent that body, which, never fully representative of the people, had lost in the course of the war any claim to stand for anything except the bourgeois and privileged classes. The second of these was the Soviet of Workmen's and Soldiers' Deputies. Every thousand workmen and every company of soldiers had the right to send one member to the Soviet. From the very first there could be no doubt in the mind of an unprejudiced observer as to which of these two bodies best represented the Russian people. I do not think I shall ever again be so happy in my life as I was during those first days when I saw working men and peasant soldiers sending representatives of their class and not of mine. I remembered Shelley's,

'Shake your chains to earth like dew
Which in sleep had fallen on you -
Ye are many - they are few',

and wondered that this thing had not come to pass before. And I though, how applicable to revolution are Sir Thomas Browne's words on the Flood when he wrote: 'That there was a Deluge once, seems not to me so great a Miracle as that there is not one always.'

Immediately there became visible a definite fissure, soon a wide gulf, between the ideals of these two bodies, the government and the Soviet. The people, the working classes and the peasants, who suffered most from the war, demanded that steps should be taken to secure peace. They did not want to fight to get territory for the sake of some phantasmagoric gain which did not affect them, which they did not understand. They were starving already, and saw worse starvation ahead. The government, on the other hand, was, if anything, except for the presence in it of Kerensky the labour member, more definitely imperialistic than the autocracy whose place it had taken.

The gulf between the working classes and the government became suddenly deeper when it was realised that the future of the revolution depended on the possession of the army. If the army were not to be swept into the revolution, if it were allowed to remain apart from politics, it would be a passive weapon in the hands of the government, who would thus be able to suppress the Soviets, and so the true expression of the people's will, whenever it should think fit. If the government had been able to retain possession of the army then Miliukov might have had his way, and the bourgeoisie would have secured the profits of the revolt of the masses.

This, however, was not to be, and immediately the contradiction between revolution and war of the imperialistic kind became evident. The army, which at that time meant practically the whole of the younger peasantry, took the share in politics it had a right to take. From that moment the future of the Soviets was assured, and the bourgeois government was doomed to be a government only by the goodwill of the Soviets which, within a few days of the beginning of the revolution, were the only real power in the country.

That they had been right in fearing retention of the army by the bourgeoisie was proved again and again, by Kerensky, Kornilov, Kaledin, Alexeiev, Dutov, at subsequent periods of the revolution, each one in turn basing his resistance to the Soviets on some part of the army which had been kept free from the contagion of free political expression.

Then began the long struggle of the summer. The Soviets, in which the moderates who desired to keep the government as a sort of executive organ, mistrusting their own abilities, were in a majority, exerted all their influence on the government in the direction of peace. The government made its representations to the Allies, but, at any rate at first, gambled on the future and pretended that things were not so bad and that Russia could still take an active part in the war. There was a decisive moment when Miliukov wrote a note to the Allies calculated to lull them into the belief that the changes in Russia meant nothing, and that Russia stood by her old claims. The soldiers and people poured into the streets in protest, and that lie had to be publicly withdrawn.

Already there was serious opposition to the moderate party in the Soviets from the Bolsheviks, who urged that coalition with the bourgeoisie was merely postponing peace, and bringing starvation and disaster nearer. The Moderates proposed a Stockholm Conference, at which socialist groups of all countries should meet and try to come to a common understanding. This was opposed by the Allied goverments and by the Bolsheviks, on the grounds that the German majority socialists would be the agents of the German government. One deadlock followed another. Each successive deadlock strengthened the party of the Bolsheviks who held that the Provisional government was an incubus, and that all authority should belong to the Soviets, to which in internal affairs, it actually did belong.

The Bolshevik leaders, Lenin and Trotsky, had come from exile in Western countries not merely to take their share in the Russian Revolution, but to use Russia in kindling the world revolution. They called for peace, but peace for them was not an end in itself. They could say with Christ, that they brought not peace but a sword. For they hoped that in stirring the working classes of the world to demand peace from their goverments, they would be putting into their hands the sword that was necessary for the social revolution in which cause they had, like many of their friends, spent the best years of their lives.

In their own country, at any rate, they have proved that they were right in their calculation. The struggle for peace and the failure to obtain it shook the government into the disastrous adventure of the Galician advance. It was shaken again by the Galician retreat and weakened with every telegram from Allied countries that emphasised the continuance of the war. Each shock for the government was also a shock for the moderate party in the Soviets. The struggle in Russia became, as the Bolsheviks wished it should become, a struggle between the classes, a struggle in which the issue became ever clearer between the working and the privileged classes. The government went to Moscow for moral support and came back without it. The Kornilov mutiny, a definite threat against the Soviets by a handful of privileged classes, (made in the guise of a patriotic movement and therefore supported by Kornilov himself and by certain of the Allies), merely strengthened the organisations it was intended to overthrow. Within the Soviets the moderate party which had already come by force of events to be a sort of annexe of the bourgeoisie, grew weaker and weaker after this illustration of the danger of their policy. Just as the government went to Moscow to seek support in a conference, so the moderate party, feeling support slipping from under it, knowing that the next meeting of the All Russian Assembly of Soviets would find it in a minority, treacherously sought a new foothold in an artificial democratic assembly. Not even these tactics shook the actual fabric of the Soviets, and when, in October, first Petrograd, then Moscow, showed a huge Bolshevik majority, the Bolshevik leaders were so confident that they had the country behind them that they made a very single arrangement for the ejection of the government openly over the telephone, and, notwithstanding, neither the government nor the old moderates (now in a minority) could muster the authority to prevent them.

The point that I wish to make is this that from the first moment of the revolution to the present day, the real authority of the Soviets has been unshaken. The October Revolution did not give authority to the Soviets. That had always been theirs, by their very nature. It was merely a public open illustration of the change of opinion brought about in the Soviets themselves by the change of opinion in the working man and soldiers who elected them. The October Revolution cleared away the waste growths that hid the true government of Russia from the world, and as the smoke of the short struggle died away, it was seen that that government had merely to formulate an authority it already possessed.

What is the republic of the Soviets?

The formulation of the Soviet constitution was a matter of actual practice guided always by the definite principle of the dictatorship of the proletariat which I have elsewhere briefly discussed in speaking of the Constituent Assembly. There had been a number of small, formal changes or readjustments, of independent parts in the machine, but I do not think either opponents or supporters of the Soviet government can quarrel very seriously with the following statement. Every workman, every peasant in Russia has the right to vote in the election of deputies to his local Soviet, which is made up of a number of deputies corresponding to the number of electors. The local Soviets can choose their delegates to an All-Russian Assembly of Soviets. This All-Russian Assembly elects its Central Executive Committee, on the basis of approximately one in five of the delegates to the assembly. This Central Executive Committee controls, appoints and dismisses the People's Commissaries, who are the actual government. All decrees of state importance are passed by the Central Executive Committee before being issued as laws by the Council of People's Commissaries.

At each successive All-Russian Assembly of Soviets, the Executive Committee automatically resigns, and the Assembly as a whole expresses its approval or disapproval of what has been done by its representatives and by the Council of Commissaries during the period since the previous All-Russian Assembly, and, electing a new Executive Committee, which in political character accurately corresponds to the party colouring of the Assembly ensures that the controlling organ shall accurately reflect the feeling of the electorate.

No limit is set to local reelection. Deputies are withdrawn and others substituted for them whenever this seems necessary to the local electorate. Thus the country is free from the danger of finding itself governed by the ghosts of its dead opinions, and, on the other hand, those ghosts find themselves expediously laid in their graves as soon as, becoming ghosts, they cease to have the right to rule.

Just as the Soviet constitution ensures that the actual law-givers shall be in the closest touch with the people, just as it ensures that indeed instead of in amiable theory the people shall be their own lawgivers, so it also provides for intercommunication in a contrary direction. The remotest atom on the periphery is not without its influence on the centre. So also the centre, through the Soviets, affects the atoms of the periphery. The institution of Soviets means that every minutest act of the Council of People's Commissaries is judged and interpreted in accordance with its own local conditions by each local Soviet. No other form of government could give this huge diverse entity of Russia, with its varying climates and races, with its plains, its steppes, its wild mountains, the free, local autonomy of interpretation which it needs. The shepherd of the Caucasus, the Cossack from the Urals and the fisherman from the Yenisei can sit together in the All-Russian Assembly, and know that the laws, whose principles they approve, are not steel bands too loose for one and throttling another, but are instruments which each Soviet can fashion in its own way for the special needs of its own community.

This constitution is one particularly apt for Russia. It is also particularly apt for a country in a time of revolution. It affords a real dictatorship to the class that is in revolt, and such dictatorship is necessary, since no one could expect from members of the class that is being ousted from its place of domination wholehearted assistance in its own undoing. Those democrats in other countries and – in Russia – who do not understand what is happening under their eyes, exclaim at the unfairness of excluding the bourgeoisie from power. They forget, or have never realised, that the object of the social revolution is to put an end to the existence of the bourgeois or exploiting class, not merely to make it powerless. If exploitation is destroyed then there can be no class of exploiters, and the present exclusion of the bourgeoisie from government is merely a means of hastening and rendering less painful the transition of the bourgeois from his parasitic position to the more honourable position of equality with his fellow workers. Once the conditions of parasitism, privilege and exploitation have been destroyed, the old divisions of the class struggle will automatically have disappeared.

By the nature of things it has so happened that practically all the foreign observers of events in Russia have belonged to the privileged classes in their respective countries, and have been accustomed to associate with the privileged classes in Russia. They have consequently found it difficult to escape from their class in judging the story happening before their eyes. Those working men sent from the Allied countries, less with the idea of studying the revolution, but of telling it to do what the Allies wanted, have also been specially chosen, and deprived by their very mandates of the clear eyes and open mind they should have. Socialists especially, who had long dreamed of revolution, found it particularly difficult to recognise in this cloudy, tremendous struggle the thing which their dreams had softened for them into something more docile, less self willed. Nothing has been more remarkable or less surprising than the fact that of all the observers sent here from abroad those men have seen the thing clearest who by their upbringing and standards of life have been furthest from the revolutionary movement.

I do not propose to recapitulate the whole programme of the Soviet government, nor to spend minutes, when I have so few, in discussing in detail their efforts towards an equitable land settlement, their extraordinarily interesting work in building up, under the stress of famine and war, an economic industrial organisation which shall facilitate the eventual socialisation of Russia. That is material for many letters, and here I have not time for one. I therefore take the two events which have been most misused in blackening the Soviet government to those who should have been its friends. These were the dissolution of the Constituent Assembly, and the negotiations which ended, temporarily at least, in a separate peace between Russia and the Central Empires. I will take these two events, and try to show what happened in each case, and why the reproaches flung at the Soviets on account of them were due either to misunderstanding or to malice.

The Constituent Assembly

I suppose in America, as in England, the dissolution of the Constituent Assembly was one of the events that best served the people who were anxious to persuade public opinion that the Soviet government was a government of usurpation, holding its own by force, and not representing the will of the people. I think that, without any special pleading, it will be possible to bring together facts which put an entirely different light on that event. The mere fact that the parties opposed to the Bolsheviks had spent eight months murdering the Constituent Assembly, putting it off day by day in hopes that the country would change, and that the revolution would come crawling home asking for a quiet life, leaving the gentlemen to do the work of the government, should be set against the short speech of the sailor who told the Assembly that it had talked enough, that its guards were tired, and that really it was time to go to bed. It should be remembered that the Constituent Assembly was for neither party an end in itself. For each party it represented a political instrument, not a political aim. It was a tool, not a task. It was thrown away when further use of it would have damaged the purpose for which it was invented.

Look back, for a moment, on its history. The very idea of a Constituent Assembly was first put forward by the Soviet, by the very body which, in the end, opposed its realisation. The Soviet, in those exhilarating days of March 1917, declared that without such an Assembly the future of Russia could not be decided. The effect of this declaration was to make impossible Miliukov's plan of choking the revolution at birth. Miliukov, in the first days of the revolution tried by means of quick jugglery with abdications, a regency, and a belated constitution, to profit by the elemental uprising of the masses to secure an exchange of authority out of the hands of the Tsar's bureaucracy, into the hands of the bourgeoisie. For him, the revolution was to be a tramcar which would stop conveniently at the point where the Cadet Party used to alight. The idea of the Constituent Assembly was a like a big label on that tramcar showing that it had a further destination. It became clear at once that that car would not stop at the point that Miliukov had chosen. The next hope of the bourgeoisie was to keep it moving to prevent it stopping anywhere else until the passengers should be so tired of moving that they would be glad to stop anywhere and would be amenable and peaceable on alighting.

The bourgeois parties deliberately postponed the meeting of the Constituent Assembly, since it was clear that, were it to meet at once, its members would be practically identical with those of the Soviet, so that the voice of the bourgeoisie would be unheard in the roar of the waking masses. The aim of the bourgeoisie was: (1) to postpone the elections until the electors had wearied of the Soviets, and (2) to postpone such reforms as most concerned the destruction of their own privileges (such as the land reforms) until they could summon a Constituent Assembly whose character would be agreeable to themselves. While the bourgeoisie held this attitude it was natural that the Soviets, and most of all the left party in the Soviets, should use the Constituent Assembly as a means of showing up the duplicity of their bourgeois opponents.

Gradually circumstances changed. The bourgeoisie lost hope

and transferred their allegiance to the moderate majority in the Soviets, because they began to realise that the marked increase of Bolshevism heralded something from their point of view even worse than the Constituent Assembly as it would have been in April or May. The extremely flexible representation of the Soviets showed that the masses were coming nearer and nearer to the position of the Bolsheviks, or rather to a readiness to support the Bolshevik leaders in view of the manifest failure of the coalition government to get peace, or indeed anything else that the masses desired. The Constituent Assembly now became the last hope of the original moderate members of the Soviet Executive, who felt the ground of real support in the active political masses slipping from beneath their feet. At this point came the October Revolution, when the coalition, already a ghost, and a discredited ghost, was laid in its grave. Immense Bolshevik majorities in the Petrograd and Moscow Soviets, and then in the All-Russian Assembly of Soviets, proved that the mass of active political opinion in the country fully approved of the step that had been taken.

Then followed the elections to the Constituent Assembly (organised and canvassed before the October Revolution) in which there was a majority against the Bolsheviks. The explanation of this is perfectly simple. It lies in the fact that a revolution is a very uncomfortable thing for everybody who takes part in it, and that great numbers of people during the preceding eight months had come to look forward to the Constituent Assembly much as children look forward to the word FINIS at the end of a difficult lesson-book. The Constituent Assembly meant for these people an end to political debate, an end even to political life, an end anyhow to revolution.

In every country it is only a small minority that really concerns itself with politics. Outside that minority is a big unconscious mass of voting material, which does not concern itself with active politics, and asks nothing from its government except to be let alone. This indifferent mass, which took very little part in the living politics of the Soviets, was ready to vote for the Constituent Assembly in a sort of dim belief that those elections would mean a return to a quiet life, and should therefore be encouraged. It voted much as rich men give alms to a charity. It voted in much the spirit of the rich man who is willing to give alms to a deserving charity for which he would be most unwilling to do any real work. It knew vaguely that the bourgeoisie were fairly bad, and it had also heard that the Bolsheviks were terrible people. It therefore put its vote on the side of those people against whom it had heard nothing in particular. And the result was that the live part of the nation was faced – almost at the moment of coming to their own – with a legacy in the form of an Assembly, the majority in which was made up of the very men whom they had just overthrown. The question was a plain one. Should the conscious workers of the country submit to the dead weight of the unconscious, even if that dead weight was artfully fashioned by their enemies into the form of the very tool with which they had themselves been successfully working? The question was put at a moment of extreme difficulty, when acceptance of the Constituent Assembly would have relieved the Bolsheviks (at the New Year) of tremendous responsibility. It would have been an easy way out, for cowards. But the Bolsheviks were not afraid of responsibility, were not looking for easy ways out, were confident that the whole of the active, conscious population was behind them, and swept the Assembly aside. Not anywhere in Russia did the indifferent mass stir in protest. The Assembly died, like the Tsardom, and the coalition before it. Not any one of the three showed in the manner of its dying that it retained any right to live.

Peace negotiations

The day after the October Revolution Lenin proposed, and the Assembly carried, the declaration on peace, with its promise to do away with the secret diplomacy that had kept Russia in the war beyond her strength, and allowed small groups to gamble with the lives of nations. On that day, October 26, the whole world was told that the new Russian government was ready to conclude peace itself, and invited all the fighting countries to put an end to the war. Without annexation (that is, without the seizure of other people's land and without the forced incorporation of other nationalities), and without indemnity. The declaration was sent out by radio on November 7. Some goverments prevented its publication, others sought to disguise its true character and to give it the appearance of an offer of separate peace. The Allies replied to it with a threat, conveyed to the Russian Commander-in-Chief Dukhonin, that further steps towards peace would have serious consequences. It should of course be remembered that the Allies were in a position of peculiar difficulty. Practically all the Russians who were able to give direct information to members of the Allied goverments belonged to the classes that had persistently fed themselves and others with lies as to the character of the Bolsheviks. They believed that the Soviets could hold authority only for a few days and they persuaded Allied goverments to share that belief.

The next step of the Sovietswas and agreement made across the front itself, stopping all military operations between the Black Sea and the Baltic. This was followed by yet another invitation to the Allies to join Russia in peace negotiations. Meanwhile the German government, with one eye on the military party and the other on the feeling of German labour, which at that time was unrestful and excited by the Russian Revolution, was hesitating over its answer. I shall not here attempt any detailed history of what followed. My only point is that the Soviet government cannot be accoused of having sought and obtained a separate peace. The first aim of the Bolsheviks was, as it always will be, a universal social revolution. They hoped to illustrate to the workers of the world the possibility of honourable peace, and nothing would have pleased them better than to find that such a peace rejected by all goverments alike, so that the workers, convinced of its possibility, should rise and overthrow them. That was their general aim. They, least of all goverments in the world, were interested in a German victory. Their proposal was for a general peace, for the peace which Russia, in agony, had been awaiting for a year.

What followed? Step by step, they published every detail of their negotiations over the armistice and every word of the German replies. Then came the first German answer as to the conditions of peace, in which Germany and her allies expressed themselves ready to make the Russian formula the basis of negotiation. The Bolsheviks believed that if the Allies had even at that late hour joined them, so that in withdrawing from that position the Germans would have been facing a continuance of the war as a whole instead of merely a failure to obtain peace with the weakest of the Allies, peace on the Russian formula would have been attainable. The Allies left them, unrecognised, ignored, to continue their struggle singlehanded. The Germans now took a bolder line, and the hand outstretched in spurious friendship became a grasping claw. The first Russian delegation came home to confer with the Soviet government at to what was to be done in this new situation; the peace they had promised their exhausted army, their tortured working classes, seemed to be fading like a mirage. Trotsky, at the head of a reinforced delegation, went to Brest with one of the most daring plans with which any David has sought to destroy his Goliath.

The absence of the Allies had deprived him of the possibility of exhibiting to the working classes of the world the inability of their present goverments to conclude a peace in which there should be neither conqueror nor conquered. He now attempted to bring about a revolution in Germany, or to obtain such a peace for Russia by making the German government itself illustrate in their negotiations with him their utter disregard for the expressed wishes of the German people. He did actually succeed in causing huge strikes in both Austria and in Germany, and it is impossible for anyone to say that he would not have finally succeeded in hitting the Goliath of force opposed to him fairly between the eyes with this shining pebble of an idea, which was the only weapon at his command, if, at the last moment, his aim had not been deflected and the target shifted by the treachery of the handful of men in the Ukraine who were resisting by every means in their power the natural development of the Soviets. These men, preferring to sell their country to Germany than to lose the reins of government themselves, opened separate negotiations, thereby breaking the unity of the ideal front which Trotsky opposed to the Germans. The Germans saw that with part of that front they could come immediately to terms. Instantly their tone in the negotiations changed. They persuaded their own people that the Russians were themselves to blame for not getting the peace they required, and that a just peace was only possible with the Ukraine. Meanwhile the soldiers and workers of the Ukraine were gradually obtaining complete power over their own country, so that when Germany actually concluded peace with the Ukraine, the so-called government whose signatures were attached to that treacherous agreement was actually in asylum in German headquarters and unable to return to its own supposed capital except under the protection of German bayonets. The Soviet triumphed in the Ukraine, and declared its solidarity with Russia. The Germans, like the Allies, preferred to recognise the better dressed persons who were ready to conclude peace with them in the name of a country which had definitely disowned them. From that moment the Brest peace negotiations were doomed to failure. Trotsky made a last desperate appeal to the workers of Germany. He said, 'We will not sign your robber's peace, but we demobilise our army and declare that Russia is no longer at war. Will the German people allow you to advance on a defenceless revolution?'

The Germans did advance, not at first in regular regiments, but in small groups of volunteers who had no scruples in the matter. Many German soldiers, to their eternal honour, refused to advance, and were shot. The demobilisation of the Russian army meant little, because it had long ceased to be anything but a danger to the peaceful population in its rear. The Soviet had only the very smallest real force, and that, as yet, unorganised, with enthusiasm but without confidence, utterly unpracticed in warfare, consisting chiefly of workmen who, as was natural, were the first to understand what it was they had to defend. It soon became clear that serious resistance was impossible. The Soviet government was faced with a choice: to collapse in a quite unequal struggle, or to sign a peace agreement of which they disapproved. Many thought that the cause of revolution would be best served by their deaths, and were ready to die. Lenin doubted the efficacy of such a rhetorical gesture, and believed that the secession of Russia from the war would ensure the continuation of the war by the imperialistic groups until such time as other countries reached the same exhaustion as had been reached by Russia, when in his opinion, revolution would be inevitable. He held that, for the future of the world revolution, the best that could be done would be the preservation, even in seriously limited territory, of the Soviet government as a nucleus of revolution, as an illustration of the possibility of revolution, until that moment when the workers of Russia should be joined by the workers of the world. His opinion carried the majority first of the Executive Committee, then of the fourth All-Russian Assembly. The Germans replied to the Russian offer to sign the peace with a statement which was an ironic parody of the Russian declaration at Brest. The Russians had said, 'We will not sign peace, but the war is ended,' the Germans said, 'We agree to peace, but the war shall continue.'

And, indeed, while the Soviet government moved to Moscow, the Germans, using in the south the pretext of the Ukrainian Rada, and in the north that of the bourgeois Finnish government, advanced through the Ukraine to the outlet of the Don, and in the north to the very gates of Petrograd. The matter stands so, as I write these lines. By the time you read them, much will have happened that it is impossible now to foresee.

The Soviet government and the Allies

From the moment of the October Revolution on, the best illustration of the fact that the Soviet government is the natural government of the Russian people, and has deep roots in the whole of the conscious responsible part of the working classes and the peasantry, has been the attitude of the defeated minorities who oppose it. Whereas the Bolsheviks worked steadily in the Soviets when the majority was against them, and made their final move for power only when assured they had the overwhelming majority of the Soviets behind them, their opponents see their best hope of regaining power not in the Soviets, not even in Russia itself, but in some extraordinary intervention from without. By asking for foreign help against the Soviet government they prove that such help should not be given, and that they do not deserve it. The Soviet has stood for six months and more, absolutely unshaken by any movement against it inside Russia. In the Ukraine the anti-Soviet minority asked for intervention and received it. German bayonets and German organisation destroyed the Soviets of the Ukraine, and then destroyed the mock government that had invited their help. We, the Allies, supported that anti-Soviet minority, and, in so far as our help was efficacious, contributed our share in obtaining for Germany a victorious progress from one end of the Black Sea coast to the other. In helping the Ukrainian minority we helped the Germans to secure the Ukrainian bread and coal and iron that would otherwise have gone to help Russia to recuperate. In Finland we repeated the mistake. We gave at least moral help to the White Finns, simply because they were opposed to the Red Finns who were supported by the Soviets, not realising that the White Finns were the pawns of Germany, and that in the defeat of the Red Finns we witnessed the defeat of the only party in Finland which was bound, by its socialistic nature, to be an enemy of imperialistic Germany. Do not let us make the same mistake in Russia. If the Allies lend help to any minority that cannot overturn the

Soviets without their help, they will be imposing on Free Russia a government which will be in perpetual need of external help, and will, for simple reasons of geography, be bound to take that help from Germany. Remember that for the German autocracy, conscious of the socialistic mass beneath it, the mere existence of the Soviet government of Russia is a serious danger. Remember that any no-Soviet government in Russia would be welcomed by Germany and, reciprocally, could not but regard Germany as its protector. Remember that the revolutionary movement in Eastern Europe, no less than the American and British navies, is an integral part of the Allied blockade of the Central Empires.

And, apart from the immediate business of the war, remember that Germany is seeking by every means, open and secret, to obtain such command over Russia's resources as will in the long run allow her to dictate her will to Russia's people. Remember that the Soviet government, fully aware of this, would be glad of your help, of your cooperation, would be glad even to give you control over some part of her resources, if only to prevent that ominous ultimate dominion within Russia of a single foreign power.

Remember all these things, if indeed you need, as I think you do not need, such selfish motives to prompt you to the support of men who, if they fail, will fail only from having hoped too much. Every true man is in some sort, until his youth dies and his eyes harden, the potential builder of a New Jerusalem. At some time or other, every one of us has dreamed of laying his brick in such a work. And even if this thing that is being built here with tears and blood is not the golden city that we ourselves have dreamed, it is still a thing to the sympathetic understanding of which each one of us is bound by whatever he owes to his own youth. And if each one of us, then all the more each nation is bound by what it owes to those first daring days of its existence, when all the world looked askance upon its presumptuous birth. America was young once, and there were men in America who would have brought in foreign aid to re-establish their dominion over a revolted nation. Are those the men to whom America now looks back with gratitude and pride?

Well, writing at speed to break my pen, and with the knowledge that in a few hours the man leaves Moscow who is to carry this letter with him to America, I have failed to say much that I would have said. I write now with my messenger waiting for my manuscript and somehow or other, incoherent, incomplete as it is, must bring it to an end. I will end, as I began, with a quotation from your own Emerson.

'What is the scholar, what is the man for, but for hospitality to every new thought of his time? Have you leisure, power, property, friends? You shall be the asylum and patron of every new thought, every unproven opinion, every untried project, which proceeds out of good will and honest seeking. All the newspapers, all the tongues of today will of course at first defame what is noble; but you who hold not of today, not of the Times, but of the Everlasting, are to stand for it; and the highest compliment man ever receives from heaven is the sending to him its disguised and discredited angels.'

No one contends that the Bolsheviks are angels. I ask only that men shall look through the fog of libel that surrounds them and see that the ideal for which they are struggling, in the only way in which they can struggle, is among those lights which every man of young and honest heart sees before him somewhere on the road, and not among those other lights from which he resolutely turns away. These men who have made the Soviet government in Russia, if they must fail, will fail with clean shields and clean hearts, having striven for an ideal which will live beyond them. Even if they fail, they will none the less have written a page of history more daring than any other which I can remember in the history of humanity. They are writing it amid slinging of mud from all the meaner spirits in their country, in yours and in my own. But when the thing is over, and their enemies have triumphed, the mud will vanish like black magic at noon, and that page will be as white as the snows of Russia, and the writing on it as bright as the gold domes that I used to see glittering in the sun when I looked from my windows in Petrograd.

And when in after years men read that page they will judge your country and mine, your race and mine, by the help or hindrance they gave to the writing of it.

Arthur Ransome
1918

Six weeks in Russia 1919

Introduction

I am well aware that there is material in this book which will be misused by fools both white and red. That is not my fault. My object has been narrowly limited. I have tried by means of a bald record of conversations and things seen, to provide material for those who wish to know what is being done and thought in Moscow at the present time, and demand something more to go upon than secondhand reports of wholly irrelevant atrocities committed by either one side or the other, and often by neither one side nor the other, but by irresponsible scoundrels who, in the natural turmoil of the greatest convulsion in the history of our civilization, escape temporarily here and there from any kind of control.

The book is in no sense of the word propaganda. For propaganda, for the defence or attack of the Communist position, is needed a knowledge of economics, both from the capitalist and socialist standpoints, to which I cannot pretend.

Very many times during the revolution it has seemed to me a tragedy that no Englishman properly equipped in this way was in Russia studying the gigantic experiment which, as a country, we are allowing to pass abused but not examined. I did my best. I got, I think I may say, as near as any foreigner who was not a Communist could get to what was going on. But I never lost the bitter feeling that the opportunities of study which I made for myself were wasted, because I could not hand them on to some other Englishman, whose education and training would have enabled him to make a better, a fuller use of them. Nor would it have been difficult for such a man to get the opportunities which were given to me when, by sheer persistence in enquiry, I had overcome the hostility which I at first encountered as the correspondent of a 'bourgeois' newspaper. Such a man could be in Russia now, for the Communists do not regard war as we regard it. The Germans would hardly have allowed an Allied Commission to come to Berlin a year ago to investigate the nature and working of the autocracy. The Russians, on the other hand, immediately agreed to the suggestion of the Berne Conference that they should admit a party of socialists, the majority of whom, as they well knew, had already expressed condemnation of them. Further, in agreeing to this, they added that they would as willingly admit a committee of enquiry sent by any of the 'bourgeois' governments actually at war with them.

I am sure that there will be many in England who will understand much better than I the drudgery of the revolution which is in this book very imperfectly suggested. I repeat that it is not my fault that they must make do with the eyes and ears of an ignorant observer. No doubt I have not asked the questions they would have asked, and have thought interesting and novel much which they would have taken for granted.

The book has no particular form, other than that given it by a more or less accurate adherence to chronology in setting down things seen and heard. It is far too incomplete to allow me to call it a journal. I think I could have made it twice as long without repetitions, and I am not at all sure that in choosing in a hurry between this and that I did not omit much which could with advantage be substituted for what is here set down. There is nothing here of my talk with the English soldier prisoners and nothing of my visit to the officers confined in the Butyrka jail. There is nothing of the plagues of typhus and influenza, or of the desperate situation of a people thus visited and unable to procure from abroad the simplest drugs which they cannot manufacture at home or even the anaesthetics necessary for their wounded on every frontier of their country. I forgot to describe the ballet which I saw a few days before leaving. I have said nothing of the talk I had with Eliava concerning the Russian plans for the future of Turkestan. I could think of a score of other omissions. Judging from what I have read since my return from Russia, I imagine people will find my book very poor in the matter of terrors. There is nothing here of the Red Terror, or of any of the terrors on the other side. But for its poverty in atrocities my book will be blamed only by fanatics, since they alone desire proofs of past terrors as justification for new ones.

On reading my manuscript through, I find it quite surprisingly dull. The one thing that I should have liked to transmit through it seems somehow to have slipped away. I should have liked to explain what was the appeal of the revolution to men like Colonel Robins and myself, both of us men far removed in origin and upbringing from the revolutionary and socialist movements in our own countries. Of course no one who was able, as we were able, to watch the men of the revolution at close quarters could believe for a moment that they were the mere paid agents of the very power which more than all others represented the stronghold they had set out to destroy. We had the knowledge of the injustice being done to these men to urge us in their defence. But there was more in it than that. There was the feeling, from which we could never escape, of the creative effort of the revolution. There was the thing that distinguishes the creative from other artists, the living, vivifying expression of something hitherto hidden in the consciousness of humanity. If this book were to be an accurate record of my own impressions, all the drudgery, gossip, quarrels, arguments, events and experiences it contains would have to be set against a background of that extraordinary vitality which obstinately persists in Moscow even in these dark days of discomfort, disillusion, pestilence, starvation and unwanted war.

Arthur Ransome

One / To Petrograd

On January 30 a party of four newspaper correspondents, two Norwegians, a Swede and myself, left Stockholm to go into Russia. We travelled with the members of the Soviet government's legation, headed by Vorovsky and Litvinov, who were going home after the breaking off of official relations by Sweden. Some months earlier I had got leave from the Bolsheviks to go into Russia to get further material for my history of the revolution, but at the last moment there was opposition and it seemed likely that I should be refused permission. Fortunately, however, a copy of the Morning Post reached Stockholm, containing a report of a lecture by Mr Lockhart in which he had said that as I had been out of Russia for six months I had no right to speak of conditions there. Armed with this I argued that it would be very unfair if I were not allowed to come and see things for myself. I had no further difficulties.

We crossed by boat to Abo, grinding our way through the ice, and then travelled by rail to the Russian frontier, taking several days over the journey owing to delays variously explained by the

Finnish authorities. We were told that the Russian White Guards had planned an attack on the train. Litvinov, half smiling, wondered if they were purposely giving time to the White Guards to organise such an attack. Several nervous folk inclined to that opinion. But at Viborg we were told that there were grave disorders in Petrograd and that the Finns did not wish to fling us into the middle of a scrimmage. Then someone obtained a newspaper and we read a detailed account of what was happening. This account was, as I learnt on my return, duly telegraphed to England like much other news of a similar character. There had been a serious revolt in Petrograd. The Semenovsky regiment had gone over to the mutineers, who had seized the town. The government, however, had escaped to Kronstadt, whence they were bombarding Petrograd with naval guns.

This sounded fairly lively, but there was nothing to be done, so we finished up the chess tournament we had begun on the boat. An Estonian won it, and I was second, by reason of a lucky win over Litvinov, who is really a better player. By Sunday night we reached Terijoki and on Monday moved slowly to the frontier of Finland close to Bieloostrov. A squad of Finnish soldiers was waiting, excluding everybody from the station and seeing that no dangerous revolutionary should break away on Finnish territory. There were no horses, but three hand sledges were brought, and we piled the luggage on them, and then set off to walk to the frontier duly convoyed by the Finns. A Finnish lieutenant walked at the head of the procession, chatting good humouredly in Swedish and German, much as a man might think it worthwhile to be kind to a crowd of unfortunates just about to be flung into a boiling cauldron. We walked a few hundred yards along the line and then turned into a road deep in snow through a little bare wood, and so down to the little wooden bridge over the narrow frozen stream that separates Finland from Russia. The bridge, not twenty yards across, has a toll bar at each end, two sentry boxes and two sentries. On the Russian side the bar was the familiar black and white of the old Russian Empire, with a sentry box to match. The Finns seemingly had not yet had time to paint their bar and box.

The Finns lifted their toll bar, and the Finnish officers leading our escort walked solemnly to the middle of the bridge. Then the luggage was dumped there, while we stood watching the trembling of the rickety little bridge under the weight of our belongings, for we were all taking in with us as much food as we decently could. We were none of us allowed on the bridge until an officer and a few men had come down to meet us on the Russian side. Only little Nina, Vorovsky's daughter, about ten years old, chattering Swedish with the Finns, got leave from them, and shyly, step by step, went down the other side of the bridge and struck up acquaintance with the soldier of the Red Army who stood there, gun in hand, and obligingly bent to show her the sign, set in his hat, of the crossed sickle and hammer of the Peasants' and Workmen's Republic. At last the Finnish lieutenant took the list of his prisoners and called out the names 'Vorovsky, wife and one bairn', looking laughingly over his shoulder at Nina flirting with the sentry. Then 'Litvinov,' and so on through all the Russians, about 30 of them. We four visitors, Grimlund the Swede, Puntervald and Stang the Norwegians, and I, came last. At last, after a general shout of farewell, and 'Helse Finland' from Nina, the Finns turned and went back into their civilization, and we went forward into the new struggling civilization of Russia. Crossing that bridge we passed from one philosophy to another, from one extreme of the class struggle to the other, from a dictatorship of the bourgeoisie to a dictatorship of the proletariat.

The contrast was noticeable at once. On the Finnish side of the frontier we had seen the grandiose new frontier station, much larger than could possibly be needed, but quite a good expression of the spirit of the new Finland. On the Russian side we came to the same grey old wooden station known to all passengers to and from Russia for polyglot profanity and passport difficulties. There were no porters, which was not surprising because there is barbed wire and an extremely hostile sort of neutrality along the frontier and traffic across has practically ceased. In the buffet, which was very cold, no food could be bought. The long tables once laden with caviar and other *zakuski* were bare. There was, however, a samovar, and we bought tea at 60 kopecks a glass and lumps of sugar at two roubles fifty each. We took our tea into the inner passport room, where I think a stove must have been burning the day before, and there made some sort of a meal off some of Puntervald's Swedish hardbread. It is difficult to me to express the curious mixture of depression and exhilaration that was given to the party by this derelict starving station combined with the feeling that we were no longer under guard but could do more or less as we liked. It split the party into two factions, of which one wept while the other sang. Madame Vorovsky, who had not been in Russia since the first revolution, frankly wept, but she wept still more in Moscow where she found that even as the wife of a high official of the government she enjoyed no privileges which would save her from the hardships of the population. But the younger members of the party, together with Litvinov, found their spirits irrepressibly rising in spite of having no dinner. They walked about the village, played with the children, and sang, not revolutionary songs, but just jolly songs, any songs that came into their heads. When at last the train came to take us into Petrograd, and we found that the carriages were unheated, somebody got out a mandolin and we kept ourselves warm by dancing. At the same time I was sorry for the five children who were with us, knowing that a country simultaneously suffering war, blockade and revolution is not a good place for childhood. But they had caught the mood of their parents, revolutionaries going home to their revolution, and trotted excitedly up and down the carriage or anchored themselves momentarily, first on one person's knee and then on another's.

It was dusk when we reached Petrograd. The Finland Station, of course, was nearly deserted, but here there were four porters, who charged 250 roubles for shifting the luggage of the party from one end of the platform to the other. We ourselves loaded it into the motor lorry sent to meet us, as at Bieloostrov we had loaded it into the van. There was a long time to wait while rooms were being allotted to us in various hotels, and with several others I walked outside the station to question people about the mutiny and the bombardment of which we had heard in Finland. Nobody knew anything about it. As soon as the rooms were allotted and I knew that I had been lucky enough to get one in the Astoria, I drove off across the frozen river by the Liteini Bridge. The trams were running. The town seemed absolutely quiet, and away down the river I saw once again in the dark, which is never quite dark because of the snow, the dim shape of the fortress, and passed one by one the landmarks I had come to know so well during the last six years—the Summer Garden, the British Embassy, and the great Palace Square where I had seen armoured cars flaunting about during the July rising, soldiers camping during the hysterical days of the Kornilov affair and, earlier, Kornilov himself reviewing the Junkers. My mind went further back to the March revolution, and saw once more the picket fire of the revolutionaries at the corner that night when the remains of the Tsar's government were still frantically printing proclamations ordering the people to go home, at the very moment while they themselves were being besieged in the Admiralty. Then it flung itself further back still, to the day of the declaration of war, when I saw this same square filled with people, while the Tsar came out for a moment on the palace balcony. By that time we were pulling up at the Astoria and I had to turn my mind to something else.

The Astoria is now a bare barrack of a place, but comparatively clean. During the war and the first part of the revolution it was tenanted chiefly by officers, and owing to the idiocy of a few of these at the time of the first revolution in shooting at a perfectly friendly crowd of soldiers and sailors, who came there at first with no other object than to invite the officers to join them, the place was badly smashed up in the resulting scrimmage. I remember with

Major Scale fixing up a paper announcing the fall of Baghdad
either the night this happened or perhaps the night before. People
rushed up to it, thinking it some news about the revolution, and
turned impatiently away. All the damage has been repaired, but the
red carpets have gone, perhaps to make banners, and many of the
electric lights were not burning, probably because of the shortage
in electricity. I got my luggage upstairs to a very pleasant room on
the fourth floor. Every floor of that hotel had its memories for me.
In this room lived that brave reactionary officer who boasted that
he had made a raid on the Bolsheviks and showed little Madame
Kollontai's hat as a trophy. In this I used to listen to Perceval
Gibbon when he was talking about how to write short stories and
having influenza. There was the room where Miss Beatty used to
give tea to tired revolutionaries and to still more tired inquirers
into the nature of revolution while she wrote the only book that
has so far appeared which gives anything like a true impressionist
picture of those unforgettable days.* Close by was the room where
poor Denis Garstin used to talk of the hunting he would have
when the war should come to an end.

I enquired for a meal, and found that no food was to be had
in the hotel, but they could supply hot water. Then, to get an
appetite for sleep, I went out for a short walk, though I did not
much like doing so with nothing but an English passport, and with
no papers to show that I had any right to be there. I had, like the
other foreigners, been promised such papers but had not yet
received them. I went round to the Regina, which used to be one
of the best hotels in the town, but those of us who had rooms
there were complaining so bitterly that I did not stay with them,
but went off along the Moika to the Nevsky and so back to my
own hotel. The streets, like the hotel, were only half lit, and hardly
any of the houses had a lighted window. In the old sheepskin coat
I had worn on the front and in my high fur hat, I felt like some

---

*The Red Heart of Russia.

ghost of the old regime visiting a town long dead. The silence and emptiness of the streets contributed to this effect. Still, the few people I met or passed were talking cheerfully together and the rare sledges and motors had comparatively good roads, the streets being certainly better swept and cleaned than they have been since the last winter of the Russian Empire.

Two / Smolni

Early in the morning I got tea, and a bread card on which I was given a very small allowance of brown bread, noticeably better in quality than the compound of clay and straw which made me ill in Moscow last summer. Then I went to find Litvinov, and set out with him to walk to the Smolni institute, once a school for the daughters of the aristocracy, then the headquarters of the soviet, then the headquarters of the Soviet government, and finally, after the government's evacuation to Moscow, bequeathed to the Northern Commune and the Petrograd Soviet. The town, in daylight, seemed less deserted, though it was obvious that the 'unloading' of the Petrograd population, which was unsuccessfully attempted during the Kerensky regime, had been accomplished to a large extent. This has been partly the result of famine and of the stoppage of factories, which in its turn is due to the impossibility of bringing fuel and raw material to Petrograd. A very large proportion of Russian factory hands have not, as in other countries, lost their connection with their native villages. There was always a considerable annual migration backwards and forwards between the villages and the town and great numbers of workmen have gone home, carrying with them the ideas of the revolution. It should also be remembered that the bulk of the earlier formed units of the

Red Army is composed of workmen from the towns who, except in the case of peasants mobilised in districts which have experienced an occupation by the counter-revolutionaries, are more determined and better understand the need for discipline than the men from the country.

The most noticeable thing in Petrograd to anyone returning after six months' absence is the complete disappearance of armed men. The town seems to have returned to a perfectly peaceable condition in the sense that the need for revolutionary patrols has gone. Soldiers walking about no longer carry their rifles, and the picturesque figures of the revolution who wore belts of machine-gun cartridges slung about their persons have gone.

The second noticeable thing, especially in the Nevsky, which was once crowded with people too fashionably dressed, is the general lack of new clothes. I did not see anybody wearing clothes that looked less than two years old, with the exception of some officers and soldiers who are as well equipped nowadays as at the beginning of the war. Petrograd ladies were particularly fond of boots, and of boots there is an extreme shortage. I saw one young woman in a well-preserved, obviously costly fur coat, and beneath it straw shoes with linen wrappings.

We had started rather late, so we took a tram halfway up the Nevsky. The tram conductors are still women. The price of tickets has risen to a rouble, usually, I noticed, paid in stamps. It used to be ten kopecks.

The armoured car which used to stand at the entrance of Smolni has disappeared and been replaced by a horrible statue of Karl Marx, who stands, thick and heavy, on a stout pedestal, holding behind him an enormous top-hat like the muzzle of an eighteen-inch gun. The only signs of preparations for defence that remain are the pair of light field guns which, rather the worse for weather, still stand under the pillars of the portico which they would probably shake to pieces if ever they should be fired. Inside the routine was as it used to be, and when I turned down the passage to get my permit to go upstairs, I could hardly believe that I had been away for so long. The place is emptier than it was. There is not the same eager crowd of country delegates pressing up and down the corridors and collecting literature from the stalls that I used to see in the old days when the serious little workman from the Viborg side stood guard over Trotsky's door, and from the alcove with its window looking down into the great hall, the endless noise of debate rose from the Petrograd Soviet that met below.

Litvinov invited me to have dinner with the Petrograd Commissars, which I was very glad to do, partly because I was hungry and partly because I thought it would be better to meet Zinoviev thus than in any other manner, remembering how sourly he had looked upon me earlier in the revolution. Zinoviev is a Jew, with a lot of hair, a round smooth face, and a very abrupt manner. He was against the November Revolution, but when it had been accomplished returned to his old allegiance to Lenin and, becoming President of the Northern Commune, remained in Petrograd when the government moved to Moscow. He is neither an original thinker nor a good orator except in debate, in answering opposition, which he does with extreme skill. His nerve was badly shaken by the murders of his friends Volodarsky and Uritzky last year, and he is said to have lost his head after the attack on Lenin, to whom he is extremely devoted. I have heard many Communists attribute to this fact the excesses which followed that event in Petrograd. I have never noticed anything that would make me consider him pro-German, though of course he is pro-Marx. He has, however, a decided prejudice against the English. He was among the Communists who put difficulties in my way as a 'bourgeois journalist' in the earlier days of the revolution, and I had heard that he had expressed suspicion and disapproval of Radek's intimacy with me. I was amused to see his face when he came in and saw me sitting at the table. Litvinov introduced me to him, very tactfully telling him of Lockhart's attack upon me, whereupon he became quite decently friendly, and said that if I could stay a few days in Petrograd on my way back from Moscow he would see that I had access to the historical material I wanted about the doings of the Petrograd Soviet during the time I had been away. I told him I was surprised to find him here and not at Kronstadt, and asked about the mutiny and the treachery of the Semenovsky regiment. There was a shout of laughter, and Pozern explained that there was no Semenovsky regiment in existence, and that the manufacturers of the story, every word of which was a lie, had no doubt tried to give realism to it by putting in the name of the regiment which had taken a chief part in putting down the Moscow insurrection of 14 years ago. Pozern, a thin, bearded man with glasses, was sitting at the other end of the table, as Military Commissar of the Northern Commune.

Dinner in Smolni was the same informal affair that it was in the old days, only with much less to eat. The Commissars, men and women, came in from their work, took their places, fed and went back to work again, Zinoviev in particular staying only a few minutes. The meal was extremely simple, soup with shreds of horse-flesh in it, very good indeed, followed by a little kasha together with small slabs of some sort of white stuff of no particular consistency or taste. Then tea and a lump of sugar. The conversation was mostly about the chances of peace, and Litvinov's rather pessimistic reports were heard with disappointment. Just as I had finished, Vorovsky, Madame Vorovsky and little Nina, together with the two Norwegians and the Swede, came in. I learnt that about half the party were going on to Moscow that night and, deciding to go with them, hurried off to the hotel.

Three / Petrograd to Moscow

There was, of course, a dreadful scrimmage about getting away. Several people were not ready at the last minute. Only one motor was obtainable for nine persons with their light luggage, and a motor lorry for the heavy things. I chose to travel on the lorry with the luggage and had a fine bumpity drive to the station, reminding me of similar though livelier experiences in the earlier days of the revolution when lorries were used for the transport of machine guns, red guards, orators, enthusiasts of all kinds, and any stray persons who happened to clamber on.

At the Nikolai Station we found perfect order until we got into our wagon, an old third-class wagon, in which a certain number of places which one of the party had reserved had been occupied by people who had no right to be there. Even this difficulty was smoothed out in a manner that would have been impossible a year or even six months ago.

The wagon was divided by a door in the middle. There were open coupés and side seats which became plank beds when necessary. We slept in three tiers on the bare boards. I had a very decent place on the second tier, and, by a bit of good luck, the topmost bench over my head was occupied only by luggage, which gave me room to climb up there and sit more or less upright under the roof with my legs dangling above the general tumult of mothers, babies, and Bolsheviks below. At each station at which the train stopped there was a general procession backwards and forwards through the wagon. Everybody who had a kettle or a coffee pot or a tin can, or even an empty meat tin, crowded through the carriage and out to get boiling water. I had nothing but a couple of thermos flasks, but with these I joined the others. From every carriage on the train people poured out and hurried to the taps. No one controlled the taps but, with the instinct for co-operation for

which Russians are remarkable, people formed themselves automatically into queues, and by the time the train started again
everybody was back in his place and ready for a general tea drinking. This performance was repeated again and again throughout the
night. People dozed off to sleep, woke up, drank more tea, and
joined in the various conversations that went on in different parts
of the carriage. Up aloft, I listened first to one and then to another.
Some were grumbling at the price of food. Others were puzzling
why other nations insisted on being at war with them. One man
said he was a co-operator who had come by roundabout ways from
Archangel and, describing the discontent there, told a story which I
give as an illustration of the sort of thing that is being said. in
Russia by non-Bolsheviks. This man, in spite of the presence of
many Communists in the carriage, did not disguise his hostility to
their theories and practice, and none the less told this story. He
said that some of the Russian troops in the Archangel district
refused to go to the front. Their commanders, unable to compel
them, resigned and were replaced by others who, since the men
persisted in refusal, appealed for help. The barracks, so he said,
were then surrounded by American troops, and the Russians, who
had refused to go to the front to fire on other Russians, were given
the choice, either that every tenth man should be shot, or that they
should give up their ringleaders. The ringleaders, 12 in number,
were given up, were made to dig their own graves, and shot. The
whole story may well be Archangel gossip. If so, as a specimen of
such gossip, it is not without significance. In another part of the
carriage an argument on the true nature of selfishness caused some
heat because the disputants insisted on drawing their illustrations
from each other's conduct. Then there was the diversion of a
swearing match at a wayside station between the conductor and
some one who tried to get into this carriage and should have got
into another. Both were fluent and imaginative swearers, and even
the man from Archangel stopped talking to listen to them. One, I
remember, prayed vehemently that the other's hand might fly off,

and the other, not to be outdone, retorted with a similar prayer with regard to the former's head. In England the dispute, which became very fierce indeed, would have ended in assault, but here it ended in nothing but the collection on the platform of a small crowd of experts in bad language who applauded verbal hits with impartiality and enthusiasm.

At last I tried to sleep, but the atmosphere in the carriage, of smoke, babies, stale clothes, and the peculiar smell of the Russian peasantry which no one who has known it can forget, made sleep impossible. But I travelled fairly comfortably, resolutely shutting my ears to the talk, thinking of fishing in England, and shifting from one bone to another as each ached in turn from contact with the plank on which I lay.

Four / First days in Moscow

It was a rare cold day when I struggled through the crowd out of the station in Moscow, and began fighting with the sledge-drivers who asked a hundred roubles to take me to the Metropole. I remembered coming here a year ago with Colonel Robins, when we made ten roubles a limit for the journey and often travelled for eight. Today, after heated bargaining, I got carried with no luggage but a typewriter for 50 roubles. The streets were white with deep snow, less well cleaned than the Petrograd streets of this year but better cleaned than the Moscow streets of last year. The tramways were running. There seemed to be at least as many sledges as usual, and the horses were in slightly better condition than last summer when they were scarcely able to drag themselves along. I asked the reason of the improvement, and the driver told me the horses were now rationed like human beings, and all got a small allowance of oats. There were crowds of people about, but the numbers of closed shops were very depressing. I did not then know that this was due to the nationalisation of trade and a sort of general stock-taking, the object of which was to prevent profiteering in manufactured goods, etc., of which there were not enough to go round. Before I left many shops were being reopened as national concerns, like our own national kitchens. Thus, one would see over a shop the inscription, 'The 5th Boot Store of the Moscow Soviet' or 'The 3rd Clothing Store of the Moscow Soviet' or 'The 11th Book Shop'. It had been found that speculators bought, for example, half a dozen overcoats, and sold them to the highest bidders, thus giving the rich an advantage over the poor. Now if a man needs a new suit he has to go in his rags to his house committee, and satisfy them that he really needs a new suit for himself. He is then given the right to buy a suit. In this way an attempt is made to prevent speculation and to ensure a more or less equitable distribution of the inadequate stocks. My greatest surprise was given me by the Metropole itself, because the old wounds of the revolution, which were left unhealed all last summer, the shell holes and bullet splashes which marked it when I was here before, have been repaired.

Litvinov had given me a letter to Karakhan of the Commissariat of Foreign Affairs, asking him to help me in getting a room. I found him at the Metropole, still smoking as it were the cigar of six months ago. Karakhan, a handsome Armenian, elegantly bearded and moustached, once irreverently described by Radek as 'a donkey of classical beauty', who has consistently used such influence as he has in favour of moderation and agreement with the Allies, greeted me very cordially, and told me that the foreign visitors were to be housed in the Kremlin. I told him I should much prefer to live in an hotel in the ordinary way, and he at once set about getting a room for me. This was no easy business, though he obtained an authorisation from Sverdlov, president of the Executive Committee, for me to live where I wished, in the

Metropole or the National, which are mostly reserved for Soviet delegates, officials and members of the Executive Committee. Both were full, and he finally got me a room in the old Loskutnaya Hotel, now the Red Fleet, partially reserved for sailor delegates and members of the Naval College.

Rooms are distributed on much the same plan as clothes. Housing is considered a State monopoly, and a general census of housing accommodation has been taken. In every district there are housing committees to whom people wanting rooms apply. They work on the rough and ready theory that until every man has one room no one has a right to two. An Englishman acting as manager of works near Moscow told me that part of his house had been allotted to workers in his factory, who, however, were living with him amicably, and had, I think, allowed him to choose which rooms he should concede. This plan has, of course, proved very hard on house owners, and in some cases the new tenants have made a horrible mess of the houses, as might, indeed, have been expected, seeing that they had previously been of those who had suffered directly from the decivilising influences of overcrowding. After talking for some time we went round the corner to the Commissariat for Foreign Affairs, where we found Chicherin who, I thought, had aged a good deal and was (though this was perhaps his manner) less cordial than Karakhan. He asked about England, and I told him Litvinov knew more about that than I, since he had been there more recently. He asked what I thought would be the effect of his note with detailed terms published that day. I told him that Litvinov, in an interview which I had telegraphed, had mentioned somewhat similar terms some time before, and that personally I doubted whether the Allies would at present come to any agreement with the Soviet government, but that, if the Soviet government lasted, my personal opinion was that the commercial isolation of so vast a country as Russia could hardly be prolonged indefinitely on that account alone. (For the general attitude to that note, see page 81).

I then met Voznesensky (Left Social Revolutionary), of the Oriental Department, bursting with criticism of the Bolshevik attitude towards his party. He secured a ticket for me to get dinner in the Metropole. This ticket I had to surrender when I got a room in the National. The dinner consisted of a plate of soup, and a very small portion of something else. There are national kitchens in different parts of the town supplying similar meals. Glasses of weak tea were sold at 30 kopecks each, without sugar. My sister had sent me a small bottle of saccharin just before I left Stockholm, and it was pathetic to see the childish delight with which some of my friends drank glasses of sweetened tea.

From the Metropole I went to the Red Fleet to get my room fixed up. Six months ago there were comparatively clean rooms here, but the sailors have demoralised the hotel and its filth is indescribable. There was no heating and very little light. A samovar left after the departure of the last visitor was standing on the table, together with some dirty curl-papers and other rubbish. I got the waiter to clean up more or less, and ordered a new samovar. He could not supply spoon, knife, or fork, and only with great difficulty was persuaded to lend me glasses.

The telephone, however, was working, and after tea I got into touch with Madame Radek, who had moved from the Metropole into the Kremlin. I had not yet got a pass to the Kremlin, so she arranged to meet me and get a pass for me from the commandant. I walked through the snow to the white gate at the end of the bridge which leads over the garden up a steep incline to the Kremlin. Here a fire of logs was burning, and three soldiers were sitting around it. Madame Radek was waiting for me, warming her hands at the fire, and we went together into the citadel of the republic.

A meeting of the People's Commissars was going on in the Kremlin, and on an open space under the ancient churches were a number of motors black on the snow. We turned to the right down the Dvortzovaya Street, between the old Cavalier House and the Potyeshny Palace, and went in through a door under the archway that crosses the road, and up some dark flights of stairs to a part of the building that used, I think, to be called the Pleasure Palace. Here, in a wonderful old room, hung with Gobelins tapestries absolutely undamaged by the revolution, and furnished with carved chairs, we found the most incongruous figure of the old Swiss internationalist, Karl Moor, who talked with affection of Keir Hardie and of Hyndman, 'in the days when he was a socialist', and was disappointed to find that I knew so little about them. Madame Radek asked, of course, for the latest news of Radek, and I told her that I had read in the Stockholm papers that he had gone to Brunswick, and was said to be living in the palace there.* She feared he might have been in Bremen when that town was taken by the government troops, and did not believe he would ever get back to Russia. She asked me, did I not feel already (as indeed I did) the enormous difference which the last six months had made in strengthening the revolution. I asked after old acquaintances, and learnt that Pyatakov, who, when I last saw him, was praying that the Allies should give him machine rifles to use against the Germans in the Ukraine, had been the first President of the Ukrainian Soviet Republic, but had since been replaced by Rakovsky. It had been found that the views of the Pyatakov government were further left than those of its supporters, and so Pyatakov had given way to Rakovsky who was better able to conduct a more moderate policy. The Republic had been proclaimed in Kharkov, but at that time Kiev was still in the hands of the Directorate.

That night my room in the Red Fleet was so cold that I went to bed in a sheepskin coat under rugs and all possible bedclothes with a mattress on the top. Even so I slept very badly.

The next day I spent in vain wrestlings to get a better room.

---

* It was not till later that we learned he had returned to Berlin, been arrested, and put in prison.

Walking about the town I found it dotted with revolutionary sculptures, some very bad, others interesting, all done in some haste and set up for the celebrations of the anniversary of the revolution last November. The' painters also had been turned loose to do what they could with the hoardings, and though the weather had damaged many of their pictures, enough was left to show what an extraordinary carnival that had been. Where a hoarding ran along the front of a house being repaired the painters had used the whole of it as a vast canvas on which they had painted huge symbolic pictures of the revolution. A whole block in the Tverskaya was so decorated. Best, I think, were the row of wooden booths almost opposite the Hotel National in the Okhotnia Ryadi. These had been painted by the futurists or kindred artists, and made a really delightful effect, their bright colours and naif patterns seeming so natural to Moscow that I found myself wondering how it was that they had never been so painted before. They used to be a uniform dull yellow. Now, in clear primary colours, blue, red, yellow, with rough flower designs, on white and chequered backgrounds, with the masses of snow in the road before them, and bright-kerchiefed women and peasants in ruddy sheepskin coats passing by, they seemed less like futurist paintings than like some traditional survival, linking new Moscow with the Middle Ages. It is perhaps interesting to note that certain staid purists in the Moscow Soviet raised a protest while I was there against the license given to the futurists to spread themselves about the town, and demanded that the art of the revolution should be more comprehensible and less violent. These criticisms, however, did not apply to the row of booths which were a pleasure to me every time I passed them.

In the evening I went to see Reinstein in the National. Reinstein is a little old grandfather, a member of the American Socialist Labour Party, who was tireless in helping the Americans last year, and is a prodigy of knowledge about the revolution. He must be nearly 70, never misses a meeting of the Moscow Soviet or the Executive Committee, gets up at seven in the morning, and goes from one end of Moscow to the other to lecture to the young men in training as officers for the Soviet Army, more or less controls the English soldier war prisoners, about whose Bolshevism he is extremely pessimistic, and enjoys an official position as head of the quite futile department which prints hundredweight upon hundredweight of propaganda in English, none of which by any chance ever reaches these shores. He was terribly disappointed that I had brought no American papers with me. He complained of the lack of transport, a complaint which I think I must have heard at least three times a day from different people the whole time I was in Moscow. Politically, he thought, the position could not be better, though economically it was very bad. When they had corn, as it were, in sight, they could not get it to the towns for lack of locomotives. These economic difficulties were bound to react sooner or later on the political position.

He talked about the English prisoners. The men are brought to Moscow, where they are given special passports and are allowed to go anywhere they like about the town without convoy of any kind. I asked about the officers, and he said that they were in prison but given everything possible, a member of the International Red Cross, who worked with the Americans when they were here, visiting them regularly and taking in parcels for them. He told me that on hearing in Moscow that some sort of fraternisation was going on on the Archangel front, he had hurried off there with two prisoners, one English and one American. With some difficulty a meeting was arranged. Two officers and a sergeant from the Allied side and Reinstein and these two prisoners from the Russian, met on a bridge midway between the opposing lines. The conversation seemed to have been mostly an argument about working class conditions in America, together with reasons why the Allies should go home and leave Russia alone. Finally the Allied representatives (I fancy Americans) asked Reinstein to come with them to Archangel and state his case, promising him safe conduct there and back. By this time two Russians had joined the group, and one of them offered his back as a desk, on which a safe-conduct for Reinstein was written. Reinstein, who showed me the safe-conduct, doubted its validity, and said that anyhow he could not have used it without instructions from Moscow. When it grew dusk they prepared to separate. The officers said to the prisoners, 'What? Aren't you coming back with us?' The two shook their heads decidedly, and said, 'No, thank you'.

I learnt that someone was leaving the National next day to go to Kharkov, so that I should probably be able to get a room. After drinking tea with Reinstein till pretty late, I went home, burrowed into a mountain of all sorts of clothes, and slept a little.

In the morning I succeeded in making out my claim to the room at the National, which turned out to be a very pleasant one, next door to the kitchen and therefore quite decently warm. I wasted a lot of time getting my stuff across. Transport from one hotel to the other, though the distance is not a hundred yards, cost 40 roubles. I got things straightened out, bought some books, and prepared a list of the material needed and the people I wanted to see.

The room was perfectly clean. The chambermaid who came in to tidy up quite evidently took a pride in doing her work properly, and protested against my throwing matches on the floor. She said she had been in the hotel since it was opened. I asked her how she liked the new regime. She replied that there was not enough to eat, but that she felt freer.

In the afternoon I went downstairs to the main kitchens of the hotel, where there is a permanent supply of hot water. One enormous kitchen is set apart for the use of people living in the hotel. Here I found a crowd of people, all using different parts of the huge stove. There was an old grey haired Cossack, with a scarlet tunic under his black, wide-skirted, narrow-waisted coat, decorated in the Cossack fashion with ornamental cartridges. He was warming his soup, side by side with a little Jewess making potato cakes. A spectacled elderly member of the Executive Committee was busy doing something with a little bit of meat. Two little girls were boiling potatoes in old tin cans. In another room set apart for washing, a sturdy little long haired revolutionary was cleaning a shirt. A woman with her hair done up in a blue handkerchief was very carefully ironing a blouse. Another was busy stewing sheets, or something of that kind, in a big cauldron. And all the time people from all parts of the hotel were coming with their pitchers and pans, from fine copper kettles to disreputable empty meat tins, to fetch hot water for tea. At the other side of the corridor was a sort of counter in front of a long window opening into yet another kitchen. Here there was a row of people waiting with their own saucepans and plates, getting their dinner allowances of soup and meat in exchange for tickets. I was told that people thought they got slightly more if they took their food in this way straight from the kitchen to their own rooms instead of being served in the restaurant. But I watched closely, and decided it was only superstition. Besides, I had not got a saucepan.

On paying for my room at the beginning of the week I was given a card with the days of the week printed along its edge. This card gave me the right to buy one dinner daily, and when I bought it that day of the week was snipped off the card so that I could not buy another. The meal consisted of a plate of very good soup, together with a second course of a scrap of meat or fish. The price of the meal varied between five and seven roubles.

One could obtain this meal any time between two and seven. Living hungrily through the morning, at two o'clock I used to experience definite relief in the knowledge that now at any moment I could have my meal. Feeling in this way less hungry, I used then to postpone it hour by hour, and actually dined about five or six o'clock. Thinking that I might indeed have been specially favoured I made investigations, and found that the dinners supplied at the public feeding houses (the equivalent of our national kitchens) were of precisely the same size and character, any difference between the meals depending not on the food but on the cook.

A kind of rough and ready co-operative system also obtained. One day there was a notice on the stairs that those who wanted could get one pot of jam apiece by applying to the provisioning committee of the hotel. I got a pot of jam in this way, and on a later occasion a small quantity of Ukrainian sausage.

Besides the food obtainable on cards it was possible to buy, at ruinous prices, food from speculators, and an idea of the difference in the prices may be obtained from the following examples: Bread is one rouble 20 kopecks per pound by card and 15 to 20 roubles per pound from the speculators. Sugar is 12 roubles per pound by card, and never less than 50 roubles per pound in the open market. It is obvious that abolition of the card system would mean that the rich would have enough and the poor nothing. Various methods have been tried in the effort to get rid of speculators, whose high profits naturally decrease the willingness of the villages to sell bread at less abnormal rates. But as a Communist said to me, 'There is only one way to get rid of speculation, and that is to supply enough on the card system. When people can buy all they want at one rouble 20 they are not going to pay an extra 14 roubles for the encouragement of speculators'. 'And when will you be able to do that?' I asked. 'As soon as the war ends, and we can use our transport for peaceful purposes.'

There can be no question about the starvation of Moscow. On the third day after my arrival in Moscow I saw a man driving a sledge laden with, I think, horseflesh, mostly bones, probably dead sledge horses. As he drove a black crowd of crows followed the sledge and perched on it, tearing greedily at the meat. He beat at them continually with his whip, but they were so famished that they took no notice whatever. The starving crows used even to force their way through the small ventilators of the windows in my hotel to pick up any scraps they could find inside. The pigeons, which formerly crowded the streets, utterly undismayed by the traffic, confident in the security given by their supposed connection with religion, have completely disappeared.

Nor can there be any question about the cold. I resented my own sufferings less when I found that the State Departments were no better off than other folk. Even in the Kremlin I found the Keeper of the Archives sitting at work in an old sheepskin coat and felt boots, rising now and then to beat vitality into his freezing hands like a London cabman of old times.

Five / The Executive Committee on the reply to the Prinkipo proposal

FEBRUARY 10

It will be remembered that a proposal was made by the Peace Conference that the various de facto governments of Russia should meet on an island in the Bosphorus to discuss matters, an armistice being arranged meanwhile. No direct invitation was sent to the Soviet government. After attempting to obtain particulars through the editor of a French socialist paper, Chicherin on February 4 sent a long note to the Allies. The note was not at first considered with great favour in Russia, although it was approved by the opposition parties on the right, the Mensheviks even going so far as to say that in sending such a note, the Bolsheviks were acting in the interest of the whole of the Russian people. The opposition on the left complained that it was a betrayal of the revolution into the hands of the Entente, and there were many Bolsheviks who said openly that they thought it went a little too far in the way of concession. On February 10, the Executive Committee met to consider the international position.

Before proceeding to an account of that meeting, it will be well to make a short summary of the note in question. Chicherin, after referring to the fact that no invitation had been addressed to them and that the absence of a reply from them was being treated as the rejection of a proposal they had never received, said that in spite of its more and more favourable position, the Russian Soviet government considered a cessation of hostilities so desirable that it was ready immediately to begin negotiations, and, as it had more than once declared, to secure agreement 'even at the cost of serious concessions in so far as these should not threaten the development of the Republic'. 'Taking into consideration that the enemies against whom it has to struggle borrow their strength of resistance exclusively from the help shown them by the powers of the Entente, and that therefore these powers are the only actual enemy of the Russian Soviet government, the latter addresses itself precisely to the powers of the Entente, setting out the points on which it considers such concessions possible with a view to the ending of every kind of conflict with the aforesaid powers.' There follows a list of the concessions they are prepared to make. The first of these is recognition of their debts, the interest on which, 'in view of Russia's difficult financial position and her unsatisfactory credit', they propose to guarantee in raw materials. Then, 'in view of the interest continually expressed by foreign capital in the question of the exploitation for its advantage of the natural resources of Russia, the Soviet government is ready to give to subjects of the powers of the Entente mineral, timber and other concessions, to be defined in detail, on condition that the economic and social structure of Soviet Russia shall not be touched by the internal arrangements of these concessions'. The last point is that which roused most opposition. It expresses a willingness to negotiate even concerning such annexations, hidden or open, as the Allies may have in mind. The words used are 'The Russian Soviet government has not the intention of excluding at all costs consideration of the question of annexations, etc ...' Then, 'by annexations must be understood the retention on this or that part of the territory of what was the Russian Empire, not including Poland and Finland, of armed forces of the Entente or of such forces as are maintained by the governments of the Entente or enjoy their financial, military, technical or other support'. There follows a statement that the extent of the concessions will depend on the military position. Chicherin proceeds to give a rather optimistic account of the external and internal situation. Finally he touches on the question of propaganda. 'The Russian Soviet government, while pointing out that it cannot limit the freedom of the revolutionary press, declares its readiness, in case of necessity, to include in the general agreement with the powers of the Entente the obligation not to interfere in their internal affairs'. The note ends thus: 'On the foregoing bases the Russian Soviet government is ready immediately to begin negotiations either on Prinkipo island or in any other place whatsoever with all the powers of the Entente together or with separate powers of their number, or with any Russian political groupings whatsoever, according to the wishes of the powers of the Entente. The Russian Soviet government begs the powers of the Entente immediately to inform it whither to send its representatives, and precisely when and by what route'. This note was dated February 4, and was sent out by wireless.

From the moment when the note appeared in the newspapers of February 5, it had been the main subject of conversation. Every point in it was criticised and counter-criticised, but even its critics, though anxious to preserve their criticism as a basis for political action afterwards, were desperately anxious that it should meet with a reply. No one in Moscow at that time could have the slightest misgiving about the warlike tendencies of the revolution. The overwhelming mass of the people and of the revolutionary leaders want peace, and only continued warfare forced upon them could turn their desire for peace into desperate, resentful aggression. Everywhere I heard the same story: 'We cannot get things straight while we have to fight all the time.' They would not admit it, I am sure, but few of the Soviet leaders who have now for 18 months been wrestling with the difficulties of European Russia have not acquired, as it were in spite of themselves, a national, domestic point of view. They are thinking less about world revolution than about getting bread to Moscow, or increasing the output of textiles, or building river power stations to free the northern industrial district from its dependence on the distant coal fields. I was consequently anxious to hear what the Executive Committee would have to say, knowing that there I should listen to some expression of the theoretical standpoint from which my hard working friends had been drawn away by interests nearer home.

The Executive Committee met as usual in the big hall of the Hotel Metropole, and it met as usual very late. The sitting was to begin at seven, and, foolishly thinking that Russians might have changed their nature in the last six months, I was punctual and found the hall nearly empty, because a party meeting of the Communists in the room next door was not finished. The hall looked just as it used to look, with a red banner over the presidium and another at the opposite end, both inscribed 'The All Russian Executive Committee', 'Proletariat of all lands, unite', and so on. As the room gradually filled, I met many acquaintances.

Old Professor Pokrovsky came in, blinking through his spectacles, bent a little, in a very old coat, with a small black fur hat, his hands clasped together, just as, so I have been told, he walked unhappily to and fro in the fortress at Brest during the second period of the negotiations. I did not think he would recognise me, but he came up at once, and reminded me of the packing of the archives at the time when it seemed likely that the Germans would take Petrograd. He told me of a mass of material they are publishing about the origin of the war. He said that England came out of it best of anybody, but that France and Russia showed in a very bad light.

Just then, Demian Biedny rolled in, fatter than he used to be (admirers from the country send him food) with a round face, shrewd laughing eye, and cynical mouth, a typical peasant, and the poet of the revolution. He was passably shaved, his little yellow moustache was trimmed, he was wearing new leather breeches, and seemed altogether a more prosperous poet than the untidy ruffian I first met about a year or more ago before his satirical poems in Pravda and other revolutionary papers had reached the heights of popularity to which they have since attained. In the old days before the revolution in Petrograd he used to send his poems to the revolutionary papers. A few were published and scandalised the more austere and serious minded revolutionaries, who held a meeting to decide whether any more were to be printed. Since the revolution, he has rapidly come into his own, and is now a sort of licensed jester, flagellating Communists and non-Communists alike. Even in this assembly he had about him a little of the manner of Robert Burns in Edinburgh society. He told me with expansive glee that they had printed 250,000 of his last book, that the whole edition was sold in two weeks, and that he had had his portrait painted by a real artist. It is actually true that of his 18 different works, only two are obtainable today.

Madame Radek, who last year showed a genius for the making of sandwiches with chopped leeks, and did good work for Russia as head of the committee for dealing with Russian war prisoners, came and sat down beside me, and complained bitterly that the authorities wanted to turn her out of the grand ducal apartments in the Kremlin and make them into a historical museum to illustrate the manner of life of the Romanovs. She said she was sure that was simply an excuse and that the real reason was that Madame Trotsky did not like her having a better furnished room than her own. It seems that the Trotskys, when they moved into the Kremlin, chose a lodging extremely modest in comparison with the gorgeous place where I had found Madame Radek.

All this time the room was filling, as the party meeting ended and the members of the Executive Committee came in to take their places. I was asking Litvinov whether he was going to speak, when a little hairy energetic man came up and with great delight showed us the new matches invented in the Soviet laboratories.

Russia is short of match-wood, and without paraffin. Besides which I think I am right in saying that the bulk of the matches used in the north came from factories in Finland. In these new Bolshevik matches neither wood nor paraffin is used. Waste paper is a substitute for one, and the grease that is left after cleaning wool is a substitute for the other. The little man, Berg, secretary of the Presidium of the Council of Public Economy, gave me a packet of his matches. They are like the matches in a folding cover that used to be common in Paris. You break off a match before striking it. They strike and burn better than any matches I have ever bought in Russia, and I do not see why they should not be made in England, where we have to import all the materials of which ordinary matches are made. I told Berg I should try to patent them and so turn myself into a capitalist. Another Communist, who was listening, laughed, and said that most fortunes were founded in just such a fraudulent way.

Then there was Steklov of the Izvestia, Madame Kollontai, and a lot of other people whose names I do not remember. Little Bukharin, the editor of Pravda and one of the most interesting talkers in Moscow, who is ready to discuss any philosophy you like, from Berkeley and Locke down to Bergson and William James, trotted up and shook hands. Suddenly a most unexpected figure limped through the door. This was the lame Eliava of the Vologda Soviet, who came up in great surprise at seeing me again, and reminded me how Radek and I, hungry from Moscow, astonished the hotel of the Golden Anchor by eating 15 eggs apiece, when we came to Vologda last summer (I acted as translator during Radek's conversations with the American Ambassador and Mr Lindley). Eliava is a fine, honest fellow, and had a very difficult time in Vologda where the large colony of foreign embassies and missions naturally became the centre of disaffection in a district which at the time was full of inflammable material. I remember when we parted from him, Radek said to me that he hardly thought he would see him alive again. He told me he had left

Vologda some three months ago and was now going to Turkestan. He did not disguise the resentment he felt towards M Noulens (the French ambassador) who, he thought, had stood in the way of agreement last year, but said that he had nothing whatever to say against Lindley.

At last there was a little stir in the raised presidium, and the meeting began. When I saw the lean, long haired Avanesov take his place as secretary, and Sverdlov, the president, lean forward a little, ring his bell, and announce that the meeting was open and that 'Comrade Chicherin has the word', I could hardly believe that I had been away six months.

Chicherin's speech took the form of a general report on the international situation. He spoke a little more clearly than he was used to do, but even so I had to walk round to a place close under the tribune before I could hear him. He sketched the history of the various steps the Soviet government has taken in trying to secure peace, even including such minor 'peace offensives' as Litvinov's personal telegram to President Wilson. He then weighed, in no very hopeful spirit, the possibilities of this last note to all the Allies having any serious result. He estimated the opposing tendencies for and against war with Russia in each of the principal countries concerned. The growth of revolutionary feeling abroad made imperialistic governments even more aggressive towards the Workers' and Peasants' Republic than they would otherwise be. It was now making their intervention difficult, but no more. It was impossible to say that the collapse of imperialism had gone so far that it had lost its teeth. Chicherin speaks as if he were a dead man or a ventriloquist's lay figure. And indeed he is half dead. He has never learnt the art of releasing himself from drudgery by handing it over to his subordinates. He is permanently tired out. You feel it is almost cruel to say 'Good morning' to him when you meet him, because of the appeal to be left alone that comes unconsciously into his eyes. Partly in order to avoid people, partly because he is himself accustomed to work at night, his section of the foreign office keeps extraordinary hours, is not to be found till about five in the afternoon and works till four in the morning. The actual material of his report was interesting, but there was nothing in its manner to rouse enthusiasm of any kind. The audience listened with attention, but only woke into real animation when with a shout of laughter it heard an address sent to Clemenceau by the emigré financiers, aristocrats and bankrupt politicians of the Russian colony in Stockholm, protesting against any sort of agreement with the Bolsheviks.

Bukharin followed Chicherin. A little eager figure in his neat brown clothes (bought, I think, while visiting Berlin as a member of the Economic Commission), he at least makes himself clearly heard, though his voice has a funny tendency to breaking. He compared the present situation with the situation before Brest. He had himself (as I well remember) been with Radek, one of the most violent opponents of the Brest peace, and he now admitted that at that time Lenin had been right and he wrong. The position was now different, because whereas then imperialism was split into two camps fighting each other, it now showed signs of uniting its forces. He regarded the League of Nations as a sort of capitalist syndicate, and said that the difference in the French and American attitude towards the League depended upon the position of French and American capital. Capital in France was so weak, that she could at best be only a small shareholder. Capital in America was in a very advantageous position. America therefore wanted a huge all-European syndicate in which each state would have a certain number of shares. America, having the greatest number of shares, would be able to exploit all the other nations. This is a fixed idea of Bukharin's, and he has lost no opportunity of putting out this theory of the League of Nations since the middle of last summer. As for Chicherin's note, he said it had at least great historical interest on account of the language it used, which was very different from the hypocritical language of ordinary diplomacy. Here were no phrases about noble motives, but a plain recognition of the facts of the case. 'Tell us what you want,' it says, 'and we are ready to buy you off, in order to avoid armed conflict.' Even if the Allies gave no answer the note would still have served a useful purpose and would be a landmark in history.

Litvinov followed Bukharin. A solid, jolly, round man, with his peaked grey fur hat on his head, rounder than ever in fur-collared, thick coat, his eye glasses slipping from his nose as he got up, his grey muffler hanging from his neck, he hurried to the tribune. Taking off his things and leaving them on a chair below, he stepped up into the tribune with his hair all rumpled, a look of extreme seriousness on his face, and spoke with a voice whose capacity and strength astonished me who had not heard him speak in public before. He spoke very well, with more sequence than Bukharin, and much vitality, and gave his summary of the position abroad. He said (and Lenin expressed the same view to me afterwards) that the hostility of different countries to Soviet Russia varied in direct proportion to their fear of revolution at home. Thus France, whose capital had suffered most in the war and was weakest, was the most uncompromising, while America, whose capital was in a good position, was ready for agreement. England, with rather less confidence, he thought was ready to follow America. Need of raw material was the motive tending towards agreement with Russia. Fear that the mere existence of a Labour government anywhere in the world strengthens the revolutionary movement elsewhere, was the motive for the desire to wipe out the Soviet at all cost. Chicherin's note, he thought, would emphasise the difference between these opposing views and would tend to make impossible an alliance of the capitalists against Russia.

Finally, Kamenev, now president of the Moscow Soviet, spoke, objecting to Bukharin's comparison of the peace now sought with that of Brest Litovsk. Then everything was in a state of experiment and untried. Now it was clear to the world that the unity of Russia could be achieved only under the soviets. The powers opposed to them could not but recognise this fact. Some parts of Russia (Ukraine) had during the last 15 months experienced every kind of government, from the soviets, the dictatorship of the proletariat, to the dictatorship of foreign invaders and the dictatorship of a general of the old regime, and they had later all returned to the soviets. Western European imperialists must realise that the only government in Russia which rested on the popular masses was the government of the soviets and no other. Even the paper of the Mensheviks, commenting on Chicherin's note, had declared that by this step the Soviet government had shown that it was actually a national government acting in the interests of the nation. He further read a statement by Right Social Revolutionaries (delegates of that group, members of the Constituent Assembly, were in the gallery) to the effect that they were prepared to help the Soviet government as the only government in Russia that was fighting against a dictatorship of the bourgeoisie.

Finally, the Committee unanimously passed a resolution approving every step taken in trying to obtain peace, and at the same time 'sending a fraternal greeting to the Red Army of workers and peasants engaged in ensuring the independence of Soviet Russia'. The meeting then turned to talk of other things.

I left, rather miserable to think how little I had foreseen when Soviet Russia was compelled last year to sign an oppressive peace with Germany, that the time would come when they would be trying to buy peace from ourselves. As I went out I saw another unhappy figure, unhappy for quite different reasons. Angelica Balabanova, after dreaming all her life of socialism in the most fervent utopian spirit, had come at last to Russia to find that a socialist state was faced with difficulties at least as real as those which confront other states, that in the battle there was little sentiment and much cynicism, and that dreams worked out in terms of humanity in the face of the opposition of the whole of the rest of the world are not easily recognised by their dreamers. Poor little Balabanova, less than five feet high, in a black coat that reached to her feet but did not make her look any taller, was wandering about like a lost and dejected spirit. Not so, she was thinking, should socialists deal with their enemies. Somehow, but not so. Had the silver trumpets blown seven times in vain, and was it really necessary to set to work and, stone by stone, with bleeding hands, level the walls of Jericho?

There was snow falling as I walked home. Two workmen, arguing, were walking in front of me. 'If only it were not for the hunger,' said one. 'But will that ever change?' said the other.

Six / Kamenev and the Moscow Soviet

FEBRUARY 11

Litvinov has been unlucky in his room in the Metropole. It is small, dark and dirty, and colder than mine. He was feeling ill and his chest was hurting him, perhaps because of his speech last night; but while I was there Kamenev rang him up on the telephone, told him he had a car below, and would he come at once to the Moscow Soviet to speak on the international situation? Litvinov tried to excuse himself, but it was no use, and he said to me that if I wanted to see Kamenev I had better come along. We found Kamenev in the hall, and after a few minutes in a little Ford car we were at the Moscow Soviet. The soviet meets in the small lecture theatre of the old Polytechnic. When we arrived, a party meeting was going on, and Kamenev, Litvinov, and I went behind the stage to a little empty room, where we were joined by a member of the soviet whose name I forget.

It was Kamenev's first talk with Litvinov after his return, and I think they forgot that I was there. Kamenev asked Litvinov what he meant to do, and Litvinov told him he wished to establish a special department of control to receive all complaints, to examine into the efficiency of different commissariats, to get rid of parallelism, etc., and, in fact, to be the most unpopular department in Moscow. Kamenev laughed. 'You need not think you are the first to have that idea. Every returning envoy without exception has the same. Coming back from abroad they notice more than we do the inefficiencies here, and at once think they will set everything right. Rakovsky sat here for months dreaming of nothing else. Joffe was the same when he came back from that tidy Berlin. Now you; and when Vorovsky comes (Vorovsky was still in Petrograd) I am ready to wager that he too has a scheme for general control waiting in his pocket. The thing cannot be done. The only way is, when something obviously needs doing, to put in someone we can trust to get it done. Soap is hard to get. Good. Establish a commission and soap instantly disappears. But put in one man to see that soap is forthcoming, and somehow or other we get it.'

'Where is the soap industry concentrated?'

'There are good factories, well equipped, here, but they are not working, partly for lack of material and partly, perhaps, because some crazy fool imagined that to take an inventory you must bring everything to a standstill.'

Litvinov asked him what he thought of the position as a whole. He said good, if only transport could be improved; but before the public of Moscow could feel an appreciable improvement it would be necessary that a hundred wagons of foodstuffs should be coming in daily. At present there are seldom more than 20. I asked Kamenev about the schools, and he explained that one of their difficulties was due to the militarism forced upon them by external attacks. He explained that the new Red Army soldiers, being mostly workmen, are accustomed to a higher standard of comfort than the old army soldiers, who were mostly peasants. They objected to the planks which served as beds in the old, abominable, over crowded and unhealthy barracks. Trotsky, looking everywhere for places to put his darlings, found nothing more suitable than the schools; and, in Kamenev's words, 'We have to fight hard for every school.' Another difficulty, he said, was the lack of school books. Histories, for example, written under the censorship and in accordance with the principles of the old regime, were now useless, and new ones were not ready, apart from the difficulty of getting paper and of printing. A lot, however, was being done. There was no need for a single child in Moscow to go hungry; 150,000 to 180,000 children got free meals daily in the schools. Over 10,000 pairs of felt boots had been given to children who needed them. The number of libraries had enormously increased. Physically workmen lived in far worse conditions than in 1912, but as far as their spiritual welfare was concerned there could be no comparison. Places like the famous Yar restaurant, where once the rich went to amuse themselves with orgies of feeding and drinking and flirting with gypsies, were now made into working men's clubs and theatres, where every working man had a right to go. As for the demand for literature from the provinces, it was far beyond the utmost efforts of the presses and the paper stores to supply.

When the party meeting ended, we went back to the lecture room where the members of the soviet had already settled themselves in their places. I was struck at once by the absence of the general public which in the old days used to crowd the galleries to overflowing. The political excitement of the revolution has passed, and today there were no more spectators than are usually to be found in the gallery of the House of Commons. The character of the soviet itself had not changed. Practically every man sitting on the benches was obviously a workman and keenly intent on what was being said. Litvinov practically repeated his speech of last night, making it, however, a little more demagogic in character, pointing out that after the Allied victory, the only corner of the world not dominated by Allied capital was Soviet Russia.

The soviet passed a resolution expressing 'firm confidence that the Soviet government will succeed in getting peace and so in opening a wide road to the construction of a proletarian state.' A note was passed up to Kamenev who, glancing at it, announced that the newly elected representative of the Chinese workmen in Moscow wished to speak. This was Chitaya Kuni, a solid little Chinaman with a big head, in black leather coat and breeches. I had often seen him before, and wondered who he was. He was received with great cordiality and made a quiet, rather shy speech in which he told them he was learning from them how to introduce socialism in China, and more compliments of the same sort. Reinstein replied, telling how at an American labour congress some years back the Americans shut the door in the face of a representative of a union of foreign workmen. 'Such,' he said, 'was the feeling in America at the time when Gompers was supreme, but that time has passed.' Still, as I listened to Reinstein, I wondered in how many other countries besides Russia, a representative of foreign labour would be thus welcomed. The reason has probably little to do with the goodheartedness of the Russians. Owing to the general unification of wages Mr Kuni could not represent the competition of cheap labour. I talked to the Chinaman afterwards. He is president of the Chinese Soviet. He told me they had just about a thousand Chinese workmen in Moscow, and therefore had a right to representation in the government of the town. I asked about the Chinese in the Red Army, and he said there were two or three thousand, not more.

Seven / An ex-capitalist

FEBRUARY 13

I drank tea with an old acquaintance from the provinces, a Russian who, before the revolution, owned a leather-bag factory which worked in close connection with his uncle's tannery. He gave me a short history of events at home. The uncle had started with small capital, and during the war had made enough to buy outright the tannery in which he had had shares. The story of his adventures since the October revolution is a very good illustration of the rough and ready way in which theory gets translated into practice. I am writing it, as nearly as possible, as it was told by the nephew.

During the first revolution, that is from March till October 1917, he fought hard against the workmen, and was one of the founders of a soviet of factory owners, the object of which was to defeat the efforts of the workers' soviets.* This, of course, was smashed by the October Revolution, and 'Uncle, after being forced, as a property owner, to pay considerable contributions, watched the newspapers closely, realised that after the nationalisa-tion of the banks resistance was hopeless, and resigned himself to do what he could, not to lose his factory altogether.'

He called together all the workmen, and proposed that they should form an *artel* or co-operative society and take the factory into their own hands, each man contributing a thousand roubles towards the capital with which to run it. Of course the workmen had not got a thousand roubles apiece, 'so uncle offered to pay it in for them, on the understanding that they would eventually pay him back.' This was illegal, but the little town was a long way from the centre of things, and it seemed a good way out of the dif-ficulty. He did not expect to get it back, but he hoped in this way to keep control of the tannery, which he wished to develop, hav-ing a paternal interest in it.

Things worked very well. They elected a committee of con-trol. 'Uncle was elected president, I was elected vice-president, and there were three workmen. We are working on those lines to this day. They give uncle 1,500 roubles a month, me a thousand and the bookkeeper a thousand. The only difficulty is that the men will treat uncle as the owner, and this may mean trouble if things go wrong; Uncle is for ever telling them, 'It's your factory, don't call

*By agreeing upon lock-outs, etc.

me Master,' and they reply, 'Yes, it's our factory all right, but you are still Master, and that must be."

Trouble came fast enough, with the tax levied on the propertied classes. 'Uncle', very wisely, had ceased to be a property owner. He had given up his house to the factory, and been allotted rooms in it, as president of the factory soviet. He was therefore really unable to pay when the people from the district soviet came to tell him that he had been assessed to pay a tax of 60,000 roubles. He explained the position. The nephew was also present and joined in the argument, whereupon the tax collectors consulted a bit of paper and retorted, 'A tax of 20,000 has been assessed on you too. Be so good as to put your coat on.'

That meant arrest, and the nephew said he had 5,000 roubles and would pay that, but could pay no more. Would that do?

'Very well,' said the tax-collector, 'fetch it.'

The nephew fetched it.

'And now put your coat on.'

'But you said it would be all right if I paid the 5,000!'

'That's the only way to deal with people like you. We recognise that your case is hard, and we dare say that you will get off. But the soviet has told us to collect the whole tax or the people who refuse to pay it, and they have decreed that if we came back without one or the other, we shall go to prison ourselves. You can hardly expect us to go and sit in prison out of pity for you. So on with your coat and come along.'

They went, and at the militia headquarters were shut into a room with barred windows where they were presently joined by most of the other rich men of the town, all in a rare state of indignation, and some of them very angry with 'Uncle', for taking things so quietly. 'Uncle was worrying about nothing in the world but the tannery and the leather works which he was afraid might get into difficulties now that both he and I were under lock and key.'

The plutocracy of the town being thus gathered in the little room at the militia house, their wives came, timorously at first, and chattered through the windows. My informant, being unmarried, sent word to two or three of his friends, in order that he might not be the only one without some one to talk with outside. The noise was something prodigious, and the head of the militia finally ran out into the street and arrested one of the women, but was so discomfited when she removed her shawl and he recognised her as his hostess at a house where he had been billeted as a soldier that he hurriedly let her go. The extraordinary parliament between the rich men of the town and their wives and friends, like a crowd of hoodie crows, chattering outside the window, continued until dark.

Next day the workmen from the tannery came to the militia house and explained that 'Uncle' had really ceased to be a member of the propertied classes, that he was necessary to them as president of their soviet, and that they were willing to secure his release by paying half of the tax demanded from him out of the factory funds. Uncle got together 30,000, the factory contributed another 30, and he was freed, being given a certificate that he had ceased to be an exploiter or a property owner, and would in future be subject only to such taxes as might be levied on the working population. The nephew was also freed, on the grounds that he was wanted at the leather works.

I asked him how things were going on. He said, 'Fairly well, only uncle keeps worrying because the men still call him "Master". Otherwise, he is very happy because he has persuaded the workmen to set aside a large proportion of the profits for developing the business and building a new wing to the tannery.'

'Do the men work?'

'Well,' he said, 'we thought that when the factory was in their own hands they would work better, but we do not think they do so, not noticeably, anyhow.'

'Do they work worse?'

'No, that is not noticeable either.'

I tried to get at his political views. Last summer he had told me that the Soviet government could not last more than another two or three months. He was then looking forward to its downfall. Now he did not like it any better, but he was very much afraid of war being brought into Russia, or rather of the further disorders which war would cause. He took a queer sort of pride in the way in which the territory of the Russian republic was gradually resuming its old frontiers. 'In the old days no one ever thought the Red Army would come to anything,' he said. 'You can't expect much from the government, but it does keep order, and I can do my work and rub along all right.' It was quite funny to hear him in one breath grumbling at the revolution and in the next anxiously asking whether I did not think they had weathered the storm, so that there would be no more disorders.

Knowing that in some country places there had been appalling excesses, I asked him how the Red Terror that followed the attempt on the life of Lenin had shown itself in their district. He laughed.

'We got off very cheaply,' he said. 'This is what happened. A certain rich merchant's widow had a fine house, with enormous stores of all kinds of things, fine knives and forks, and too many of everything. For instance, she had 22 samovars of all sizes and sorts. Typical merchant's house, so many tablecloths that they could not use them all if they lived to be a hundred. Well, one fine day, early last summer, she was told that her house was wanted and that she must clear out. For two days she ran hither and thither trying to get out of giving it up. Then she saw it was no good, and piled all those things, samovars and knives and forks and dinner services and table cloths and overcoats (there were over a dozen fur overcoats) in the garrets which she closed and sealed, and got the president of the soviet to come and put his seal also. In the end things were so friendly that he even put a sentinel there to see that the seal should not be broken. Then came the news from Petrograd and Moscow about the Red Terror, and the soviet, after holding a meeting and deciding that it ought to do something, and being on too good terms with all of us to do any thing very bad, suddenly remembered poor Maria Nicolaevna's garrets. They broke the seals and tumbled out all the kitchen things, knives, forks, plates, furniture, the 22 samovars and the overcoats, took them in carts to the soviet and declared them national property. National property! And a week or two later there was a wedding of a daughter of one of the members of the soviet, and somehow or other the knives and forks were on the table, and as for samovars, there were enough to make tea for a hundred.'

Eight / A theorist of revolution

FEBRUARY 13

After yesterday's talk with a capitalist victim of the revolution, I am glad for the sake of contrast to set beside it a talk with one of the revolution's chief theorists. The leather worker illustrated the revolution as it affects an individual. The revolutionary theorist was quite incapable of even considering his own or any other individual interests and thought only in terms of enormous movements in which the experiences of an individual had only the significance of the adventures of one ant among a myriad. Bukharin, member of the old economic mission to Berlin, violent opponent of the Brest peace, editor of Pravda, author of many books on economics and revolution, indefatigable theorist, found me drinking tea at a table in the Metropole.

I had just bought a copy of a magazine which contained a map of the world, in which most of Europe was coloured red or pink for actual or potential revolution. I showed it to Bukharin and said, 'You cannot be surprised that people abroad talk of you as of the new imperialists.'

Bukharin took the map and looked at it.

'Idiotism, rank idiotism!' he said. 'At the same time,' he added, 'I do think we have entered upon a period of revolution which may last 50 years before the revolution is at last victorious in all Europe and finally in all the world.'

Now, I have a stock theory which I am used to set before revolutionaries of all kinds, nearly always with interesting results. (See p. 119)

I tried it on Bukharin. I said:

'You people are always saying that there will be revolution in England. Has it not occurred to you that England is a factory and not a granary, so that in the event of revolution we should be immediately cut off from all food supplies. According to your own theories, English capital would unite with American in ensuring that within six weeks the revolution had nothing to eat. England is not a country like Russia where you can feed yourselves somehow or other by simply walking to where there is food. Six weeks would see starvation and reaction in England. I am inclined to think that a revolution in England would do Russia more harm than good.'

Bukharin laughed. 'You old counter-revolutionary !' he said. 'That would be all true, but you must look further. You are right in one thing. If the revolution spreads in Europe, America will cut off food supplies. But by that time we shall be getting food from Siberia.'

'And is the poor Siberian railway to feed Russia, Germany, and England?'

'Before then Pichon and his friends will have gone. There will be France to feed too. But you must not forget that there are the cornfields of Hungary and Rumania. Once civil war ends in Europe, Europe can feed herself. With English and German engineering assistance we shall soon turn Russia into an effective grain supply for all the working men's republics of the continent. But even then the task will be only beginning. The moment there is revolution in England, the English colonies will throw themselves eagerly into the arms of America. Then will come America's turn, and, finally, it is quite likely that we shall all have to combine to overthrow the last stronghold of capitalism in some South African bourgeois republic. I can well imagine,' he said, looking far away with his bright little eyes through the walls of the dark dining room, 'that the working men's republics of Europe may have to have a colonial policy of an inverse kind. Just as now you conquer backward races in order to exploit them, so in the future you may have to conquer the colonists to take from them the means of exploitation. There is only one thing I am afraid of.'

'And what is that?'

'Sometimes I am afraid that the struggle will be so bitter and so long drawn out that the whole of European culture may be trampled under foot.'

I thought of my leather worker of yesterday, one of thousands experiencing in their own persons the appalling discomforts, the turn over and revaluation of all established values that revolution, even without death and civil war, means to the ordinary man; and, being perhaps a little faint hearted, I finished my tea in silence. Bukharin, after carelessly opening these colossal perspectives, drank his tea in one gulp, prodigiously sweetened with my saccharin, reminded me of his illness in the summer, when Radek scoured the town for sweets for him, curing him with no other medicine, and then hurried off, fastening his coat as he went, a queer little De Quincey of revolution, to disappear into the dusk, before, half running, half walking, as his way is, he reached the other end of the big dimly lit, smoke filled dining room.

Nine / Effects of isolation

I had a rather grim talk with Meshtcheriakov at dinner. He is an old Siberian exile, who visited England last summer. He is editing a monthly magazine in Moscow, mostly concerned with the problems of reconstruction, and besides that doing a lot of educational work among the labouring classes. He is horrified at the economic position of the country. Isolation, he thinks, is forcing Russia backwards towards a primeval state.

'We simply cannot get things. For example, I am lecturing on mathematics. I have more pupils than I can deal with. They are as greedy for knowledge as sponges for water, and I cannot get even the simplest text books for them. I cannot even find in the second hand book stores an old course of mathematics from which I could myself make a series of copies for them. I have to teach like a teacher of the Middle Ages. But, like him, I have pupils who want to learn.'

'In another three years,' said someone else at the table, 'we shall be living in ruins. Houses in Moscow were always kept well warmed. Lack of transport has brought with it lack of fuel, and water pipes have burst in thousands of houses. We cannot get what is needed to mend them. In the same way we cannot get paints for the walls, which are accordingly rotting. In another three years we shall have all the buildings of Moscow tumbling about our ears.'

Some one else joined in with a laugh: 'In ten years we shall be running about on all fours.'

'And in 20 we shall begin sprouting tails.'

Meshtcheriakov finished his soup and laid down his wooden spoon.

'There is another side to all these things,' he said. 'In Russia, even if the blockade lasts, we shall get things established again sooner than anywhere else, because we have all the raw materials in our own country. With us it is a question of transport only, and of transport within our own borders. In a few years, I am convinced, in spite of all that is working against us, Russia will be a better place to live in than anywhere else in Europe. But we have a bad time to go through. And not we alone. The effects of the war are scarcely visible as yet in the West, but they will become visible. Humanity has a period of torment before it …'

'Bukharin says 50 years,' I said, referring to my talk of yesterday.

'Maybe. I think less than that. But the revolution will be far worse for you nations of the West than it has been for us. In the West, if there is revolution, they will use artillery at once, and wipe out whole districts. The governing classes in the west are determined and organised in a way our home grown capitalists never were. The autocracy never allowed them to organise, so, when the autocracy itself fell, our task was comparatively easy. There was nothing in the way. It will not be like that in Germany.'

Ten / An evening at the opera

I READ IN ONE of the newspapers that a member of the American Commission in Berlin reasoned from the fact that the Germans were crowding to theatres and spectacles that they could not be hungry. There can be no question about the hunger of the people of Moscow, but the theatres are crowded, and there is such demand for seats that speculators acquire tickets in the legitimate way and sell them illicitly near the doors of the theatre to people who have not been able to get in, charging, of course, double the price or even more. Interest in the theatre, always keen in Moscow, seems to me to have rather increased than decreased. There is a School of Theatrical Production, with lectures on every subject connected with the stage, from stage carpentry upwards. A

Theatrical Bulletin is published three times weekly, containing the programmes of all the theatres and occasional articles on theatrical subjects. I had been told in Stockholm that the Moscow theatres were closed. The following is an incomplete list of the plays and spectacles to be seen at various theatres on February 13 and February 14, copied from the Theatrical Bulletin of those dates. Just as it would be interesting to know what French audiences enjoyed at the time of the French revolution, so I think it worthwhile to record the character of the entertainments at present popular in Moscow.

Opera at the Great Theatre—'Sadko' by Rimsky-Korsakov and 'Samson and Delilah' by Saint-Saens.

Small State Theatre—'Besheny Dengi' by Osrovsky and 'Starik' by Gorky.

Moscow Art Theatre—'The Cricket on the Hearth' by Dickens and 'The Death of Pazuchin' by Saltykov-Shtchedrin.

Opera—'Selo Stepantchiko' and 'Coppelia.'

People's Palace—'Dubrovsky' by Napravnik and 'Demon' by Rubinstein.

Zamoskvoretzky Theatre—'Groza' by Ostrovsky and 'Meshtchane' by Gorky.

Popular Theatre—'The Miracle of Saint Anthony' by Maeterlinck.

Komissarzhevskaya Theatre—'A Christmas Carol' by Dickens and 'The Accursed Prince' by Remizov.

Korsh Theatre—'Much Ado about Nothing' by Shakespeare and 'Le Misanthrope' and 'Georges Dandin' by Moliere.

Dramatic Theatre—'Alexander I' by Merezhkovsky.

Theatre of Drama and Comedy—'Little Dorrit' by Dickens and 'The King's Barber' by Lunacharsky.

Besides these, other theatres were playing K R (Konstantin Romanov), Ostrovsky, Potapenko, Vinitchenko, etc. The two studios of the Moscow Art Theatre were playing 'Rosmersholm' and a repertoire of short plays. They, like the Art Theatre Company, occasionally play in the suburban theatres when their place at home is taken by other performers.

I went to the Great State Theatre to Saint-Saens' 'Samson and Delilah'. I had a seat in the box close above the orchestra, from which I could obtain a view equally good of the stage and of the house. Indeed, the view was rather better of the house than of the stage. But that was as I had wished, for the house was what I had come to see.

It had certainly changed greatly since the pre-revolutionary period. The Moscow plutocracy of bald merchants and bejewelled fat wives had gone. Gone with them were evening dresses and white shirt fronts. The whole audience was in the monotone of everyday clothes. The only contrast was given by a small group of Tartar women in the dress circle, who were shawled in white over head and shoulders, in the Tartar fashion. There were many soldiers, and numbers of men who had obviously come straight from their work. There were a good many grey and brown woollen jerseys about, and people were sitting in overcoats of all kinds and ages, for the theatre was very cold. (This, of course, was due to lack of fuel, which may in the long run lead to a temporary stoppage of the theatres if electricity cannot be spared for lighting them). The orchestra was also variously dressed. Most of the players of brass instruments had evidently been in regimental bands during the war, and still retained their khaki-green tunics with a very mixed collection of trousers and breeches. Others were in every kind of everyday clothes. The conductor alone wore a frock coat, and sat in his place like a specimen from another age, isolated in fact by his smartness alike from his ragged orchestra and from the stalls behind him.

I looked carefully to see the sort of people who fill the stalls under the new regime, and decided that there has been a general transfer of brains from the gallery to the floor of the house. The same people who in the old days scraped kopecks and waited to get a good place near the ceiling now sat where formerly were the people who came here to digest their dinners. Looking from face to face that night I thought there were very few people in the theatre who had had anything like a good dinner to digest. But, as for their keenness, I can imagine few audiences to which, from the actor's point of view, it would be better worthwhile to play. Applause, like brains, had come down from the galleries.

Of the actual performance I have little to say except that ragged clothes and empty stomachs seemed to make very little difference to the orchestra. Helzer, the ballerina, danced as well before this audience as ever before the bourgeoisie. As I turned up the collar of my coat I reflected that the actors deserved all the applause they got for their heroism in playing in such cold. Now and then during the evening I was unusually conscious of the unreality of opera generally, perhaps because of the contrast in magnificence between the stage and the shabby, intelligent audience. Now and then, on the other hand, stage and audience seemed one and indivisible. For 'Samson and Delilah' is itself a poem of revolution, and gained enormously by being played by people every one of whom had seen something of the sort in real life. Samson's stirring up of the Israelites reminded me of many scenes in Petrograd in 1917, and when, at last, he brings the temple down in ruins on his triumphant enemies, I was reminded of the words attributed to Trotsky: 'If we are, in the end, forced to go, we shall slam the door behind us in such a way that the echo shall be felt throughout the world.'

Going home afterwards through the snow, I did not see a single armed man. A year ago the streets were deserted after ten in the evening except by those who, like myself, had work which took them to meetings and such things late at night. They used to be empty except for the military pickets round their log fires. Now they were full of foot passengers going home from the theatres, utterly forgetful of the fact that only 12 months before they had thought the streets of Moscow unsafe after dark. There could be no question about it. The revolution is settling down, and people now think of other matters than the old question, will it last one week or two?

Eleven / The Committee of State Constructions

I went by appointment to see Pavlovitch, President of the Committee of State Constructions. It was a very jolly morning and the streets were crowded. As I walked through the gate into the Red Square I saw the usual crowd of peasant women at the little chapel of the Iberian Virgin, where there was a blaze of candles. On the wall of what used, I think, to be the old town hall, close by the gate, some fanatic agnostic has set a white inscription on a tablet, 'Religion is opium for the People'. The tablet, which has been there a long time, is in shape not unlike the customary frame for a sacred picture. I saw an old peasant, evidently unable to read, cross himself solemnly before the chapel, and then, turning to the left, cross himself as solemnly before this anti-religious inscription. It is perhaps worth while to remark in passing that the new Communist programme, while insisting, as before, on the definite separation of church and state, and church and school, now includes the particular statement that 'care should be taken in no way to hurt the feelings of the religious'. Churches and chapels are open, church processions take place as before, and Moscow's as in the old days, is still a city of church bells.

A long line of sledges with welcome bags of flour was passing through the square. Soldiers of the Red Army were coming off parade, laughing and talking, and very noticeably smarter than the men of six months ago. There was a bright clear sky behind the fantastic Cathedral of Saint Basil, and the rough graves under the Kremlin wall, where those are buried who died in the fighting at the time of the November Revolution, have been tidied up. There was scaffolding round the gate of the Kremlin which was damaged at that time and is being carefully repaired.

The Committee of State Constructions was founded last spring to co-ordinate the management of the various engineering and other constructive works previously carried on by independent departments. It became an independent organ with its own finances about the middle of the summer. Its headquarters are in the Nikolskaya, in the Chinese town, next door to the old building of the Anglo-Russian Trading Company, which still bears the Lion and the Unicorn sculptured above its green and white facade some time early in the 17th century.

Pavlovitch is a little, fat, spectacled man with a bald head, fringed with the remains of red hair, and a little reddish beard. He was dressed in a black leather coat and trousers. He complained bitterly that all his plans for engineering works to improve the productive possibilities of the country were made impracticable by the imperious demands of war. As an old Siberian exile he had been living in France before the revolution and, as he said, had seen there how France made war. 'They sent her locomotives, and rails for the locomotives to run on, everything she needed they sent her from all parts of the world. When they sent horses, they sent also hay for their food, and shoes for their feet, and even nails for the shoes. If we were supplied like that, Russia would be at peace in a week. But we have nothing, and can get nothing, and are forced to be at war against our will.

'And war spoils everything,' he continued. 'This committee should be at work on affairs of peace, making Russia more useful to herself and to the rest of the world. You know our plans. But with fighting on all our fronts, and with all our best men away, we are compelled to use 90 percent of our energy and material for the immediate needs of the army. Every day we get masses of telegrams from all fronts, asking for this or that. For example, Trotsky telegraphs here simply 'We shall be in Orenburg in two days', leaving us to do what is necessary. Then with the map before me, I have to send what will be needed, no matter what useful work has to be abandoned meanwhile, engineers, railway gangs for putting right the railways, material for bridges, and so on.

'Indeed, the biggest piece of civil engineering done in Russia for many years was the direct result of our fear lest you people or the Germans should take our Baltic fleet. Save the dreadnoughts we could not, but I decided to save what we could. The widening and deepening of the canal system so as to shift boats from the Baltic to the Volga had been considered in the time of the Tsar. It was considered and dismissed as impracticable. Once, indeed, they did try to take two torpedo boats over, and they lifted them on barges to make the attempt. Well, we said that as the thing could be planned, it could be done, and the canals are deepened and widened, and we took through them, under their own power, seven big destroyers, six small destroyers and four submarine boats, which, arriving unexpectedly before Kazan, played a great part in our victory there. But the pleasure of that was spoilt for me by the knowledge that I had had to take men and material from the building of the electric power station, with which we hope to make Petrograd independent of the coal supply.

'The difficulties we have to fight against are, of course, enormous, but much of what the old regime failed to do, for want of initiative or for other reasons, we have done and are doing. Some of the difficulties are of a most unexpected kind. The local inhabitants, partly, no doubt, under the influence of our political opponents, were extremely hostile with regard to the building of the power station, simply because they did not understand it. I went there myself, and explained to them what it would mean, that their river would become a rich river, that they would be able to get cheap power for all sorts of works, and that they would have electric light in all their houses. Then they carried me shoulder high through the village, and sent telegrams to Lenin, to Zinoviev, to everybody they could think of, and since then we have had nothing but help from them.

'Most of our energy at present has to be spent on mending and making railways and roads for the use of the army. Over 11,000 versts of railway are under construction, and we have finished the railway from Arzamas to Shikhran. Twelve hundred versts of highroad are under construction. And to meet the immediate needs of the army we have already repaired or made 8,000 versts of roads of various kinds. As a matter of fact the internal railway net of Russia is by no means as bad as people make out. By its means, hampered as we are, we have been able to beat the counter-revolutionaries, concentrating our best troops, now here, now there, wherever need may be. Remember that the whole way round our enormous frontiers we are being forced to fight groups of reactionaries supported at first mostly by the Germans, now mostly by yourselves, by the Rumanians, by the Poles, and in some districts by the Germans still. Troops fighting on the Ural front are fighting a month later south of Voronezh, and a month later again are having a holiday, marching on the heels of the Germans as they evacuate the occupied provinces. Some of our troops are not yet much good. One day they fight, and the next they think they would rather not. So that our best troops, those in which there are most workmen, have to be flung in all directions. We are at work all the time enabling this to be done, and making new roads to enable it to be done still better. But what waste, when there are so many other things we want to do!

'All the time the needs of war are pressing on us. Today is the first day for two months that we have been able to warm this building. We have been working here in overcoats and fur hats in a temperature below freezing point. Why? Wood was already on its way to us, when we had suddenly to throw troops northwards. Our wood had to be flung out of the wagons, and the Red Army put in its place, and the wagons sent north again. The thing had to be done, and we have had to work as best we could in the cold. Many of my assistants have fallen ill. Two only yesterday had to be taken home in a condition something like that of a fit, the result of prolonged sedentary work in unheated rooms. I have lost the use of my right hand for the same reason.' He stretched out his right hand, which he had been keeping in the pocket of his coat. It was an ugly sight, with swollen, immovable fingers, like the roots of a vegetable.

At this moment someone came in to speak to Pavlovitch. He stood at the table a little behind me, so that I did not see him, but Pavlovitch, noticing that he looked curiously at me, said, 'Are you acquaintances?' I looked round and saw Sukhanov, Gorky's friend, formerly one of the cleverest writers on the Novaya Jizn. I jumped up and shook hands with him.

'What, have you gone over to the Bolsheviks?' I asked.

'Not at all,' said Sukhanov, smiling, 'but I am working here.'

'Sukhanov thinks that we do less harm than anybody else,' said Pavlovitch, and laughed. 'Go and talk to him and he'll tell you all there is to be said against us. And there's lots to say.'

Sukhanov was an extremely bitter enemy of the Bolsheviks, and was very angry with me when, over a year ago, I told him I was convinced that sooner or later he would be working with them. I told Pavlovitch the story, and he laughed again. 'A long time ago,' he said, 'Sukhanov made overtures to me through Miliutin. I agreed, and everything was settled, but when a note appeared in Pravda to say that he was going to work in this Committee, he grew shy, and wrote a contradiction. Miliutin was very angry and asked me to publish the truth. I refused, but wrote on that day in my diary, "Sukhanov will come". Three months later he was already working with us. One day he told me that in the big diary of the revolution which he is writing, and will write very well, he had some special abuse for me. "I have none for you," I said, "but I will show you one page of my own diary", and I showed him that page, and asked him to look at the date. Sukhanov is an honest fellow, and was bound to come.'

He went on with his talk.

'You know, hampered as we are by lack of everything, we could not put up the fight we are putting up against the reactionaries if it were not for the real revolutionary spirit of the people as a whole. The reactionaries have money, munitions, supplies of all kinds, instructors, from out side. We have nothing, and yet we beat them. Do you know that the English have given them tanks? Have you heard that in one place they used gases or something of the kind, and blinded 800 men? And yet we win. Why? Because from every town we capture we get new strength. And any town they take is a source of weakness to them, one more town to garrison and hold against the wishes of the population.'

'And if you do get peace, what then?'

'We want from abroad all that we cannot make ourselves. We want a 100,000 *versts* of rails. Now we have to take up rails in one place to lay them in another. We want new railways built. We want dredgers for our canals and river works. We want excavators.'

'And how do you expect people to sell you these things when your foreign credit is not worth a farthing?'

'We shall pay in concessions, giving foreigners the right to take raw materials. Timber, actual timber, is as good as credit. We have huge areas of forest in the north, and every country in Europe needs timber. Let that be our currency for foreign purchases. We are prepared to say, "You build this, or give us that, and we will give you the right to take so much timber for yourselves." And so on. And concessions of other kinds also. As a matter of fact negotiations are now proceeding with a foreign firm for the building of a railway from the Obi to Kotlas.'

'But part of that district is not in your hands.'

'If we get peace we shall be able to arrange that without difficulty.'

Just as I was going he stopped me, and evidently not in the least realising that English people generally have come to think of him and his friends as of some strange sort of devils, if not with horns and tails, certainly far removed from human beings, he asked: 'If we do get peace, don't you think there will be engineers and skilled labourers in England who will volunteer to come out to Russia and help us? There is so much to do that I can promise they will have the best we can give them. We are almost as short of skilled men as we are of locomotives. We are now taking simple unskilled workmen who show any signs of brains and training them as we go along. There must be engineers, railwaymen, mechanics among English socialists who would be glad to come. And of course they need not be socialists, so long as they are good engineers.'

That last suggestion of his is entirely characteristic. It is impossible to make the Bolsheviks realise that the English people feel any hostility towards them. Nor do they feel hostility towards the English as such. On my way back to the hotel I met a party of English soldiers, taken prisoners on the northern front, walking free, without a convoy, through the streets.

Twelve / The Executive Committee and the Terror

February 17

My general impression that the Soviet revolution has passed through its period of internal struggle and is concentrating upon constructive work so far as that is allowed by war on all its frontiers, and that the population is settling down under the new regime, was confirmed by the meeting of the Executive Committee which definitely limited the powers of the Extraordinary Commission. Before the sitting was opened I had a few words with Peters and with Krylenko. The excitement of the internal struggle was over. It had been bitterly fought within the party, and both Krylenko of the Revolutionary Tribunal and Peters of the Extraordinary Commission were here merely to witness the official act that would define their new position. Peters talked of his failure to get away for some shooting; Krylenko jeered at me for having refused to believe in the Lockhart conspiracy. Neither showed any traces of the bitter struggle waged within the party for and against the almost dictatorial powers of the Extraordinary Commission for dealing with counter-revolution.

The sitting opened with a report by Dzerzhinsky, that strange ascetic who, when in prison in Warsaw, insisted on doing the dirty work of emptying the slops and cleaning other people's cells besides his own, on a theory that one man should where possible take upon himself the evil which would otherwise have to be shared by all; and in the dangerous beginning of the revolution had taken upon himself the most unpopular of all posts, that of President of the Extraordinary Commission. His personal uprightness is the complement of an absolute personal courage, shown again and again during the last 18 months. At the time of the Left Social Revolutionary mutiny he went without a guard to the headquarters of the mutineers, believing that he could bring them to reason, and when arrested by them dared them to shoot him and showed so bold a front that in the end the soldiers set to watch him set him free and returned to their allegiance. This thin, tallish man, with a fanatic face not un like some of the traditional portraits of Saint Francis, the terror of counter-revolutionaries and criminals alike, is a very bad speaker. He looks into the air over the heads of his audience and talks as if he were not addressing them at all but someone else unseen. He talks even of a subject which he knows perfectly with curious inability to form his sentences; stops, changes words, and often, recognising that he cannot finish his sentence, ends where he is, in the middle of it, with a little odd, deprecating emphasis, as if to say: 'At this point there is a full stop. At least so it seems.'

He gave a short colourless sketch of the history of the

Extraordinary Commission. He referred to the various crises with which it had had to deal, beginning with the drunken pogroms in Petrograd, the suppression of the combined anarchists and criminals in Moscow (he mentioned that after that four hours' struggle which ended in the clearing out of the anarchists' strongholds, criminality in Moscow decreased by 80 percent), to the days of the Terror when, now here, now there, armed risings against the soviet were engineered by foreigners and by counter-revolutionaries working with them. He then made the point that throughout all this time the revolution had been threatened by largescale revolts. Now the revolution was safe from such things and was threatened only by individual treacheries of various kinds, not by things which needed action on a large scale. They had traitors, no doubt, in the Soviet institutions who were waiting for the day (which would never come) to join with their enemies, and meanwhile were secretly hampering their work. They did not need on that account to destroy their institutions as a whole. The struggle with counter-revolution had passed to a new stage. They no longer had to do open battle with open enemies; they had merely to guard themselves against individuals. The laws of war by which, meeting him on the field of battle, the soldier had a right to kill his enemy without trial, no longer held good. The situation was now that of peace, where each offender must have his guilt proved before a court. Therefore the right of sentencing was removed from the Extraordinary Commission; but if, through unforeseen circumstances, the old conditions should return, they intended that the dictatorial powers of the Commission should be restored to it until those conditions had ceased.

Thus if, in case of armed counter-revolution, a district were declared to be in a state of war, the Extraordinary Commission would resume its old powers. Otherwise its business would be to hand offenders, such as Soviet officials who were habitually late (here there was a laugh, the only sign throughout his speech that Dzerzhinsky was holding the attention of his audience), over to the Revolutionary Tribunal, which would try them and, should their guilt be proved, put them in concentration camps to learn to work. He read point by point the resolutions establishing these changes and providing for the formation of Revolutionary Tribunals. Trial to take place within 48 hours after the conclusion of the investigation, and the investigation to take not longer than a month. He ended as he ended his sentences, as if by accident, and people scarcely realised he had finished before Sverdlov announced the next speaker.

Krylenko proposed an amendment to ensure that no member of the Revolutionary Tribunal could be also a member of the Extraordinary Commission which had taken up and investigated a case. His speech was very disappointing. He is not at his best when addressing a serious meeting like that of the Executive Committee. The Krylenko who spoke tonight, fluently, clearly, but without particular art, is a very different Krylenko from the virtuoso in mob oratory, the little, dangerous, elderly man in ensign's uniform who swayed the soldiers' mass meetings in Petrograd a year and a half ago. I remember hearing him speak in barracks soon after the murder of Shingarev and Kokoshkin, urging class struggle and at the same time explaining the difference between that and the murder of sick men in bed. He referred to the murder and, while continuing his speech, talking already of another subject, he went through the actions of a man approaching a bed and killing a sleeper with a pistol. It was a trick, of course, but the thrilling, horrible effect of it moved the whole audience with a shudder of disgust. There was nothing of this kind in his short lecture on jurisprudence tonight.

Avanesov, the tall, dark secretary of the Executive Committee, with the face of a big, benevolent hawk hooded in long black hair, opposed Krylenko on the ground that there were not enough trustworthy workers to ensure that in country districts such a provision could be carried out. Finally the resolution was passed as a whole and the amendment was referred to the judgment of the presidium.

The committee next passed to the consideration of the Extraordinary Tax levied on the propertied classes. Krestinsky, Commissary of Finance, made his report to a grim audience, many of whom quite frankly regarded the tax as a political mistake. Krestinsky is a short, humorous man, in dark spectacles, dressed more like a banker than like a Bolshevik. It was clear that the collection of the tax had not been as successful as he had previously suggested. I was interested in his reference to the double purpose of the tax and in the reasons he gave for its comparative failure. The tax had a fiscal purpose, partly to cover deficit, partly by drawing in paper money to raise the value of the rouble. It had also a political purpose. It was intended to affect the propertied classes only, and thus to weaken the kulaks (hardfists, rich peasants) in the villages and to teach the poorer peasants the meaning of the revolution. Unfortunately some soviets, where the minority of the kulaks had retained the unfair domination given it by its economic strength, had distributed the tax-paying equally over the whole population, thus very naturally raising the resentment of the poor who found themselves taxed to the same amount as those who could afford to pay. It had been necessary to send circular telegrams emphasising the terms of the decree. In cases where the taxation had been carried out as intended there had been no difficulty. The most significant reason for the partial unsuccess was that the propertied class, as such, had already diminished to a greater extent than had been supposed, and many of those taxed, for example, as factory owners were already working, not as factory owners, but as paid directors in nationalised factories, and were therefore no longer subject to the tax. In other words, the partial failure of the tax was a proof of the successful development of the revolution. (This is illustrated by the concrete case of 'Uncle' recorded on p.95) Krestinsky believed that the revolution had gone so far that no further tax of this kind would be either possible or necessary.

Thirteen / Notes of conversations with Lenin

Whatever else they may think of him, not even his enemies deny that Vladimir Ilich Ulyanov (Lenin) is one of the greatest personalities of his time. I therefore make no apology for writing down such scraps of his conversation as seem to me to illustrate his manner of mind.

He was talking of the lack of thinkers in the English labour movement, and said he remembered hearing Shaw speak at some meeting. Shaw, he said, was 'A good man fallen among Fabians' and a great deal further left than his company. He had not heard of 'The Perfect Wagnerite', but was interested when I told him the general idea of the book, and turned fiercely on an interrupter who said that Shaw was a clown. 'He may be a clown for the bourgeoisie in a bourgeois state, but they would not think him a clown in a revolution.'

He asked whether Sidney Webb was consciously working in the interests of the capitalists, and when I said I was quite sure that he was not, he said, 'Then he has more industry than brains. He certainly has great knowledge.'

He was entirely convinced that England was on the eve of revolution, and pooh-poohed my objections. 'Three months ago I thought it would end in all the world having to fight the centre of reaction in England. But I do not think so now. Things have gone further there than in France, if the news as to the extent of the strikes is true.'

I pointed out some of the circumstances, geographical and economical, which would make the success of a violent revolution in England problematical in the extreme, and put to him the same suggestion that I put to Bukharin (see page 100), namely, that a suppressed movement in England would be worse for Russia than our traditional method of compromise. He agreed at once, but said, 'That is quite true, but you cannot stop a revolution … although Ramsay MacDonald will try to at the last minute. Strikes and soviets. If these two habits once get hold, nothing will keep the workmen from them. And soviets, once started, must sooner or later come to supreme power.' Then, 'But certainly it would be much more difficult in England. Your big clerk and shop keeping class would oppose it, until the workmen broke them. Russia was indeed the only country in which the revolution could start. And we are not yet through our troubles with the peasantry.'

I suggested that one reason why it had been possible in Russia was that they had had room to retreat.

'Yes,' he said. 'The distances saved us. The Germans were frightened of them, at the time when they could indeed have eaten us up, and won peace, which the Allies would have given them in gratitude for our destruction. A revolution in England would have nowhere whither to retire.'

Of the soviets he said, 'In the beginning I thought they were and would remain a purely Russian form; but it is now quite clear that under various names they must be the instruments of revolution everywhere.'

He expressed the opinion that in England they would not allow me to tell the truth about Russia, and gave as an example the way in which Colonel Robins had been kept silent in America. He asked about Robins, 'Had he really been as friendly to the Soviet government as he made out?' I said, 'Yes, if only as a sportsman admiring its pluck and courage in difficulties.' I quoted Robins' saying, 'I can't go against a baby I have sat up with for six months. But if there were a Bolshevik movement in America I'd be out with my rifle to fight it every time.' 'Now that,' said Lenin, 'is an honest man and more far seeing than most. I always liked that man.' He shook with laughter at the image of the baby, and said, 'That baby had several million other folk sitting up with it too.'

He said he had read in an English socialist paper a comparison of his own theories with those of an American, Daniel De Leon. He had then borrowed some of De Leon's pamphlets from Reinstein (who belongs to the party which De Leon founded in America), read them for the first time, and was amazed to see how far and how early De Leon had pursued the same train of thought as the Russians. His theory that representation should be by industries, not by areas, was already the germ of the Soviet system. He remembered seeing De Leon at an International Conference. De Leon made no impression at all, a grey old man, quite unable to speak to such an audience: but evidently a much bigger man than he looked, since his pamphlets were written before the experience of the Russian Revolution of 1905. Some days afterwards I noticed that Lenin had introduced a few phrases of De Leon, as if to do honour to his memory, into the draft for the new programme of the Communist Party.

Talking of the lies that are told about Russia, he said it was interesting to notice that they were mostly perversions of truth and not pure inventions, and gave as an example the recent story that he had recanted. 'Do you know the origin of that?' he said. 'I was wishing a happy New Year to a friend over the telephone, and said "And may we commit fewer stupidities this year than last!" Someone overheard it and told someone else. A newspaper announced "Lenin says we are committing stupidities" and so the story started.'

More than ever, Lenin struck me as a happy man. Walking home from the Kremlin, I tried to think of any other man of his calibre who had had a similar joyous temperament. I could think of none. This little, bald headed, wrinkled man, who tilts his chair this way and that, laughing over one thing or another, ready any minute to give serious advice to any who interrupt him to ask for it, advice so well reasoned that it is to his followers far more compelling than any command, every one of his wrinkles is a wrinkle of laughter, not of worry. I think the reason must be that he is the first great leader who utterly discounts the value of his own personality. He is quite without personal ambition. More than that, he believes, as a Marxist, in the movement of the masses which, with or without him, would still move. His whole faith is in the elemental forces that move people, his faith in himself is merely his belief that he justly estimates the direction of those forces. He does not believe that any man could make or stop the revolution which he thinks inevitable. If the Russian Revolution fails, according to him, it fails only temporarily, and because of forces beyond any man's control. He is consequently free with a freedom no other great man has ever had. It is not so much what he says that inspires confidence in him. It is this sensible freedom, this obvious detachment. With his philosophy he cannot for a moment believe that one man's mistake might ruin all. He is, for himself at any rate, the exponent, not the cause, of the events that will be for ever linked with his name.

Fourteen / The Supreme Council of Public Economy

FEBRUARY 20

Today was an unlucky day. I felt tired, ill and hungry, and had arranged to talk with both Rykov, the President of the Supreme Council of People's Economy, and Krestinsky, the Commissar of Finance, at such awkward times that I got no tea and could get nothing to eat until after four o'clock. Two such talks on an empty stomach (for the day before I had had only a plate of soup and a little scrap of fish) were a little too much for me, and I fear I did not gather as much information as I should have collected under better conditions.

I had a jolly drive, early in the morning, through the Chinese Town, and out by the gate in the old wall, up Myasnitzkaya Street, and round to the right to a building that used to be the Grand Hotel of Siberia, a loathsome place where I once stayed. Here in the old days provincial merchants put up, who did not mind high prices and a superfluity of bugs. It has now been turned into a hive of office work, and is the headquarters of the Supreme Council of Public Economy, which, controlling production and distribution alike, is the centre of the constructive work going on throughout the country.

This council, the theorists tell me, is intended to become the central organization of the state. The soviets will naturally become less and less important as instruments of political transition as that transition is completed and the struggle against reaction within and without comes to an end. Then the chief business of the state will no longer be to protect itself against enemies but to develop its economic life, to increase its productivity and to improve the material conditions of the workers of whom it is composed. All these tasks are those of the Supreme Council of Public Economy, and as the bitterness of the struggle dies away this body, which came into being almost unnoticed in the din of battle, will become more and more important in comparison with the soviets, which were in origin not constructive organisations but the instruments of a revolution, the hardest stages of which have already been accomplished.

It is perhaps worth while to set out here the constitution of this council. It is considered at present as the economic department of the All-Russian Central Executive Committee, to which, and to the Council of People's Commissaries, it is responsible. It regulates all production and distribution. It reports on the various estimates of the state budget and, in conjunction with the Commissariats of Finance and State Control, carries out the financing of all branches of public economy. It consists of 69 members, and is composed as follows: Ten representatives from the All-Russian Executive

Committee, 30 from the All-Russian Industrial Productive Union (a union of trade unions), 20 from the ten District Councils of Public Economy, two from the All Russian Council of Workers' Co-operative Societies, and one representative each from the Commissariats of Supply, Ways of Communication, Labour, Agriculture, Finance, Trade and Industry, and Internal Affairs. It meets as a whole at least once in every month. The work of its members is directed by a Presidium of nine members, of which it elects eight, the President being elected by the All-Russian Central Executive Committee, and enjoying the rank of a People's Commissar or Minister.

I had a long talk with Rykov, the President, or rather listened to a long lecture by him, only now and then succeeding in stopping him by forcing a question into the thread of his harangue. He stammers a little, and talks so indistinctly that for the first time (No. The first time was when Chicherin gabbled through the provisions of the Brest Treaty at the fourth All-Russian Assembly) I felt willing to forgive normal Russians, who nearly always talk as if they were in Petrograd and their listener in Vladivostok.

Part of what he said is embodied in what I have already written. But besides sketching the general aims of the council, Rykov talked of the present economic position of Russia. At the moment Russian industry was in peculiar difficulties owing to the fuel crisis. This was partly due to the fact that the Czechs and the reactionaries, who had used the Czechs to screen their own organisation, had control of the coalfields in the Urals, and partly to the fact that the German occupation of the Ukraine and the activities of Krasnov had cut off Soviet Russia from the Donetz coal basin, which had been a main source of supply, although in the old days Petrograd had also got coal from England. It was now, however, clear that, with a friendly Ukraine, they would have the use of the Donetz basin much sooner than they had expected.

The Brest peace and the deprivations it involved had made them consider the position of the industrial districts from a new standpoint, and they were determined to make Petrograd and Moscow as far as possible independent of all fuel which had to be brought from a distance. He referred to the works in progress for utilising water power to provide electrical energy for the Petrograd factories, and said that similar electrification, on a basis of turf fuel, is planned for Moscow.

I asked how they were going to get the machines. He said that of course they would prefer to buy them abroad, but that, though this was impossible, the work would not be delayed on that account, since they could make a start with the machines they had. Turbines for the Petrograd works they still hoped to obtain from abroad when peace had been arranged. If the worst came to the worst he thought they could make their own. 'That is one unexpected result of Russia's long isolation. Her dependence on imports from abroad is lessening.' He gave an example in salt, the urgent need of which has led to the opening of a new industry, whose resources are such as to enable Russia not only to supply herself with salt, but the rest of the world as well if need should be.

I asked what were their immediate plans with regard to the electrification of Moscow. He said that there was no water power near Moscow but big turf deposits which would be used as fuel. In order not to interfere with the actual lighting of the town from the power station already in existence, they are taking the electric plant from the Provodnik works, which will supply enough electricity for the lighting of the town. As soon as that is set up and working, they will use it for the immediate needs of Moscow, and set about transferring the existing power-station to the new situation near the turf beds. In this way they hope to carry out the change from coal to turf without interfering with the ordinary life of the town. Eventually when things settle down they will get a larger plant.

I said, 'Of course you have a double object in this, not only to lessen the dependence of the industrial districts on fuel that has to be brought from a distance, and of which you may be deprived, but also to lessen the strain on transport?'

'Yes,' he said. 'Indeed at the present moment the latter is our greatest difficulty, hampering everything we would wish to do. And transport we cannot put right without help from abroad. Therefore we do everything we can to use local resources, and are even developing the coal deposits near Moscow, which are of inferior quality to the Donetz coal, and were in the old days purposely smothered by the Donetz coal owners, who wished to preserve their monopoly.'

I asked him if in his opinion Russia could organise herself without help from abroad. He said, 'I rather think she will have to. We want steam dredgers, steam excavators, and locomotives most of all, but we have small hope of getting them in the immediate future, because the effects of the war have been so serious in the disorganisation of industry in the Western countries that it is doubtful whether they will be in a position to supply even their own needs.'

While we were talking Berg, the secretary, came in. I asked him how his Soviet matches were progressing, and he said that the labels were being printed and that the first lot would soon be ready. They will be distributed on the card system, and he had calculated that they could sell them at 12 kopecks a packet. I paid a rouble for a box of ordinary matches at Bieloostrov, and a rouble and a half here.

Fifteen / The race with ruin

After leaving Rykov I went to see Krestinsky, the Commissar of Finance, the curious little optimist whose report on the Extraordinary Tax I had heard at the last meeting of the Executive Committee. I found him in the Ilyinka Street, in the Chinese town. I began by telling him that I did not believe that they meant to pay the loans. He laughed and gave me precisely the answer I had expected: 'Of course we hope there will be a revolution in other countries, in which case they will repudiate their debts and forgive us ours. But if that does not happen we know very well that we shall have to pay, and we are prepared to pay, and shall be able to pay, in concessions, in raw material which they need more than they need gold.'

Then, being myself neither an economist nor a theoretical socialist, I put before him what had been said to me in Stockholm by an Englishman who was both one and the other; namely, that, being isolated from European finance, the Soviet government of Russia was bound to come to an end on economic and financial grounds alone.

He said: 'That would certainly be so, if rising prices, rising wages, were to mean indefinitely increased demands on the printing machines for paper money. But, while we are at present forced to print more and more money, another process is at work which, in the long run, will bring this state of things to an end. Just as in our dealings with other countries we exchange goods instead of paying in money, so within our own frontiers money is ceasing to be the sole medium of exchange. Gradually the workmen are coming to receive more and more in other forms than money. Houses, for example, lighting and heating are only a beginning. These things being state monopolies, the task of supplying the workman's needs without the use of money is comparatively easy. The chief difficulty is, of course, food supplies, which depend on our ability to keep up an exchange of goods with the villages. If we can supply the villages with manufactured goods, they will supply us with food. You can fairly say that our ruin or salvation depends on a race between the decreasing value of money (with the consequent need for printing notes in ever greater quantities) and our growing ability to do without money altogether. That is of course, a broad view, and you must not for a moment suppose that we expect to do without money in the immediate future. I am merely showing you the two opposing tendencies on which our economic fate depends.'

I will not set down here what he said about the Extraordinary Tax, for it was merely a repetition of what I had heard him say in committee. In connection with it, however, he admitted that capitalism and profiteering were hard things to root out, saying that they had great difficulty in getting at what he called 'the new bourgeoisie', namely the speculators who have made fortunes since the revolution by selling scarce food products at fantastic prices. It was difficult to tax them because they carried on their operations secretly and it was next to impossible to find out who they were. They did not bank their money, and though an attempt had been made to get at them through the house committees, it was found that even these committees were unable to detect them. They will, however, be made to disgorge their ill-gotten gains when the measure first proposed by Sokolnikov last summer is put into practice. This is a general exchange of new money for old, after which the old will be declared invalid. 'Of course,' said Krestinsky, 'they will cheat in every possible way, scattering out the money among a number of friends and relations. But something will have been done in cleaning them up, and that process will be completed by a second exchange of money later on.'

Fifteen milliards of new notes for the first exchange are already printed, but they think that 20 milliards will be necessary.

I asked if the new money was better looking than the old, if it looked more like money that was worth having than the wretched little notes printed by the Provisional government and scornfully called 'Kerenkies' by the populace. Krestinsky said he was afraid not, but that the second and final exchange would be made in notes which they expected to be permanent. They did not expect the notes of the first exchange to circulate abroad, but the notes of the second would carry with them state obligation and they expected them to go into general currency. He added, smiling, that the words 'Proletariat of all lands, unite,' were to appear on the notes in eight languages. The question of the look of the notes, of their ability to inspire confidence by their mere appearance, is of real importance in a country where so many of the peasantry will judge their value by nothing else.

I reminded him of the hostility roused in some villages by mistakes in the assessment and collecting of the Extraordinary Tax, mistakes which (so other Communists had assured me) would cost them more, politically, than the tax was worth to them, and asked him, 'Will you not have great difficulty in getting the exchange made, and are you not running the risk of providing the reactionaries with a new profitable basis of agitation?'

He said that of course they would not make the attempt unless they felt sure they were politically strong enough to carry it through. 'If it is properly explained to the villages there will be nothing to fear, because the measure will not threaten any but the rich and therefore the small minority of the peasantry. It would be a different matter if the same thing were to be tried by the counter-revolutionaries, because they would not discriminate in favour of the poor. If Kolchak and company overthrow us and try to substitute their money for ours, their action would affect rich and poor alike, minority and majority together. If there were not a hundred other causes guaranteeing the insecurity of their position, the fact that they will be unable to get rid of our money without rousing the most violent opposition in the masses throughout the country would alone be sufficient to do it.'

I asked whether that was the reason why they intended to print on the notes 'proletariat of all lands, unite', so that the counter-revolutionaries, unable to tolerate money bearing that hated phrase, should be forced to a step disastrous for themselves.

He laughed, and said that he did not think counter-revolution in the least likely unless brought in by invasion, which he did not think politically possible.

Sixteen / A play of Chekhov

FEBRUARY 21

I saw Chekhov's 'Uncle Vanya' acted by the cast of the Art Theatre in the First Studio. This is a little theatre holding just over 200 people. It was of course full. It was curious to see how complete the revolution had been in a social sense. It was impossible to tell to what class in pre-revolutionary days any particular member of the audience had belonged. I was struck by the new smartness of the boy officers of the Red Army, of whom a fair number were present. As we waited for the curtain to rise, I thought how the mental attitude of the people had changed. A year ago, we lived with exhilaration or despair on a volcano which might any day erupt and sweep away the new life before any one had become accustomed to live it. Now the danger to the revolution was a thousand miles away on the various fronts. Here, in the centre, the revolution was an established fact. People had ceased to wonder when it would end, were settling into their places in the new social order, and took their pleasures not as if they were plucking flowers on their way to execution, but in the ordinary routine of life.

The play is well known, a drama of bourgeois society in a small country place. A poor landowner scraping money for an elder brother in the town, realizing at last that the brother was not the genius for whom such sacrifice was worth while; a doctor with a love for forestry and dreams of the future; the old mock genius's young wife; his sister; his adoring mother; the old nurse and the ancient dependent adopted, as it were, with the estate; all these people in their own way make each other suffer. Chekhov's irony places before us wasted lives, hopelessness, exaggerated interest in personalities, vain strugglings after some better outlet for the expression of selves not worth expressing.

That play, acted today, seemed as remote as a play of the old regime in France would have seemed five years ago. A gulf seemed to have passed. The play had become a play of historical interest; the life it represented had gone for ever. People in Russia no longer have time for private lives of such a character. Such people no longer exist; some of them have been swept into the floodtide of revolution and are working as they never hoped to have the chance to work; others, less generous, have been broken and thrown aside. The revolution has been hard on some, and has given new life to others. It has swept away that old life so absolutely that, come what may, it will be a hundred years at least before anywhere in Russia people will be able to be unhappy in that particular way again.

The subject of 'Uncle Vanya' was a great deal more remote from the Russian audience of today than was the opera of 'Samson and Delilah' which I heard last week. And, if I realized that the revolution had come to stay, if I realized that Chekhov's play had become a play of historical interest, I realized also that Chekhov was a great master in that his work carried across the gulf between the old life and the new, and affected a revolutionary audience of today as strongly as it affected that very different audience of a few years ago. Indeed, the play seemed almost to have gained by the revolution, which had lent it, perhaps, more irony than was in Chekhov's mind as he wrote. Was this the old life? I thought, as I stepped out into the snow. If so, then thank God it has gone!

Seventeen / The Centro-Textile

This morning I drove to the Dielovoi Dvor, the big house on the Varvarskaya Square which is occupied by the central organisation of the textile industry. The head of this organisation is Nogin, an extremely capable, energetic Russian, so capable, indeed, that I found it hard to believe he could really be a Russian. He is a big man, with a mass of thick brown shaggy hair, so thick that the little bald patch on the top of his head seems like an artificial tonsure. Nogin sketched the lines on which the Russian textile industry was being reorganised, and gave orders that I should be supplied with all possible printed matter in which to find the details.

The Centro-Textile is the actual centre of the economic life of Russia, because, since textiles are the chief materials of exchange between the towns and the villages, on its success depends the success of everything else. The textile industry is, in any case, the most important of all Russian industries. Before the war it employed 500,000 workmen, and Nogin said that in spite of the disorganisation of the war and of the revolution 400,000 are employed today. This may be so in the sense that 400,000 are receiving pay, but lack of fuel or of raw material must have brought many factories to a standstill.

All the big factories have been nationalised. Formerly, although in any one town there might be factories carrying out all the different processes, these factories belonged to different owners. A single firm or bank might control factories scattered over Russia and, so that the whole process should be in its hands, the raw material travelled from factory to factory through the country, instead of merely moving about a single town. Thus a roll of material might have gone through one process at Jaroslav, another at Moscow, and a third at Tula, and finally come back to Jaroslav to be finished, simply because the different factories which worked upon it, though widely scattered, happened to be under one control. Nationalisation has made possible the rational regrouping of factories so that the complete process is carried out in one place, consequently saving transport. There are 23 complete groups of this kind, and in the textile industry generally about 50 groups in all.

There has been a similar concentration of control. In the old days there were hundreds of different competitive firms with their buildings and offices in the Ilyinka, the Varvarka, and the Nikolskaya. The Chinese town was a mass of little offices of different textile firms. The whole of that mass of struggling competitive units of direction had now been concentrated in the house in which we were talking. The control of the workers had been carried through in such a way that the technical experts had proper weight. (See p. 145) There were periodical conferences of elected representatives of all the factories, and Nogin believed that the system of combined elective workmen's and appointed experts' representation could hardly be improved upon.

Nationalisation had had the effect of standardising the output. Formerly, an infinite variety of slightly different stuffs were produced, the variations being often merely for the sake of being different in the competitive trade. Useless varieties had now been done away with, with the result of greater economy in production.

I asked what he could tell me about their difficulties in the matter of raw material. He said they no longer get anything from America, and while the railway was cut at Orenburg by the Cossacks, they naturally could get no cotton from Turkestan. In fact, last autumn they had calculated that they had only enough material to keep the factories going until December. Now they found they could certainly keep going to the end of March, and probably longer. Many small factories, wishing to make their cases out worse than they were, had underestimated their stocks. Here, as in other things, the isolation of the revolution had the effect of teaching the Russians that they were less dependent upon the outside world than they had been in the habit of supposing. He asked me if I knew it had been considered impossible to combine flax and cotton in such a way that the mixture could be worked in machines intended for cotton only. They had an infinite supply of flax, much of which in the old days had been exported. Investigations carried on for the Centro-Textile by two professors, the brothers Chilikin, had ended in the discovery of three different processes for the cottonising of flax in such a way that they could now mix not only a small percentage of their flax with cotton and use the old machines, but were actually using 50 percent flax and had already produced material experimentally with as much as 75 percent.

(Some days later two young technicians from the Centro-Textile brought me a neatly prepared set of specimens illustrating these new processes and asked me to bring them anything of the same sort from England in return. They were not Bolsheviks—were, in fact, typical non-politicals. They were pleased with what the Centro-Textile was doing, and said that more encouragement was given to research than ever formerly. But they were very despondent about the economic position. I could not make them understand why Russia was isolated, and that I might be unable to bring them technical books from England).

Nogin rather boastfully said that the Western linen industry would suffer from the isolation of Russia, whereas in the long run the Russians would be able to do without the rest of the world. With regard to wool, they would have no difficulty now that they were again united with a friendly Ukraine. The silk industry was to be developed in the Astrakhan district where climatic conditions are particularly favourable.

I asked about the fate of the old textile manufacturers and was told that though many had gone abroad many were working in the nationalised factories. The engineering staff, which mostly struck work at the beginning of the revolution, had almost without exception returned, the younger engineers in particular realising the new possibilities opening before the industry, the continual need of new improvements, and the immediate welcome given to originality of any kind. Apart from the question of food, which was bad for everybody, the social standard of the workers had risen. Thus one of their immediate difficulties was the provision of proper houses. The capitalists and manufacturers kept the workers in barracks. 'Nowadays the men want better dwellings and we mean to give them better. Some have moved into the old houses of the owners and manufacturers, but of course there are not enough of these to go round, and we have extensive plans in the way of building villages and garden cities for the workmen.'

I asked Nogin what, in his opinion, was most needed by Russia from abroad, and he said that as far as the textile industries were concerned they wanted machinery. Like everyone else to whom I put this question, he said that every industry in Russia would be in a better position if only they had more locomotives. 'Some of our factories are stopping now for lack of fuel, and at Saratov, for example, we have masses of raw material which we are unable to get to Moscow.'

Eighteen / Modification
in the agrarian programme

In the afternoon I met Sereda, the Commissar of Agriculture. He insisted that the agrarian policy had been much misrepresented by their enemies for the purposes of agitation. They had no intention of any such idiocy as the attempt to force the peasants to give up private ownership. The establishment of communes was not to be compulsory in any way; it was to be an illustrative means of propaganda of the idea of communal work, not more. The main task before them was to raise the standard of Russian agriculture, which under the old system was extremely low. By working many of the old estates on a communal system with the best possible methods they hoped to do two things at once: to teach the peasant to realise the advantages of communal labour, and to show him that he could himself get a very great deal more out of his land than he does. 'In other ways also we are doing everything we can to give direct help to the small agriculturists. We have mobilised all the agricultural experts in the country. We are issuing a mass of simply written pamphlets explaining better methods of farming.'

(I have seen scores of these pamphlets on forestry, potatoes, turf, rotation of crops, and so on, besides the agricultural journals issued by the Commissariat and sent in large quantities to the villages).

I told Sereda I had heard that the peasants were refusing to sow more than they wanted for their own needs. He said that on the contrary the latest reports gave them the right to hope for a greater sown area this year than ever before, and that even more would have been sown if Denmark had not been prevented from letting them have the seed for which they had actually paid. I put the same question to him that I put to Nogin as to what they most needed, he replied, 'tractors'.

Nineteen / Foreign trade and munitions of war

FEBRUARY 25

I had a talk in the Metropole with Krasin, who is Commissar for Trade and Industry and also President of the Committee for Supplying the Needs of the Army. He had disapproved of the November Revolution, but last year, when things looked like going badly, he came to Russia from Stockholm feeling that he could not do otherwise than help. He is an elderly man, an engineer, and very much of a European. We talked first of the Russian plans with regard to foreign trade. All foreign trade, he said, is now concentrated in the hands of the state, which is therefore able to deal as a single customer. I asked how that would apply to purchase, and whether they expected that countries dealing with them would organise committees through which the whole Russian trade of each such country should similarly pass. Krasin said, 'Of course that would be preferable, but only in the case of socialist countries. As things are now it would be very much to our disadvantage. It is better for us to deal with individual capitalists than with a ring. The formation of a committee in England, for example, with a monopoly of trade with Russia, would have the effect of raising prices against us, since we could no longer go from a dear shop to a cheaper one. Besides, as socialists we naturally wish to do nothing to help in the trustification of English manufacturers.'

He recognised that foreign trade on any large scale was impossible until their transport had been improved. Russia proposed to do her paying in raw material, in flax, timber, etc., in materials of which she had great quantities although she could not bring them to the ports until her transport should be restored. It would, therefore, be in the foreigner's own interests to help them in this matter. He added that they were confident that in the long run they could, without foreign help, so far restore their transport as to save themselves from starvation; but for a speedy return to normal conditions foreign help was essential.

The other question we touched was that of munitions. I expressed some surprise that they should be able to do so well although cut off from the West. Krasin said that as far as that was concerned they had ample munitions for a long fight. Heavy artillery is not much use for the kind of warfare waged in Russia; and as for light artillery, they were making and mending their own. They were not bothering with three-inch shells because they had found that the old regime had left scattered about Russia supplies of three-inch shells sufficient to last them several years. Dynamite also they had in enormous quantities. They were manufacturing gunpowder. The cartridge output had trebled since August when Krasin's committee was formed. He thought even as things were they could certainly fight for a year.

Twenty / The proposed delegation from Berne

I do not remember the exact date when the proposal of the Berne International Conference to send a Commission of Enquiry to Russia became known in Moscow, but on February 20 everybody who came to see me was talking about it, and from that date the question as to the reception of the delegates was the most urgently debated of all political subjects. Chicherin had replied immediately to Berne, saying that 'though they did not consider the Berne Conference either socialist or in any degree representative of the working-class they nevertheless would permit the commission's journey into Russia, and would give it every opportunity of becoming acquainted from all sides with the state of affairs, just as they would any bourgeois commission directly or indirectly connected with any of the bourgeois governments, even with those then attacking Russia.' It may well be imagined that a reply in this style infuriated the Mensheviks who consider themselves more or less affiliated to the parties represented at Berne. What, they shrieked, Kautsky not a socialist? To which their opponents replied, 'The government which Kautsky supports keeps Radek in irons in a gaol.' But to me the most interesting thing to observe was that Chicherin's reply was scarcely more satisfactory to some of the Communists. It had been sent off before any general consultation, and it appeared that the Communists themselves were widely divided as to the meaning of the proposal. One party believed that it was a first step towards agreement and peace. The other thought it an ingenious ruse by Clemenceau to get 'so-called' socialist condemnation of the Bolsheviks as a basis for Allied intervention. Both parties were, of course, wrong in so far as they thought the Allied governments had anything to do with it. Both the French and English delegates were refused passports. This, however, was not known in Moscow until after I left, and by then much had happened. I think the conference which founded the Third International in Moscow had its origin in a desire to counter any ill effects that might result from the expected visit of the people of Berne.

Litvinov said he considered the sending of the commission from Berne the most dangerous weapon yet conceived by their opponents. He complained that he had been unable to get either Lenin or Chicherin to realise that this delegation was a preparation for hostilities, not a preparation for peace. 'You do not understand that since the beginning of the war there has been a violent struggle between two Internationals, one of which does not believe in revolution while the other does. In this case a group of men already committed to condemn the revolution are coming to pass judgment on it. If they were not to condemn the revolution they would be condemning themselves. Chicherin ought to have put a condition that a delegation of left socialists should also come. But he replied within an hour of getting the telegram from Berne. These idiots here think the delegation is coming to seek a ground for peace. It is nothing of the sort. It is bound to condemn us, and the bourgeois governments will know how to profit by the criticism, however mild, that is signed by men who still retain authority as socialists. Henderson, for example (Henderson was at first named as one of the delegates, later replaced by MacDonald), will judge simply by whether people are hungry or not. He will not allow for reasons which are not in our control. Kautsky is less dangerous, because, after all, he will look below the obvious.'

Reinstein remembered the old personal hostility between Lenin and Kautsky, whom Lenin, in a book which Reinstein thought unworthy of him, had roundly denounced as a renegade and traitor. The only man in the delegation who could be counted on for an honest effort to understand was Longuet.

As the days went on, it became clear that the expected visit had provided a new bone of contention between the Russian parties. The Communists decided that the delegates should not be treated with any particular honour in the way of a reception. The Mensheviks at once set about preparing a triumphal reception on a large scale for the people whom they described as the representatives of genuine socialism. Demian Biedny retorted in an extremely amusing poetic dialogue, representing the Mensheviks rehearsing their parts to be ready for the reception. Other Communists went to work to prepare a retort of a different kind. They arranged a house for the Berne delegates to live in, but at the same time they prepared to emphasise the difference between the two Internationals by the calling of an anti-Berne conference which should disclaim all connection with that old International which they considered had gone into political bankruptcy at the outbreak of the European war.

Twentyone / The Executive Committee on the rival parties

February 26

In the afternoon I got to the Executive Committee in time to hear the end of a report by Rykov on the economic position. He said there was hope for a satisfactory conclusion to the negotiations for the building of the Obi-Kotlas railway, and hoped that this would soon be followed by similar negotiations and by other concessions. He explained that they did not want capitalism in Russia but that they did want the things that capital could give them in exchange for what they could give capital. This was, of course, referring to the opposition criticism that the Soviet was prepared to sell Russia into the hands of the 'Anglo-American Imperialistic bandits'. Rykov said that the main condition of all concessions would be that they should not effect the international structure of the Soviet Republic and should not lead to the exploitation of the workmen. They wanted railways, locomotives, and machines, and their country was rich enough to pay for these things out of its natural resources without sensible loss to the state or the yielding of an inch in their programme of internal reconstruction.

He was followed by Krestinsky, who pointed out that whereas the commissariats were, in a sense, altered forms of the old ministries, links with the past, the Council of Public Economy, organising the whole production and distribution of the country, building the new socialist state, was an entirely new organ and a link, not with the past, but with the future.

The two next speeches illustrated one of the main difficulties of the revolution. Krasin criticised the council for insufficient confidence in the security of the revolution. He said they were still hampered by fears lest here or there capitalism should creep in again. They were unnecessarily afraid to make the fullest possible use of specialists of all kinds who had taken a leading part in industry under the old regime and who, now that the old regime, the old system, had been definitely broken, could be made to serve the new. He believed that unless the utmost use was made of the resources of the country in technical knowledge, etc., they could not hope to organise the maximum productivity which alone could save them from catastrophe.

The speaker who followed him, Glebov, defended precisely the opposite point of view and represented the same attitude with regard to the reorganisation of industry as is held by many who object to Trotsky's use of officers of the old army in the reorganisation of the new, believing that all who worked in high places under the old regime must be and remain enemies of the revolution, so that their employment is a definite source of danger. Glebov is a trade union representative, and his speech was a clear indication of the non-political undercurrent towards the left which may shake the Bolshevik position and will most certainly come into violent conflict with any definitely bourgeois government that may be brought in by counter-revolution.

In the resolution on the economic position which was finally passed unanimously, one point reads as follows: 'It is necessary to strive for just economic relations with other countries in the form of state regulated exchange of goods and the bringing of the productive forces of other countries to the working out of the untouched natural resources of Soviet Russia'. It is interesting to notice the curiously mixed character of the opposition. Some call for 'a real socialism', which shall make no concessions whatsoever to foreign capital, others for the cessation of civil war and peace with the little governments which have obtained Allied support. In a single number of the Printers' Gazette, for example, there was a threat to appeal against the Bolsheviks to the delegation from Berne and an attack on Chicherin for being ready to make terms with the Entente.

The next business on the programme was the attitude to be adopted towards the repentant Social Revolutionaries of the Right. Kamenev made the best speech I have ever heard from him, for once in a way not letting himself be drawn into agitational digressions, but going point by point through what he had to say and saying it economically. The SRs had had three watchwords: 'War and alliance with the Allies', 'Coalition with the bourgeoisie', and 'The Constituent Assembly'. For over a year they had waged open war with the Soviet government over these three points. They had been defeated in the field. But they had suffered a far more serious moral defeat in having to confess that their very watchwords had been unsound. 'War and alliance with the Allies' had shown itself to mean the occupation of Russian territory by foreign troops in no way concerned to save the revolution, but ready, as they had shown, to help every force that was working for its suppression. 'Coalition with the bourgeoisie' had shown itself to be a path the natural ending to which was the dictatorship of the bourgeoisie through military force. 'The Constituent Assembly' had been proved to be no more than a useful mask behind which the enemies of the revolution could prepare their forces and trick the masses to their own undoing.

He read the declaration of the Right Social Revolutionaries, admitting that the Soviet government was the only force working against a dictatorship of the bourgeoisie, and calling upon their troops to overthrow the usurping governments in Siberia, and elsewhere. This repentance, however, had come rather late and there were those who did not share it. He said finally that the Executive Committee must remember that it was not a party considering its relations with another party, but an organ of government considering the attitude of the country towards a party which in the most serious moment of Russian history had admittedly made grave mistakes and helped Russia's enemies. Now, in this difficult moment, everyone who was sincerely ready to help the working masses of Russia in their struggle had the right to be given a place in the ranks of the fighters. The Social Revolutionaries should be allowed to prove in deeds the sincerity of their recantation. The resolution which was passed recapitulated the recantations, mentioned by name the members of the party with whom discussions had been carried on, withdrew the decision of June 14 (excluding the SRs from the Executive Committee on the ground of their counter-revolutionary tendencies) with regard to all groups of the party which held themselves bound by the recently published declarations, gave them the right equally with other parties to share in the work of the soviets, and notified the administrative and judicial organs of the Republic to free the arrested SRs who shared the point of view expressed in the recantations. The resolution was passed without enthusiasm but without opposition.

There followed the reading by Avanesov of the decree concerning the Menshevik paper Vsegda Vpered ('Forever Forward', but usually described by critics of the Mensheviks as 'Forever Backward'). The resolution pointed out that in spite of the Mensheviks having agreed on the need of supporting the Soviet government they were actually carrying on an agitation, the effect of which could only be to weaken the army. An example was given of an article, 'Stop the Civil War', in which they had pointed out that the war was costing a great deal, and that much of the food supplies went to the army. On these grounds they had demanded the cessation of the civil war. The committee pointed out that the Mensheviks were making demagogic use of the difficulties of the food supply, due in part to the long isolation from the Ukraine, the Volga district and Siberia, for which those Mensheviks who had worked with the White Guard were themselves partly responsible. They pointed out that Russia was a camp besieged from all sides, that Kolchak had seized the important centre of Perm, that Petrograd was threatened from Finland, that in the streets of Rostov and Novo Tcherkassk gallows with the bodies of workmen were still standing, that Denikin was making a destructive raid in the northern Caucasus, that the Polish legionnaires were working for the seizure of Vilna and the suppression of Lithuania and the White Russian proletariat, and that in the ports of the Black Sea the least civilised colonial troops of the Entente were supporting the White Guards. They pointed out that the Soviet government had offered concessions in order to buy off the imperialistic countries and had received no reply. Taking all this into consideration the demand to end civil war amounted to a demand for the disarming of the working class and the poor peasantry in the face of bandits and executioners advancing from all sides. In a word, it was the worst form of state crime, namely, treason to a state of workers and peasants. The committee considered useful every kind of practical criticism of the work of the Soviet government in all departments, but it could not allow that in the rear of the Red Army of workers and peasants, under that army's protection, should be carried on unrestrained an agitation which could have only one result, the weakening of Soviet Russia in the face of its many enemies. Therefore Vsegda Vpered would be closed until the Mensheviks should show in deed that they were ready to stand to the defence and support of the revolution. At the same time, the committee reminded the Mensheviks that a continuation of their counter-revolutionary work would force the Soviet government 'to expel them to the territories of Kolchak's democracy.' This conclusion was greeted with laughter and applause, and with that the meeting ended.

Twenty two / Commissariat of Labour

FEBRUARY 28

This morning I went round to the Commissariat of Labour, to see Schmidt, the Commissar. Schmidt is a clean shaven, intelligent young man, whose attention to business methods is reflected in his Commissariat, which, unlike that of foreign affairs, is extremely clean and very well organised. I told him I was particularly interested to hear what he could say in answer to the accusations made both by the Mensheviks and by the extremists on the left that control by the workers has become a dead letter, and that a time will come when the trades unions will move against the state organisations.

Schmidt answered: 'Those accusations and suggestions are all very well for agitational purposes, but the first to laugh at them would be the trade unions themselves. This commissariat, for example, which is the actual labour centre, is controlled directly by the unions. As Commissar of Labour, I was elected directly by the General Council of the Trade Unions. Of the college of nine members which controls the whole work of the commissariat, five are elected directly by the General Council of the Trades Unions and four appointed by the Council of People's Commissaries, thus giving the unions a decisive majority in all questions concerning labour. All nine are confirmed by the Council of People's Commissaries, representing the state as a whole, and the Commissar is confirmed by the All-Russian Executive Committee.'

Of course control by the workers, as it was first introduced, led speedily to many absurdities and, much to the dissatisfaction of the extreme elements, has been considerably modified. It was realised that the workers in any particular factory might by considering only their own interests harm the community as a whole, and so, in the long run, themselves. The manner of its modification is an interesting example of the way in which, without the influence of tanks, aeroplanes or bayonets, the cruder ideas of communism are being modified by life. It was reasoned that since the factory was the property, not of the particular workmen who work in it, but of the community as a whole, the community as a whole should have a considerable voice in its management. And the effect of that reasoning has been to ensure that the technical specialist and the expert works manager are no longer at the caprice of a hastily called gathering of the workmen who may, without understanding them, happen to disapprove of some of their dispositions. Thus the economical, administrative council of a nationalised factory consists of representatives of the workmen and clerical staff, representatives of the higher technical and commercial staffs, the directors of the factory (who are appointed by the Central Direction of National Factories), representatives of the local council of trade unions, the Council of Public Economy, the local soviet, and the industrial union of the particular industry carried on in the factory, together with a representative of the workers' co-operative society and a representative of the peasants' soviet of the district in which the factory is situated. In this council not more than half of the members may be representatives of the workmen and clerical staff of the factory. This council considers the internal order of the factory, complaints of any kind, and the material and moral conditions of work and so on. On questions of a technical character it has no right to do more than give advice.

The night before I saw Schmidt, little Finberg had come to my room for a game of chess in a very perturbed state of mind, having just come from a meeting of the union to which he belonged (the union of clerks, shop assistants and civil servants) where there had been a majority against the Bolsheviks after some fierce criticism over this particular question. Finberg had said that the ground basis of the discontent had been the lack of food, but that the outspoken criticism had taken the form, first, of protests against the offer of concessions in Chicherin's note of February 4th, on the ground that concessions meant concessions to foreign capitalism and the formation in Russia of capitalist centres which would eventually spread; and second, that the Communists themselves, by their modifications of workers' control, were introducing state capitalism instead of socialism.

I mentioned this union to Schmidt, and asked him to explain its hostility. He laughed, and said: 'Firstly, that union is not an industrial union at all, but includes precisely the people whose interests are not identical with those of the workmen. Secondly, it includes all the old civil servants who, as you remember, left the ministries at the November Revolution, in many cases taking the money with them. They came back in the end, but though no longer ready to work openly against the revolution as a whole, they retain much of their old dislike of us, and, as you see, the things they were objecting to last night were precisely the things which do not concern them in particular. Any other stick would be as good to them. They know well that if they were to go on strike now they would be a nuisance to us, no more. If you wish to know the attitude of the trades unions, you should look at the

Trade Union Congress which wholly supported us, and gave a very different picture of affairs. They know well that in all questions of labour, the trades unions have the decisive voice. I told you that the unions send a majority of the members of the college which controls the work of this commissariat. I should have added that the three most important departments—the department for safeguarding labour, the department for distributing labour, and that for regulating wages —are entirely controlled by the unions.'

'How do politics affect the commissariat?'

'Not at all. Politics do not count with us, just because we are directly controlled by the unions, and not by any political party. Mensheviks, Maximalists and others have worked and are working in the commissariat. Of course if a man were opposed to the revolution as a whole we should not have him here, because he would be working against us instead of helping.'

I asked whether he thought the trade unions would ever disappear in the soviet organisations. He thought not. On the contrary, they had grown steadily throughout the revolution. He told me that one great change had been made in them. Trade unions have been merged together into industrial unions, to prevent conflict between individual sections of one industry. Thus boilermakers and smiths do not have separate unions, but are united in the metalworkers' union. This unification has its effect on reforms and changes. An increase in wages, for example, is simultaneous all over Russia. The price of living varies very considerably in different parts of the country, there being as great differences between the climates of different parts as there are between the countries of Europe. Consequently a uniform absolute increase would be grossly unfair to some and grossly favourable to others. The increase is therefore proportional to the cost of living. Moscow is taken as a norm of 100, and when a new minimum wage is established for Moscow other districts increase their minimum wage proportionately. A table for this has been worked out, whereby in comparison with 100 for Moscow, Petrograd is set down as 120, Voronezh or

Kursk as 70, and so on.

We spoke of the new programme of the Communists, rough drafts of which were being printed in the newspapers for discussion, and he showed me his own suggestions in so far as the programme concerned labour. He wished the programme to include, among other aims, the further mechanisation of production, particularly the mechanisation of all unpleasant and dirty processes, improved sanitary inspection, shortening of the working day in employments harmful to health, forbidding women with child to do any but very light work, and none at all for eight weeks before giving birth and for eight weeks afterwards, forbidding overtime, and so on. 'We have already gone far beyond our old programme, and our new one steps far ahead of us. Russia is the first country in the world where all workers have a fortnight's holiday in the year, and workers in dangerous or unhealthy occupations have a month's.'

I said, 'Yes, but don't you find that there is a very long way between the passing of a law and its realisation?'

Schmidt laughed and replied: 'In some things certainly, yes. For example, we are against all overtime, but, in the present state of Russia we should be sacrificing to a theory the good of the revolution as a whole if we did not allow and encourage overtime in transport repairs. Similarly, until things are further developed than they are now, we should be criminal slaves to theory if we did not, in some cases, allow lads under 16 years old to be in the factories when we have not yet been able to provide the necessary schools where we would wish them to be. But the programme is there, and as fast as it can be realised we are realising it.'

Twenty three / Education

At the Commissariat of Public Education I showed Professor Pokrovsky a copy of *The German-Bolshevik Conspiracy*, published in America, containing documents supposed to prove that the German General Staff arranged the November Revolution, and that the Bolsheviks were no more than German agents. The weak point about the documents is that the most important of them have no reason for existence except to prove that there was such a conspiracy. These are the documents bought by Mr Sisson. I was interested to see what Pokrovsky would say of them. He looked through them, and while saying that he had seen forged documents better done, pointed as evidence to the third of them which ends with the alleged signatures of Zalkind, Polivanov, Mekhanoshin and Joffe. He observed that whoever forged the things knew a good deal, but did not know quite enough, because these persons, described as 'plenipotentiaries of the Council of Peoples' Commissars', though all actually in the service of the Soviet government, could not all, at that time, have been what they were said to be. Polivanov, for example, was a very minor official. Joffe, on the other hand, was indeed a person of some importance. The putting of the names in that order was almost as funny as if they had produced a document signed by Lenin and the Commandant of the Kremlin, putting the latter first.

Pokrovsky told me a good deal about the organisation of this commissariat, as Lunacharsky, the actual head of it, was away in Petrograd. The routine work is run by a college of nine members appointed by the Council of People's Commissars. The Commissar of Education himself is appointed by the All-Russian Executive Committee. Besides this, there is a Grand College which meets rarely for the settlement of important questions. In it are representatives of the trade unions, the workers' co-operatives, the teachers' union, various commissariats such as that for affairs of nationality, and other public organisations. He also gave me then and at a later date a number of figures illustrating the work that has been done since the revolution. Thus whereas there used to be six universities there are now 16, most of the new universities having been opened on the initiative of the local soviets, as at Astrakhan, Nijni, Kostroma, Tambov, Smolensk and other places. New polytechnics are being founded. At Ivano-Vosnesensk the new polytechnic is opened and that at Briansk is being prepared. The number of students in the universities has increased enormously though not to the same proportion as the number of universities, partly because the difficulties of food supply keep many students out of the towns, and partly because of the newness of some of the universities which are only now gathering their students about them. All education is free. In August last a decree was passed abolishing preliminary examinations for persons wishing to become students. It was considered that very many people who could attend the lectures with profit to themselves had been prevented by the war or by pre-revolution conditions from acquiring the sort of knowledge that could be tested by examination. It was also believed that no one would willingly listen to lectures that were of no use to him. They hoped to get as many working men into the universities as possible. Since the passing of that decree the number of students at Moscow University, for example, has more than doubled. It is interesting to notice that of the new students a greater number are studying in the faculties of science and history and philosophy than in those of medicine or law. Schools are being unified on a new basis in which labour plays a great part. I frankly admit I do not understand, and I gather that many teachers have also failed to understand, how this is done. Crafts of all kinds take a big place in the scheme. The schools are divided into two classes—one for children from seven to 12 years old, and one for those aged from 13 to 17. A milliard roubles has been assigned to feeding children in the schools, and those who most need them are supplied with clothes and footwear. Then there are many classes for working men, designed to give the worker a general scientific knowledge of his own trade and so prevent him from being merely a machine carrying out a single uncomprehended process. Thus a boilermaker can attend a course on mechanical engineering, an electrical worker a course on electricity, and the best agricultural experts are being employed to give similar lectures to the peasants. The workmen crowd to these courses. One course, for example, is attended by a thousand men in spite of the appalling cold of the lecture rooms. The hands of the science professors, so Pokrovsky told me, are frostbitten from touching the icy metal of their instruments during demonstrations.

The following figures represent roughly the growth in the number of libraries. In October 1917, there were 23 libraries in Petrograd, 30 in Moscow. Today there are 49 in Petrograd and 85 in Moscow, besides a hundred book distributing centres. A similar growth in the number of libraries has taken place in the country districts. In Ousolsky *ouezd*, for example, there are now 73 village libraries, 35 larger libraries and 500 hut libraries or reading rooms. In Moscow, educational institutions, not including schools, have increased from 369 to 1,357.

There are special departments for the circulation of printed matter, and they really have developed a remarkable organisation. I was shown over their headquarters on the Tverskaya, and saw huge maps of Russia with all the distributing centres marked with reference numbers so that it was possible to tell in a moment what number of any new publication should be sent to each. Every post office is a distributing centre to which is sent a certain number of all publications, periodical and other. The local soviets ask through the post offices for such quantities as are required, so that the supply can be closely regulated by the demand. The bookselling kiosks send in reports of the sale of the various newspapers, etc., to eliminate the waste of over-production, a very important matter in a country faced simultaneously by a vigorous demand for printed matter and an extreme scarcity of paper.

It would be interesting to have statistics to illustrate the character of the literature in demand. One thing can be said at once. No one reads sentimental romances. As is natural in a period of tremendous political upheaval pamphlets sell by the thousand, speeches of Lenin and Trotsky are only equalled in popularity by Demian Biedny's more or less political poetry. Pamphlets and books on Marx, on the war, and particularly on certain phases of the revolution, on different aspects of economic reconstruction, simply written explanations of laws or policies vanish almost as soon as they are put on the stalls. The reading of this kind has been something prodigious during the revolution. A great deal of poetry is read, and much is written. It is amusing to find in a red hot revolutionary paper serious articles and letters by well meaning persons advising would be proletarian poets to stick to Pushkin and Lermontov. There is much excited controversy both in magazine and pamphlet form as to the distinguishing marks of the new proletarian art which is expected to come out of the revolution and no doubt will come, though not in the form expected. But the Communists cannot be accused of being unfaithful to the Russian classics. Even Radek, a foreign fosterchild and an adopted Russian, took Gogol as well as Shakespeare with him when he went to annoy General Hoffmann at Brest. The Soviet government has earned the gratitude of many Russians who dislike it for everything else it has done by the resolute way in which it has brought the Russian classics into the bookshops. Books that were out of print and unobtainable, like Kliutchevsky's *Courses in Russian History*, have been reprinted from the stereotypes and set afloat again at most reasonable prices. I was also able to buy a book of his which I have long wanted, his *Foreigners' Accounts of the Muscovite State*, which had also fallen out of print. In the same way the government has reprinted, and sells at fixed low prices that may not be raised by retailers, the works of Koltzov, Nikitin, Krylov, Saltykov-Shtchedrin, Chekhov, Goncharov, Uspensky, Tchernyshevsky,

Pomyalovsky and others. It is issuing Chukovsky's edition of Nekrasov, reprints of Tolstoy, Dostoevsky and Turgenev, and books by Professor Timiriazev, Karl Pearson and others of a scientific character, besides the complete works of Lenin's old rival, Plekhánov. It is true that most of this work is simply done by reprinting from old stereotypes, but the point is that the books are there, and the sale for them is very large.

Among the other experts on the subject of the Soviet's educational work I consulted two friends, a little boy, Glyeb, who sturdily calls himself a Cadet though three of his sisters work in soviet institutions, and an old and very wise porter. Glyeb says that during the winter they had no heating, so that they sat in school in their coats, and only sat for a very short time, because of the great cold. He told me, however, that they gave him a good dinner there every day, and that lessons would be all right as soon as the weather got warmer. He showed me a pair of felt boots which had been given him at the school. The old porter summed up the similar experience of his sons. 'Yes,' he said, 'they go there, sing the Marseillaise twice through, have dinner and come home.' I then took these expert criticisms to Pokrovsky who said, 'It is perfectly true. We have not enough transport to feed the armies, let alone bringing food and warmth for ourselves.

'And if, under these conditions, we forced children to go through all their lessons we should have corpses to teach, not children. But by making them come for their meals we do two things, keep them alive, and keep them in the habit of coming, so that when the warm weather comes we can do better.'

Twenty four / A Bolshevik
fellow of the Royal Society

At Sukhanov's suggestion I went to see Professor Timiriazev, the greatest Russian Darwinian, well known to many scientific men in this country, a foreign member of the Royal Society, a Doctor of Cambridge University and a Bolshevik. He is about 80 years old. His left arm is paralysed, and, as he said, he can only work at his desk and not be out and about to help as he would wish. A venerable old savant, he was sitting writing with a green dressing gown about him, for his little flat was very cold. On the walls were portraits of Darwin, Newton and Gilbert, besides portraits of contemporary men of science whom he had known. English books were everywhere. He gave me two copies of his last scientific book and his latest portrait to take to two of his friends in England.

He lives with his wife and son. I asked if his son were also a Bolshevik.

'Of course,' he replied.

He then read me a letter he had written, protesting against intervention. He spoke of his old love for England and for the English people. Then, speaking of the veil of lies drawn between Soviet Russia and the rest of the world, he broke down altogether, and bent his head to hide his tears.

'I suffer doubly,' he said, after excusing himself for the weakness of a very old man. 'I suffer as a Russian, and, if I may say so, I suffer as an Englishman. I have English blood in my veins. My mother, you see, looks quite English,' pointing to a daguerreotype on the wall, 'and my grandmother was actually English. I suffer as an Englishman when I see the country that I love misled by lies, and I suffer as a Russian because those lies concern the country to which I belong, and the ideas which I am proud to hold.'

The old man rose with difficulty, for he, like every one else in Moscow, is half starved. He showed me his Byron, his Shakespeare, his *Encyclopaedia Britannica*, his English diplomas. He pointed to the portraits on the wall. 'If I could but let them know the truth,' he said, 'those friends of mine in England, they would protest against actions which are unworthy of the England we have loved together.'

Twenty five / Digression

At this point the chronological arrangement of my book, already weak, breaks down altogether. So far I have set down, almost day by day, things seen and heard which seemed to me characteristic and clear illustration of the mentality of the Communists, of the work that has been done or that they are trying to do, and of the general state of affairs. I spent the whole of my time in ceaseless investigation, talking now with this man, now with that, until at the end of a month I was so tired (besides being permanently hungry) that I began to fear rather than to seek new experiences and impressions. The last two weeks of my stay were spent, not in visiting Commissariats, but in collecting masses of printed material, in talking with my friends of the opposition parties, and, while it was in progress, visiting daily the conference in the Kremlin which, in the end, definitely announced itself as the Third International. I have considered it best to treat of that conference more or less as a whole, and am therefore compelled to disregard chronology altogether in putting down on paper the results of some of my talks with the opposition. Some of these took place on the same days as my visits to the Kremlin conference, and during those days I was also partly engaged in getting to see the British prisoners in the Butyrka prison, in which I eventually succeeded. This is my excuse for the inadequacy of my account of the conference, an inadequacy which I regret the more as I was the only non-Communist who was able to be there at all.

Twenty six / The opposition

No man likes being hungry. No man likes being cold.
Everybody in Moscow, as in Petrograd, is both hungry and cold.
There is consequently very general and very bitter discontent. This
is of course increased, not lessened, by the discipline introduced
into the factories and the heavy burden of the army, although the
one is intended to hasten the end of hunger and cold and the other
for the defence of the revolution. The Communists, as the party in
power, naturally bear the blame and are the objects of the discontent, which will certainly within a short time be turned upon any
other government that may succeed them. That government must
introduce sterner discipline rather than weaker, and the transport
and other difficulties of the country will remain the same, unless
increased by the disorder of a new upheaval and the active or passive resistance of many who are convinced revolutionaries or will
become so in answer to repression.

The Communists believe that to let power slip from their
hands at this moment would be treachery to the revolution. And,
in the face of the advancing forces of the Allies and Kolchak many
of the leaders of the opposition are inclined to agree with them,
and temporarily to submit to what they undoubtedly consider rank
tyranny. A position has been reached after these 18 months not
unlike that reached by the English Parliament party in 1643. I am
reminded of a passage in Guizot, which is so illuminating that I
make no apology for quoting it in full:

'The party had been in the ascendant for three years:
whether it had or had not, in church and state, accomplished its
designs, it was at all events by its aid and concurrence that, for
three years, public affairs had been conducted; this alone was sufficient to make many people weary of it; it was made responsible for
the many evils already endured, for the many hopes frustrated; it
was denounced as being no less addicted to persecution than the

bishops, no less arbitrary than the king; its inconsistencies, its weaknesses, were recalled with bitterness; and, independently of this, even without factions or interested views, from the mere progress of events and opinions, there was felt a secret need of new principles and new rulers.'

New rulers are advancing on Moscow from Siberia, but I do not think that they claim that they are bringing with them new principles. Though the masses may want new principles, and might for a moment submit to a reintroduction of very old principles in desperate hope of less hunger and less cold, no one but a lunatic could imagine that they would for very long willingly submit to them. In the face of the danger that they may be forced to submit not to new principles but to very old ones, the non-Communist leaders are unwilling to use to the full the discontent that exists. Hunger and cold are a good enough basis of agitation for anyone desirous of overturning any existing government. But the Left Social Revolutionaries, led by the hysterical but flamingly honest Spiridonova, are alone in having no scruples or hesitation in the matter, the more responsible parties fearing the anarchy and consequent weakening of the revolution that would result from any violent change.

The Left Social Revolutionaries

The Left Social Revolutionaries want something so much like anarchy that they have nothing to fear in a collapse of the present system. They are for a partisan army, not a regular army. They are against the employment of officers who served under the old regime. They are against the employment of responsible technicians and commercial experts in the factories. They believe that officers and experts alike, being ex-bourgeois, must be enemies of the people, insidiously engineering reaction. They are opposed to any agreement with the Allies, exactly as they were opposed to any agreement with the Germans. I heard them describe the

Communists as 'the bourgeois gendarmes of the Entente', on the ground that having offered concessions they would be keeping order in Russia for the benefit of Allied capital. They blew up Mirbach, and would no doubt try to blow up any successors he might have. Not wanting a regular army (a low bourgeois weapon) they would welcome occupation in order that they, with bees in their bonnets and bombs in their hands, might go about revolting against it.

I did not see Spiridonova, because on February 11, the very day when I had an appointment with her, the Communists arrested her, on the ground that her agitation was dangerous and anarchist in tendency, fomenting discontent without a programme for its satisfaction. Having a great respect for her honesty, they were hard put to it to know what to do with her, and she was finally sentenced to be sent for a year to a home for neurasthenics, 'where she would be able to read and write and recover her normality.' That the Communists were right in fearing this agitation was proved by the troubles in Petrograd, where the workmen in some of the factories struck, and passed Left Social Revolutionary resolutions which, so far from showing that they were awaiting reaction and General Yudenitch, showed simply that they were discontented and prepared to move to the left.

The Mensheviks

The second main group of opposition is dominated by the Mensheviks. Their chief leaders are Martov and Dan. Of these two, Martov is by far the cleverer, Dan the more garrulous, being often led away by his own volubility into agitation of a kind not approved by his friends. Both are men of very considerable courage. Both are Jews.

The Mensheviks would like the reintroduction of capitalists, of course much chastened by experience, and properly controlled by themselves. Unlike Spiridonova and her romantic supporters they approved of Chicherin's offer of peace and concessions to the Allies (see page 81). They have even issued an appeal that the Allies should come to an agreement with 'Lenin's government.' As may be gathered from their choice of a name for the Soviet government, they are extremely hostile to it, but they fear worse things, and are consequently a little shy of exploiting as they easily could the dislike of the people for hunger and cold. They fear that agitation on these lines might well result in anarchy, which would leave the revolution temporarily defenceless against Kolchak, Denikin, Yudenitch or any other armed reactionary. Their non-Communist enemies say of the Mensheviks: 'They have no constructive programme; they would like a bourgeois government back again, in order that they might be in opposition to it, on the left.'

On March 2, I went to an election meeting of workers and officials of the Moscow Co-operatives. It was beastly cold in the hall of the university where the meeting was held, and my nose froze as well as my feet. Speakers were announced from the Communists, Internationalists, Mensheviks, and Right Social Revolutionaries. The last named did not arrive. The presidium was for the most part non-Communist, and the meeting was about equally divided for and against the Communists. A Communist led off with a very bad speech on the general European situation and to the effect that there was no salvation for Russia except by the way she was going. Lozovsky, the old Internationalist, spoke next, supporting the Bolsheviks' general policy but criticising their suppression of the press. Then came Dan, the Menshevik, to hear whom I had come. He is a little, sanguine man, who gets very hot as he speaks. He conducted an attack on the whole Bolshevik position combined with a declaration that so long as they are attacked from without he is prepared to support them. The gist of his speech was: 1. He was in favour of fighting Kolchak. 2. But the Bolshevik policy with regard to the peasants will, since as the army grows it must contain more and more peasants, end in the creation of an army with counter-revolutionary sympathies 3. He objected to the Bolshevik criticism of the Berne delegation on very curious grounds, saying that though Thomas, Henderson, etc., backed their own imperialists during the war, all that was now over, and that union with them would help, not hinder, revolution in England and France. 4. He pointed out that 'All power to the soviets' now means 'All power to the Bolsheviks', and said that he wished that the soviets should actually have all power instead of merely supporting the Bolshevik bureaucracy. He was asked for his own programme, but said he had not time to give it. I watched the applause carefully. General dissatisfaction with the present state of affairs was obvious, but it was also obvious that no party would have a chance that admitted its aim was extinction of the soviets (which Dan's ultimate aim certainly is, or at least the changing of them into non-political industrial organisations) or that was not prepared to fight against reaction from without.

I went to see Sukhanov (the friend of Gorky and Martov, though his political opinions do not precisely agree with those of either), partly to get the proofs of his first volume of reminiscences of the revolution, partly to hear what he had to say. I found him muffled up in a dressing gown or overcoat in an unheated flat, sitting down to tea with no sugar, very little bread, a little sausage and a surprising scrap of butter, brought in, I suppose, from the country by a friend. Nikitsky, a Menshevik, was also there, a hopeless figure, prophesying the rotting of the whole system and of the revolution. Sukhanov asked me if I had noticed the disappearance of all spoons (there are now none but wooden spoons in the Metropole) as a symbol of the falling to pieces of the revolution. I told him that though I had not lived in Russia 30 years or more, as he had, I had yet lived there long enough and had, before the revolution, sufficient experience in the loss of fishing tackle, not to be surprised that Russian peasants, even delegates, when able, as in such a moment of convulsion as the revolution, stole spoons if only as souvenirs to show that they had really been to Moscow.

We talked, of course, of their attitude towards the

Bolsheviks. Both work in soviet institutions. Sukhanov (Nikitsky agreeing) believed that if the Bolsheviks came further to meet the other parties, Mensheviks, etc., 'Kolchak and Denikin would commit suicide and your Lloyd George would give up all thought of intervention.' I asked, What if they should be told to hold a Constituent Assembly or submit to a continuance of the blockade? Sukhanov said, 'Such a Constituent Assembly would be impossible, and we should be against it.' Of the Soviets, one or other said, 'We stand absolutely on the platform of the Soviet government now: but we think that such a form cannot be permanent. We consider the soviets perfect instruments of class struggle, but not a perfect form of government.' I asked Sukhanov if he thought counter-revolution possible. He said 'No', but admitted that there was a danger lest the agitation of the Mensheviks or others might set fire to the discontent of the masses against the actual physical conditions, and end in pogroms destroying Bolsheviks and Mensheviks alike. Their general theory was that Russia was not so far developed that a socialist state was at present possible. They therefore wanted a state in which private capital should exist, and in which factories were not run by the state but by individual owners. They believed that the peasants, with their instincts of small property holders, would eventually enforce something of the kind, and that the end would be some form of democratic republic. These two were against the offering of concessions to the Allies, on the ground that those under consideration involved the handing over to the concessionaires of the whole power in northern Russia—railways, forests, the right to set up their own banks in the towns served by the railway, with all that this implied. Sukhanov was against concessions on principle, and regretted that the Mensheviks were in favour of them.

I saw Martov at the offices of his newspaper, which had just been suppressed on account of an article, which he admitted was a little indiscreet, objecting to the upkeep of the Red Army (see page 143). He pointed eloquently to the seal on some of the doors, but told me that he had started a new paper, of which he showed me the first number, and told me that the demand for it was such that although he had intended that it should be a weekly he now expected to make it a daily. Martov said that he and his party were against every form of intervention for the following reasons: 1. The continuation of hostilities, the need of an army and of active defence were bound to intensify the least desirable qualities of the revolution, whereas an agreement, by lessening the tension, would certainly lead to moderation of Bolshevik policy. 2. The needs of the army overwhelmed every effort at restoring the economic life of the country. He was further convinced that intervention of any kind favoured reaction even supposing that the Allies did not wish this. 'They cannot help themselves,' he said, 'the forces that would support intervention must be dominated by those of reaction, since all of the non-reactionary parties are prepared to sink their differences with the Bolsheviks, in order to defend the revolution as a whole.' He said he was convinced that the Bolsheviks would either have to alter or go. He read me, in illustration of this, a letter from a peasant showing the unreadiness of the peasantry to go into communes (compulsion in this matter has already been discarded by the central government). 'We took the land,' wrote the peasant in some such words, 'not much, just as much as we could work, we ploughed it where it had not been ploughed before, and now, if it is made into a commune, other lazy fellows who have done nothing will come in and profit by our work.' Martov argued that life itself, the needs of the country and the will of the peasant masses, would lead to the changes he thinks desirable in the soviet regime.

The Right Social Revolutionaries

The position of the Right Social Revolutionaries is a good deal more complicated than that of the Mensheviks. In their later declarations they are as far from their romantic anarchist left wing as they are from their romantic reactionary extreme right. They stand, as they have always stood, for a Constituent Assembly, but they have thrown over the idea of instituting a Constituent Assembly by force. They have come into closer contact with the Allies than any other party to the left of the Cadets. By doing so, by associating themselves with the Czech forces on the Volga and minor revolts of a reactionary character inside Russia, they have pretty badly compromised themselves. Their change of attitude towards the Soviet government must not be attributed to any change in their own programme, but to the realisation that the forces which they imagined were supporting them were actually being used to support something a great deal further right. The Printers' Gazette, a non-Bolshevik organ, printed one of their resolutions, one point of which demands the overthrow of the reactionary governments supported by the Allies or the Germans, and another condemns every attempt to overthrow the Soviet government by force of arms, on the ground that such an attempt would weaken the working class as a whole and would be used by the reactionary groups for their own purposes.

Volsky is a Right Social Revolutionary, and was President of that Conference of Members of the Constituent Assembly from whose hands the directorate which ruled in Siberia received its authority and Admiral Kolchak his command, his proper title being Commander of the Forces of the Constituent Assembly. The Constituent Assembly members were to have met on January 1 of this year, then to retake authority from the directorate and organise a government on an All-Russian basis. But there was continual friction between the directorate and the Conference of Members of the Constituent Assembly, the directorate being more reactionary than they. In November came Kolchak's coup d'etat, followed by a declaration against him and an appeal for his overthrow issued by members of the Constituent Assembly. Some were arrested by a group of officers. A few are said to have been killed. Kolchak, I think, has denied responsibility for this, and probably was unaware of the intentions of the reactionaries under his command. Others of the members escaped to Ufa. On December 5, 25 days before that town was taken by the Bolsheviks, they announced their intention of no longer opposing the Soviet government in the field. After the capture of the town by the Soviet troops, negotiations were begun between the representatives of the Conference of Members of the Constituent Assembly, together with other Right Social Revolutionaries, and representatives of the Soviet government, with a view to finding a basis for agreement. The result of those negotiations was the resolution passed by the Executive Committee on February 26 (see page 142). A delegation of the members came to Moscow, and were quaintly housed in a huge room in the Metropole, where they had put up beds all round the walls and big tables in the middle of the room for their deliberations. It was in this room that I saw Volsky first, and afterwards in my own.

I asked him what exactly had brought him and all that he represented over from the side of Kolchak and the Allies to the side of the Soviet government. He looked me straight in the face, and said: 'I'll tell you. We were convinced by many facts that the policy of the Allied representatives in Siberia was directed not to strengthening the Constituent Assembly against the Bolsheviks and the Germans, but simply to strengthening the reactionary forces behind our backs.'

He also complained: 'All through last summer we were holding that front with the Czechs, being told that there were two divisions of Germans advancing to attack us, and we now know that there were no German troops in Russia at all.'

He criticised the Bolsheviks for being better makers of programmes than organisers. They offered free electricity, and presently had to admit that soon there would be no electricity for lack of fuel. They did not sufficiently base their policy on the study of actual possibilities. 'But that they are really fighting against a bourgeois dictatorship is clear to us. We are, therefore, prepared to help them in every possible way.'

He said, further: 'Intervention of any kind will prolong the regime of the Bolsheviks by compelling us to drop opposition to the Soviet government, although we do not like it, and to support it because it is defending the revolution.'

With regard to help given to individual groups or governments fighting against Soviet Russia, Volsky said that they saw no difference between such intervention and intervention in the form of sending troops.

I asked what he thought would happen. He answered in almost the same words as those used by Martov, that life itself would compel the Bolsheviks to alter their policy or to go. Sooner or later the peasants would make their will felt, and they were against the bourgeoisie and against the Bolsheviks. No bourgeois reaction could win permanently against the Soviet, because it could have nothing to offer, no idea for which people would fight. If by any chance Kolchak, Denikin and Co were to win, they would have to kill in tens of thousands where the Bolsheviks have had to kill in hundreds, and the result would be the complete ruin and the collapse of Russia in anarchy. 'Has not the Ukraine been enough to teach the Allies that even six months' occupation of non-Bolshevik territory by half a million troops has merely the effect of turning the population into Bolsheviks?'

Twenty seven / The Third International

One day near the end of February, Bukharin, hearing that I meant to leave quite soon, said rather mysteriously, 'Wait a few days longer, because something of international importance is going to happen which will certainly be of interest for your history.' That was the only hint I got of the preparation of the Third International. Bukharin refused to say more. On March 3 Reinstein looked in about nine in the morning and said he had got me a guest's ticket for the conference in the Kremlin, and wondered why I had not been there the day before, when it had opened. I told·him I knew nothing whatever about it;.Litvinov and Karakhan, whom I had seen quite recently, had never mentioned it, and guessing that this must be the secret at which Bukharin had hinted, I supposed that they had purposely kept silence. I therefore rang up Litvinov, and asked if they had had any reason against my going. He said that he had thought it would not interest me. So I went. The conference was still a secret. There was nothing about it in the morning papers.

The meeting was in a smallish room, with a dais at one end, in the old Courts of Justice built in the time of Catherine the Second, who would certainly have turned in her grave if she had known the use to which it was being put. Two very smart soldiers of the Red Army were guarding the doors. The whole room, including the floor, was decorated in red. There were banners with 'Long Live the Third International' inscribed upon them in many languages. The presidium was on the raised dais at the end of the room, Lenin sitting in the middle behind a long red covered table with Albrecht, a young German Spartacist, on the right and Platten, the Swiss, on the left. The auditorium sloped down to the foot of the dais. Chairs were arranged on each side of an alleyway down the middle, and the four or five front rows had little tables for convenience in writing. Everybody of importance was there; Trotsky, Zinoviev, Kamenev, Chicherin, Bukharin, Karakhan, Litvinov, Vorovsky, Steklov, Rakovsky, representing here the Balkan Socialist Party, Skripnik, representing the Ukraine. Then there were Stang (Norwegian Left Socialists), Grimlund (Swedish Left), Sadoul (France), Finberg (British Socialist Party), Reinstein (American Socialist Labour Party), a Turk, a German-Austrian, a Chinese, and so on. Business was conducted and speeches were made in all languages, though where possible German was used, because more of the foreigners knew German than knew French. This was unlucky for me.

When I got there people were making reports about the situation in the different countries. Finberg spoke in English, Rakovsky in French, Sadoul also. Skripnik, who, being asked, refused to talk German and said he would speak in either Ukrainian or Russia, and to most people's relief chose the latter, made several interesting points about the new revolution in the Ukraine. The killing of the leaders under the Skoropadsky regime had made no difference to the movement, and town after town was falling after internal revolt. (This was before they had Kiev and, of course, long before they had taken Odessa, both of which gains they confidently prophesied). The sharp lesson of German occupation had taught the Ukrainian Social Revolutionaries what their experiences during the last 15 months had taught the Russian, and all parties were working together.

But the real interest of the gathering was in its attitude towards the Berne conference. Many letters had been received from members of that conference, Longuet for example, wishing that the Communists had been represented there, and the view taken at Moscow was that the left wing at Berne was feeling uncomfortable at sitting down with Scheidemann and company; let them definitely break with them, finish with the Second International and join the Third. It was clear that this gathering in the Kremlin was meant as the nucleus of a new International opposed to that which had split into national groups, each supporting its own government in the prosecution of the war. That was the leit motif of the whole affair.

Trotsky, in a leather coat, military breeches and gaiters, with a fur hat with the sign of the Red Army in front, was looking very well, but a strange figure for those who had known him as one of the greatest anti-militarists in Europe. Lenin sat quietly listening, speaking when necessary in almost every European language with astonishing ease. Balabanova talked about Italy and seemed happy at last, even in Soviet Russia, to be once more in a 'secret meeting'. It was really an extraordinary affair and, in spite of some childishness, I could not help realising that I was present at something that will go down in the histories of socialism, much like that other strange meeting convened in London in 1848.

The vital figures of the conference, not counting Platten, whom I do not know and on whom I can express no opinion, were Lenin and the young German, Albrecht, who, fired no doubt by the events actually taking place in his country, spoke with brain and character. The German-Austrian also seemed a real man. Rakovsky, Skripnik, and Sirola the Finn really represented something. But there was a make-believe side to the whole affair, in which the English Left Socialists were represented by Finberg, and the Americans by Reinstein, neither of whom had or was likely to have any means of communicating with his constituents.

MARCH 4

In the Kremlin they were discussing the programme on which the new International was to stand. This is, of course, dictatorship of the proletariat and all that that implies. I heard Lenin make a long speech, the main point of which was to show that Kautsky and his supporters at Berne were now condemning the very tactics which they had praised in 1906. When I was leaving the Kremlin I met Sirola walking in the square outside the building without a hat, without a coat, in a cold so intense that I was putting snow on my nose to prevent frost-bite. I exclaimed. Sirola smiled his ingenuous smile. 'It is March,' he said, 'spring is coming.'

MARCH 5

Today all secrecy was dropped, a little prematurely, I fancy, for when I got to the Kremlin I found that the first note of opposition had been struck by the man who least of all was expected to strike it. Albrecht, the young German, had opposed the immediate founding of the Third International, on the double ground that not all nations were properly represented and that it might make difficulties for the political parties concerned in their own countries. Everyone was against him. Rakovsky pointed out that the same objections could have been raised against the founding of the First International by Marx in London. The German-Austrian combatted Albrecht's second point. Other people said that the different parties concerned had long ago definitely broken with the Second International. Albrecht was in a minority of one. It was decided therefore that this conference was actually the Third International. Platten announced the decision, and the 'International' was sung in a dozen languages at once. Then Albrecht stood up, a little red in the face, and said that he, of course, recognised the decision and would announce it in Germany.

MARCH 6

The conference in the Kremlin ended with the usual singing and a photograph. Some time before the end, when Trotsky had just finished speaking and had left the tribune, there was a squeal of protest from the photographer who had just trained his apparatus. Some one remarked 'The dictatorship of the photographer,' and, amid general laughter, Trotsky had to return to the tribune and stand silent while the unabashed photographer took two pictures. The founding of the Third International had been proclaimed in the morning papers, and an extraordinary meeting in the Great

Theatre announced for the evening. I got to the theatre at about five, and had difficulty in getting in, though I had a special ticket as a correspondent. There were queues outside all the doors. The Moscow Soviet was there, the Executive Committee, representatives of the trade unions and the factory committees, etc. The huge theatre and the platform were crammed, people standing in the aisles and even packed close together in the wings of the stage. Kamenev opened the meeting by a solemn announcement of the founding of the Third International in the Kremlin. There was a roar of applause from the audience, which rose and sang the 'International' in a way that I have never heard it sung since the All-Russian Assembly when the news came of the strikes in Germany during the Brest negotiations. Kamenev then spoke of those who had died on the way, mentioning Liebknecht and Rosa Luxemburg, and the whole theatre stood again while the orchestra played, 'You fell as victims'. Then Lenin spoke. If I had ever thought that Lenin was losing his personal popularity, I got my answer now. It was a long time before he could speak at all, everybody standing and drowning his attempts to speak with roar after roar of applause. It was an extraordinary, overwhelming scene, tier after tier crammed with workmen, the parterre filled, the whole platform and the wings. A knot of workwomen were close to me, and they almost fought to see him, and shouted as if each one were determined that he should hear her in particular. He spoke as usual, in the simplest way, emphasising the fact that the revolutionary struggle everywhere was forced to use the soviet forms. 'We declare our solidarity with the aims of the Sovietists', he read from an Italian paper, and added, 'and that was when they did not know what our aims were, and before we had an established programme ourselves.' Albrecht made a very long reasoned speech for Spartacus, which was translated by Trotsky. Guilbeau, seemingly a mere child, spoke of the socialist movement in France. Steklov was translating him when I left. You must remember that I had had nearly two years of such meetings, and am not a Russian. When I got outside the theatre, I found at each door a disappointed crowd that had been unable to get in.

The proceedings finished up next day with a review in the Red Square and a general holiday.

If the Berne delegates had come, as they were expected, they would have been told by the Communists that they were welcome visitors, but that they were not regarded as representing the International. There would then have ensued a lively battle over each one of the delegates, the Mensheviks urging him to stick to Berne, and the Communists urging him to express allegiance to the Kremlin. There would have been demonstrations and counter-demonstrations, and altogether I am very sorry that it did not happen and that I was not there to see.

Twenty eight / Last talk with Lenin

I went to see Lenin the day after the review in the Red Square, and the general holiday in honour of the Third International. The first thing he said was: 'I am afraid that the jingoes in England and France will make use of yesterday's doings as an excuse for further action against us. They will say "How can we leave them in peace when they set about setting the world on fire?" To that I would answer, "We are at war, Messieurs! And just as during your war you tried to make revolution in Germany, and Germany did her best to make trouble in Ireland and India, so we, while we are at war with you, adopt the measures that are open to us. We have told you we are willing to make peace." '

He spoke of Chicherin's last note, and said they based all their hopes on it. Balfour had said somewhere, 'Let the fire burn itself out.' That it would not do. But the quickest way of restoring good conditions in Russia was, of course, peace and agreement with the Allies. 'I am sure we could come to terms, if they want to come to terms at all. England and America would be willing, perhaps, if their hands were not tied by France. But intervention in the large sense can now hardly be. They must have learnt that Russia could never be governed as India is governed, and that sending troops here is the same thing as sending them to a Communist university.'

I said something about the general hostility to their propaganda noticeable in foreign countries.

Lenin. 'Tell them to build a Chinese wall round each of their countries. They have their customs-officers, their frontiers, their coast-guards. They can expel any Bolsheviks they wish. Revolution does not depend on propaganda. If the conditions of revolution are not there no sort of propaganda will either hasten or impede it. The war has brought about those conditions in all countries, and I am convinced that if Russia today were to be swallowed up by the sea, were to cease to exist altogether, the revolution in the rest of Europe would go on. Put Russia under water for 20 years, and you would not affect by a shilling or an hour a week the demands of the shop stewards in England.'

I told him, what I have told most of them many times, that I did not believe there would be a revolution in England.

Lenin. 'We have a saying that a man may have typhoid while still on his legs. Twenty, maybe 30 years ago I had abortive typhoid, and was going about with it, had had it some days before it knocked me over. Well, England and France and Italy have caught the disease already. England may seem to you to be untouched, but the microbe is already there.'

I said that just as his typhoid was abortive typhoid, so the disturbances in England to which he alluded might well be abortive revolution, and come to nothing. I told him the vague, disconnected character of the strikes and the generally *liberal* as opposed to socialist character of the movement, so far as it was political at all, reminded me of what I had heard of 1905 in Russia and not at all of 1917, and that I was sure it would settle down.

Lenin. 'Yes, that is possible. It is, perhaps, an educative period, in which the English workmen will come to realize their political needs, and turn from liberalism to socialism. Socialism is certainly weak in England. Your socialist movements, your socialist parties ... when I was in England I zealously attended everything I could, and for a country with so large an industrial population they were pitiable, pitiable ... a handful at a street corner ... a meeting in a drawingroom ... a schoolclass ... pitiable. But you must remember one great difference between Russia of 1905 and England of today. Our first soviet in Russia was made during the revolution. Your shop stewards committees have been in existence long before. They are without programme, without direction, but the opposition they will meet will force a programme upon them.'

Speaking of the expected visit of the Berne delegation, he asked me if I knew MacDonald, whose name had been substituted for that of Henderson in later telegrams announcing their coming. He said: 'I am very glad MacDonald is coming instead of Henderson. Of course MacDonald is not a Marxist in any sense of the word, but he is at least interested in theory, and can therefore be trusted to do his best to understand what is happening here. More than that we do not ask.'

We then talked a little on a subject that interests me very much, namely, the way in which insensibly, quite apart from war, the Communist theories are being modified in the difficult process of their translation into practice. We talked of the changes in 'workers' control', which is now a very different thing from the wild committee business that at first made work almost impossible. We talked then of the antipathy of the peasants to compulsory communism, and how that idea also had been considerably whittled away. I asked him what were going to be the relations between the Communists of the towns and the property loving peasants, and whether there was not great danger of antipathy between them, and said I regretted leaving too soon to see the elasticity of the Communist theories tested by the inevitable pressure of the peasantry.

Lenin said that in Russia there was a pretty sharp distinction between the rich peasants and the poor. 'The only opposition we have here in Russia is directly or indirectly due to the rich peasants. The poor, as soon as they are liberated from the political domination of the rich, are on our side and are in an enormous majority.'

I said that would not be so in the Ukraine, where property among the peasants is much more equally distributed.

Lenin. 'No. And there, in the Ukraine, you will certainly see our policy modified. Civil war, whatever happens, is likely to be more bitter in the Ukraine than elsewhere, because there the instinct of property has been further developed in the peasantry, and the minority and majority will be more equal.'

He asked me if I meant to return, saying that I could go down to Kiev to watch the revolution there as I had watched it in Moscow. I said I should be very sorry to think that this was my last visit to the country which I love only second to my own. He laughed, and paid me the compliment of saying that, 'although English', I had more or less succeeded in understanding what they were at, and that he should be pleased to see me again.

Twenty nine / The journey out

There is nothing to record about the last few days of my visit, fully occupied as they were with the collection and packing of printed material and preparations for departure. I left with the two Americans, Messrs Bullitt and Steffens, who had come to Moscow some days previously, and travelled up in the train with Bill Shatov, the Commandant of Petrograd, who is not a Bolshevik but a fervent admirer of Prince Kropotkin, for the distribution of whose works in Russia he has probably done as much as any man. Shatov was an emigre in New York, returned to Russia, brought law and order into the chaos of the Petrograd-Moscow railway, never lost a chance of doing a good turn to an American, and with his levelheadedness and practical sense became one of the hardest worked servants of the Soviet, although, as he said, the moment people stopped attacking them he would be the first to pull down the Bolsheviks. He went into the occupied provinces during the German evacuation of them, to buy arms and ammunition from the German soldiers. Prices, he said, ran low. You could buy rifles for a mark each, field guns for 150 marks, and a field wireless station for 500. He had then been made Commandant of Petrograd, although there had been some talk of setting him to reorganise transport. Asked how long he thought the Soviet government could hold out, he replied, 'We can afford to starve another year for the sake of the Revolution.'

The End

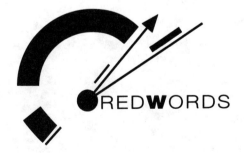

Introduction by Paul Foot
Shelley's revolutionary year

This book includes for the first time in one volume the
ten political poems which Shelley wrote in the months
after Peterloo, including The Mask of Anarchy and the
Ode to Liberty, and the essay in which he grappled
with the problems of repression and liberty, reform and
revolution, and the Philosophical View of Reform.

ISBN 1 872208 00 2

£3.95

REDWORDS

Leon Trotsky
Literature and Revolution

This book, written in the years immediately after
the Russian workers' revolution of 1917, looks at
the relationship between revolution, literature, art
and society — and at the role of literature and art
in the construction of a future socialist society.
A Marxist classic.

ISBN 1 872208 01 0

£7.85

REDWORDS